EDUCATIONAL ASPECTS OF THE LEGISLATION OF THE COUNCILS OF BALTIMORE

This is a volume in the
Arno Press collection

THE AMERICAN
CATHOLIC TRADITION

Advisory Editor
Jay P. Dolan

Editorial Board
Paul Messbarger
Michael Novak

*See last pages of this volume
for a complete list of titles.*

EDUCATIONAL ASPECTS
OF THE LEGISLATION
OF THE COUNCILS
OF BALTIMORE
1829-1884

Bernard Julius Meiring

ARNO PRESS
A New York Times Company
New York • 1978

Editorial Supervision: JOSEPH CELLINI

———◆———

First publication 1978 by Arno Press Inc.

Copyright © 1978 by Bernard Julius Meiring

Reprinted from a copy in the
  University of California, Berkeley, Library

THE AMERICAN CATHOLIC TRADITION
ISBN for complete set: 0-405-10810-9
See last pages of this volume for titles.

Manufactured in the United States of America

———◆———

Library of Congress Cataloging in Publication Data

Meiring, Bernard Julius.
  Educational aspects of the legislation of the
Councils of Baltimore, 1829-1884.

  (The American Catholic tradition)
  Originally presented as the author's thesis,
University of California, Berkeley, 1963.
    1. Catholic Church in Baltimore--Education--History.
2. Baltimore (Ecclesiastical Province). Councils--
History. I. Title. II. Series.
  LC503.B3M44 1978   377'.8'273   77-11301
  ISBN 0-405-10844-3

Educational Aspects
of the Legislation of the Councils of Baltimore, 1829-1884

By

Bernard Julius Meiring
A.B. (University of Dayton) 1951
M.A. (University of Detroit) 1957

DISSERTATION

Submitted in partial satisfaction of the requirements for
the degree of
DOCTOR OF PHILOSOPHY

in

Education

in the

GRADUATE DIVISION

of the

UNIVERSITY OF CALIFORNIA, BERKELEY

Approved: ....

....

....

Committee in charge

TABLE OF CONTENTS

Chapter I

Introduction

The Statement of the Problem

In the preface to his analysis of the educational
philosophy of the three giants of the nineteenth century
American educational scene, Neil Gerard McCluskey points
out that the Church-State issues involved in cases like the
McCollum decision, the Everson case, and the Engels conclusion, engender a fervor of controversy which can hardly be
accounted for by the issues and arguments which are aired
in public. Two basic value systems seem to be in conflict
and no solution is in sight. Americans have rejected the
solutions offered in various European countries and their
own solution is as yet incomplete. A study of the arguments
presented in the many prayer and Bible cases suggests that
the complete secularization of the school is shortly to be
completed. The definitive position of opposition to any
prayer or other evidence of Christianity within the school
framework seems indicated by the court brief in the Engels
dispute. Inherent in these decisions is the attempt of
the courts to deal with a basic issue in the American public
school system: can a common school truly serve a pluralis-
tic society?[1] The coexistence of different religious groups

---

[1]Neil Gerard McCluskey, Public Schools and Moral Education (New York: Columbia University Press, 1958), p. vii.
For a general discussion of the court cases cf. Joseph Tussman (ed.), The Supreme Court on Church and State (New York:
Oxford University Press, 1962).

1

holding at one and the same time widely disparate views regarding the nature and destiny of man makes the teaching of
these areas a practical impossibility.[1] Just as the nineteenth century witnessed the Catholic-Protestant debate when
one group was unable to obtain a hearing within the public
schools, so the twentieth witnesses the attempts of fundamental Christianity to hold the line against the secularist.
And whereas in the nineteenth century the most commonly offered solution was the pledge of a non-denominational Bible,
so in the twentieth a widely proposed solution is the ignor-
ing of the conflicted premises. A strong point in the thinking of Columbia's professor of educational history and
philosophy, Lawrence A. Cremin, has been the demonstration
of the evolution of the idea of the educational program of
the United States. In his discussion on this point he indicates that the common school was, indeed, an ideal--an
ideal which may not yet be completely realized. In its early
history, of course, the common school was co-relative with
the poor school. The cause and course of development from
poor school to public school is the inspiring story of the
attempt of a democratic society to educate all its constituents to fulfill their function of enlightened participation

---

[1]For a complete discussion of the framework of Church
and State relationships cf. Anson P. Stokes, Church and State
in the United States (New York: Harper and Bros., 1950). A
more recent bibliography is: Edmond G. Drouin, A Bibliography
on Church-State Relationships in American Education, 1940-
1960 (Washington, D. C.: Catholic University Press, 1963).

in government. As the school exercised its leveling influence on rich and poor, immigrant and native, Yankee and cowhand, Catholic and Protestant, clerk and cobbler, the school
did in actual fact become common--the possession of all men.[1]
But it also follows that in becoming common the public school
not only gave to its adherents the benefits of education,
but it asked of them certain things in return. Only in the
millenium will lions leave little lambs undisturbed, and
when the public school united diverse interests within its
ranks, it did so by compromising the diversity. Cowhand
learned arithmetic and bookkeeping but the clerk learned
of life beneath the stars. It is an oft-repeated truism
that the less the agreement in society over ultimate values,
the less the common school can reflect a unified philosophy
of values.[2] What happened in the unifying process when certain elements were unwilling to make the adjustments necessary to function within the common framework? Specifically,
what solution could the public school offer to a group who
refused to commonize? Was there room within the unity of
commonness for such diversity? It was in the sensitive
sphere of religious training that the public school met its
most decisive challenge. Two solutions were indeed possible.

---

[1]Lawrence A. Cremin and Merle L. Borrowman, _Public
Schools in Our Democracy_ (New York: Macmillan, 1956), p. 75.

[2]McCluskey, _Public Schools and Moral Education_, p. 3.

The churches could surrender their control over education
and function peacefully within the limits set by education.
This was the solution accepted by the majority of the Protestant churches in the United States.[1] During the crucial
years of the struggle for common schools, they voluntarily
relinquished their control and any claim to future control
over elementary and secondary education. The schools and
academies which they had built became the nucleus of the
emerging common school system, and many Protestant ministers
became prominent leaders in the public school movement. Inherent, perhaps, in their surrender was the recognition or
hope that they would continue to dominate public education
and the fact is that well on into the final decades of that
century public schools continued to reflect the Protestant
ethic. Leo Pfeffer comments:[2]

> Catholic hostility to the public schools
> arose out of the bitter experiences that Cath-
> olic children suffered in them. When Jews
> began to come to this country in large numbers,
> the secularization of the schools had already
> been completed; when the Catholics first came
> in numbers it was just beginning. The transi-
> tion from a Protestant to a secular school
> system was a difficult one in the course of
> which there arose considerable tension and
> friction. Catholic children were the prin-
> cipal victims. For refusing to participate
> in Protestant religious exercises or the reading
> of the Protestant Bible, Catholic public
> school children frequently suffered cruel per-
> secution. They were often subjected to physi-

[1]Francis X. Curran, The Churches and the Schools
(Chicago: University of Loyola Press, 1954), p. 5.

[2]Leo Pfeffer, Creeds in Competition: A Creative Force
in American Culture (New York: Harper and Bros., 1958), p. 61.

cal punishment, expulsion, and other indig-
nities merely because they took seriously
the guaranty of religious freedom of which
the Protestants so proudly boasted. The
transition from Protestant to secular public
education, moreover, took place during a
period when anti-Catholic bigotry was strong
and extensive, when Nativism and Know-
Nothingism flourished over a large part of
the country.

As the Protestant solution was to surrender all control to the state and to function as a controlling agent
within, the Catholics in America chose the other alternative.
As a minority group[1] they did not have the hope of influence
within the public schools that Protestant leaders enter-
tained. As a minority group composed of diverse nationali-
ties and immigrant groups they had likewise within their
own ranks strong pressure groups who while not actively at
least passively resisted the commonizing movement.[2] In
choosing to designate Catholics as a minority group in the
nineteenth century struggle one must avoid the implication

---

[1]A detailed analysis of Catholics as a minority
group in the United States has been done by Thomas T. McAvoy
in a series of articles on the question. "The Catholic
Minority in the United States, 1789-1821," Historical Records
and Studies, XXXIX-XL (1952), pp. 33-50. "The Formation of
the Catholic Minority in the United States, 1820-1860," Review of Politics, X (January, 1948), pp. 13-34. "Bishop John
Lancaster Spalding and the Catholic Minority (1877-1908),"
Review of Politics, XII (January, 1950), pp. 3-19. "The
Anguish of the Catholic Minority," American Ecclesiastical
Review, CXXI (November, 1949), pp. 380-385. "The American
Catholic Minority in the Later Nineteenth Century," Review
of Politics, XV (July, 1953), pp. 275-302.

[2]The Cahensly movement was the ultimate conclusion
of the pressure of a nationalist group with the American
Church, to receive individual social recognition. Fortunately for the Catholic Church in America, the movement was
solved peacefully, largely through the efforts of James
Cardinal Gibbons and his pacific leadership.

that the group was a unified and coherent mass. Certainly
the American Catholic Church has presented a solid and formidable front in this country. Relatively untroubled by
dogmatic conflicts, the American Catholics were never called
upon to refute painful heretical moves. The Hogan Schism
passed without serious harm to unity and even the terrible
struggle over Americanism failed to divide the American
Catholics. Yet this is not the same as saying that the
American Catholic Church presented a unified front in
political, social and economic questions. Prominent Catholics
were found on either side of most of the significant debates
in the social and political sphere. The Catholic Church in
the second quarter of the nineteenth century had the difficult
task of shaping a Catholic cultural and religious entity from
its membership of Irish, French and German immigrants. Later
generations absorbed incoming central Europeans and the
Italians with much more ease. One of the strongest agencies
in the acculturation process was the Catholic school. Consequently, we have the two-fold framework for discussing the
Catholic school movement. The first is its scope as an outside agency in the commonizing of the public school; and the
second is its role as a unifying agent within the Catholic
Church itself in forming a single Church from among the
groups of faithful, all strongly national in character.

The fact that the various national groups were willing,
nay, even eager, to set up their own language schools was
both a blessing and a curse for Church schoolmen of this
period; a blessing, because without this strong natural in-
centive, Bishops would have had an impossible task in urging
separate schools; a curse, because by dividing the Catholic
body into nationalistic groups, this tendency slowed the
program of solidifying the immigrant bodies into an American Catholic group.

The central task of this study is to trace the suc-
cessive implementation by the Catholic hierarchy of these
Church schools. The tradition of education within the Church
had a long and a varied history; consequently, it is not
surprising that here in America priests and Bishops should
be intimately involved in the educational patterns of the
American Catholic Church. This study is an analysis of the
legislation which the hierarchy of that period promulgated
and enforced. During the period from the Revolution to the
end of the nineteenth century, the Bishops of the Catholic
Church held more or less regular meetings, in which all
gathered together to discuss the problems of Church order
and discipline. These councils roughly parallel the decades
during which the common school system was in the process of
formation and development. Accordingly, the legislation

enacted by these leaders sitting in council represents the
reaction of these men to public education as they saw it
and their means for remedying what they considered its de-
ficiencies. Viewed in sequential fashion, the legislation
of the Church fathers reflects the progress also of the
common school program. In the early years, the Church legislation was simply a development of the Church's traditional
concern for education; as the conflict between secular and
religious education became more pronounced, the hierarchy
spoke more and more in terms of a reaction to undesirable
elements in public education. If the nineteenth century
can be called the era of public education, it can with equal
propriety be called the century of decision for private education in this country. The difference between the present
crisis in private education and that of the previous century
is that in the earlier century private education had to establish its right to exist in the face of the strong movement for a common school; present-day private education is
fighting the economic battle in contrast to the ideological
battle of the previous stage. Private education has become
more and more aware of its own lack of resources; today,
therefore, we are witnessing attempts to reestablish many
of the relief measures attempted during the early period of
the development of the public system. The concept of shared
time, which is attracting much attention in our larger cities,

had its forerunner in the denominational programs.[1] The
following report indicates most drastically the economic
pressure under which private education is functioning:

> European observers of the American
> Catholic scene often look to the Midwest for
> signs of the future. In the important Arch-
> diocese of St. Louis what do they see? On
> order from Joseph Cardinal Ritter, Archbishop
> of St. Louis, plans for new parish schools
> have been "indefinitely postponed." The post-
> ponement will last until pastors can organize
> schools with 49 or fewer pupils in each class-
> room.
> Also, Cardinal Ritter ordered, there will
> be no new schools -- and no old ones will be ex-
> panded -- until a ratio of at least three nun
> (or brother) teachers to each lay teacher can
> be guaranteed.
> Behind Cardinal Ritter's decision lie
> these facts: the Catholic school population
> in St. Louis has increased 100 per cent in
> the last 15 years; the number of lay teachers
> has gone from 48 to 802; but the number of
> teaching sisters and brothers has remained al-
> most the same -- 1,958 today as compared with
> 1,770 in 1945.
> What, then, has the Cardinal decided to
> do? Children who cannot be enrolled in paro-
> chial schools will have a parish "school of
> religion," with qualified principal and
> teachers and an eight-grade system (with kin-
> dergarten to be added, if possible). These
> schools will have a modern curriculum in
> catechetics. They will be organized as part
> of the Confraternity of Christian Doctrine,
> but under the direction of the archdiocesean
> school office.
> The large-scale development of schools
> of religion in St. Louis could be a giant
> step in the direction of "shared-time."[2]

---

[1]For a general report of the success of a modern
shared-time experiment, cf. John G. Deedy, "Shared Time --
The Pittsburgh Area's Experiment," Ave Maria, vol. 97
(March 2, 1963), pp. 5-9.

[2]America, vol. 107 (September 16, 1962), p. 710.

In other areas a determined effort for state-supported
programs and other expedients have been offered as substitutes for the traditional pattern of total Catholic private
education. Programs of this nature suggest a willingness by
Church authorities to reassess the traditional values believed
to be involved in the parochial system of Catholic education.
Specifically, the question is being asked: are parochial
schools solving a problem, are they meeting the need for
which they were erected? Quite obviously, questions such
as these involve a huge complex of problems and issues. Basic, however, to any understanding of the issues involved
is a thorough appreciation of the historical development of
this system. Basic, moreover, to the system is the history
of the legislation of the Councils of Baltimore. More than
any other agency, these Episcopal meetings shaped and formed
the nineteenth century Catholic mind. Therefore the pronouncements of these councils on educational matters are of
supreme importance. Just as public education derived its
form from the thought of Horace Mann and his New England
co-workers, so Catholic educational programs were shaped by
the ideas of ecclesiastical leaders in council. The influence of men like John Hughes, Peter Kenrick, John Purcell
and John Lancaster Spalding was thus magnified and spread.

The work of the Councils of Baltimore has been touched
upon in many previous works. The basic facts of the meetings
have been gathered together in the volume compiled by Peter
Guilday and his church history seminar group at the Catholic
University of America.[1] This is the only work which contains a discussion of all the councils. The educational
phases of the provincial councils have been studied by Jerome
E. Diffley[2] in his dissertation directed by Bernard Kohlbrenner of Notre Dame. This work concentrates on the factors
which forced the Catholic hierarchy in America to decide upon
a separate, privately-supported system as the only alternative to the common school system as they knew it. His chief
point is that the council of 1840 was crucial in the development of the parochial system. Little mention is made of the
legislation of the three plenary councils, which are outside
the time scope of his study. He includes a thorough and
masterful study of the Protestant nature of public education
during this period and of the prevailing philosophies of
education. In view of some of the information contained
in the present study it is felt that Diffley antedates the
formal policy of Catholic education somewhat. In assigning

[1] Peter K. Guilday, A History of the Councils of
Baltimore (New York; Macmillan, 1932).

[2] Jerome E. Diffley, "Catholic Reaction to American
Public Education, 1792-1852" (Unpublished Ph.D. dissertation, Dept. of Education, University of Notre Dame, 1959).

the rank of importance to the council of 1840, he seems to be interpreting the acts of this council in the light of later development. As he aptly demonstrates, however, the Catholic system was well under way by this time, but it is my conclusion that further subsequent developments of common school education were of prime importance in shaping later Catholic thinking. These pertinent developments in public education were not yet completed by the period in question and, consequently, the Catholic reaction was not complete. The constant repetition of the Church legislation itself is a factor indicative of the conflict which raged in the minds of the authors of these edicts. It is almost an axiom that constant and repeated decrees usually reflect the ineffectiveness of previous decisions in remedying abuses.

William Kailer Dunn has written his dissertation on the decline of religious education in the schools, under the direction of John Walton and Beulah Tatum at Johns Hopkins.[1] Dunn, with admirable research techniques, has uncovered many heretofore unnoticed pamphlets and articles. Like Diffley, he terminates his study with the work of the First Plenary Council. His study originates from the following quotation from the history of education by Brubacher:

---

[1]William K. Dunn, "The Decline of the Teaching of Religion in the American Public Elementary School in the States Originally the Thirteen Colonies, 1776-1861" (Unpublished Ph.D. dissertation, Dept. of Education, Johns Hopkins University, 1956). A slightly abridged form of the thesis was published: What Happened to Religious Education (Baltimore: The Johns Hopkins Press, 1958).

The educational counterpart of the
political divorce of church and state was
the exclusion of religion from the public
school curriculum. This secularization of
public education did not occur immediately
following the divorce of church and state,
nor did it take the same course in each of
the states. . . .[1]

As a conclusion to his own study, Dunn lists, among others,

the following points:

1. Christian doctrinal religious instruction
was a basic and integral part of the elementary
school curriculum during the colonial period
of American history. This was an inheritance
from the Old World tradition. Religion,
the colonists believed, belonged in life, and,
accordingly, it belonged in education which
was a preparation for life both here and hereafter. . . .
5. Under the leadership of Harace Mann,
Massachusetts vigorously applied the 1827
anti-sectarian textbook law, extending the
letter of the law to prohibit teaching by any
method the sectarian tenets of any religious
group. Mann's policy, avowedly a program to
keep religion in but to keep sectarianism out,
met bitter and prolonged opposition, but eventually triumphed and became the accepted Massachusetts practice. The resulting phenomenon
in the elementary school curriculum was a program which urged the imparting of ethical instruction and such "basic Christianity" as
might be gleaned from the reading of the Bible
to the pupils, a program which was not unlike
the sectarian position of Harace Mann as a
member of the Unitarian Church, and seems to
have been an epitome of the Secretary's own
religious creed. . . .
7. By the outbreak of the Civil War
(1861), the elementary public schools of these
thirteen states and the District of Columbia
had abandoned almost entirely the inculcation
of Christian doctrinal teachings. They continued to give some moral instruction and, in

---

[1]John S. Brubacher, A History of the Problems of
Education (New York: McGraw Hill Book Co., 1947), p. 334.
Dunn, What Happened to Religious Education, p. 10.

many elementary schools, continued to read the
Bible to the students or have it read by them,
as a part of the opening exercises of each day.

8. Church groups did not acquiesce completely, nor did they give up the effort to have
their children taught the doctrines of their
faiths as a part of the daily curriculum. Several Protestant Churches made ineffectual attempts to create lasting schools of their own.
Catholics tried here and there to have the use
of the Douay version allowed for their children.
The main answer of the Catholic Bishops, however,
was a decision to expand their parochial school
system and make it stick. Bishop Hughes' effort
to get public financial support failed, but he
and his fellow Bishops stayed at the task, and
at the outbreak of the Civil War were witnessing the gradual unfolding of the Catholic school
system as a lasting phenomenon in American
life.[1]

As a consequence of his own investigation Dunn takes

Brubacher to task for his interpretation of the exclusion

of religion from the schools:

> In the light of its thesis, this study,
> then, must take issue with those historians of
> education who speak as does Dr. Brubacher:
> "The educational counterpart of the political
> divorce of church and state was the exclusion
> of religion from the public school curriculum."
> As we interpret this statement, it means that
> there was an absolute Church-State separation,
> a "divorce," and it was followed by a "divorce"
> or a purposeful expulsion of religious teaching,
> as such, from the public school. It has been
> the deduction of this study that there was no
> intentional expulsion of religious teaching
> as such from the public schools, at least in
> the area and time-span examined.[2]

---

[1]Dunn, What Happened to Religious Education, pp.
304-306.

[2]Dunn, What Happened to Religious Education, p. 309.

A third closely related study was done by Sr. M.
Laurina Kaiser at the Catholic University of America.[1] Sr.
M. Laurina parallels in many cases the steps taken in this
study. However, the emphasis in her work is on printed
documents and materials, whereas this study focuses its
attention on the conciliar decrees and related materials,
with scarcely no emphasis on related synodal and conciliar
legislation. Sr. Laurina studied the development of the
parish school from earliest times to the present. The legislation of Baltimore is told in brief fashion and only
insofar as it contributed to the formation of the parish
school.

The primary materials used in this study have been
gathered in large part from the eastern archives, especially
that of Baltimore itself, where the remaining papers of the
meetings are preserved. Since Baltimore was the first diocese to be created in the United States and served as the
only archdiocese until the creation of Oregon in 1847, it
is natural that these archives should contain many important
papers. Likewise, because of its primacy in the American
Church and its designation as the site of the subsequent
plenary councils, the Baltimore archives remain the most
important in the American Catholic Church. Other letters

---

[1]Sr. M. Laurina Kaiser, The Development of the Concept and Function of the Catholic Elementary School in the
American Parish (Washington: Catholic University of America Press, 1955).

and reports were consulted at the archives of the Catholic
University of America; Georgetown; St. Mary's Seminary, Roland Park; St. Joseph's College, Emittsburg; St. Mary's Seminary, Emittsburg; St. Charles Seminary, Overbrook; and
Notre Dame University.

The historical significance of this problem is immediately evident. The critical worsening of the Church-State
problem pursuant to the Engels decision has caused a flurry
of attacks and counter-charges. This study hopes, in some
small measure, to contribute to the critical reappraisal of
the Catholic position in the present day school issue.
By a surveillance of the forces and factors which brought
about its development, one can be led to an understanding
of the tenacity with which Catholics defend their private
system. Secondly, it is a secondary intention of this study
to demonstrate that the Catholic parochial system was a planned
response to a critical challenge. As a response, therefore,
it admits of change and alteration if it can be demonstrated
that the forces which elicited the original response are
no longer active and influential. Studies of this sort may
well lead the way to a third alternative in the above mentioned either-or solution to the problem of the role of religion in the school. Finally, it seems to me to be of major
importance to gather into one volume the many decisions re-

garding education which were enacted by the Councils of Baltimore.   Important as they are in the study of Catholic education, they are available to readers only in the abbre-
viated study of Sr. M. Laurina.   True, they are found in
their untranslated sources, but their importance merits better
availability.   By presenting these decrees in sequential
fashion, the author hopes that more attention will be given
to the definitive role these councils played in the development of American Catholic education.

Chapter II

The General Background

In seeking to explain the presence of a well-organized
system of private education, differing from the public program only in the matter of religious education of its members
one can rather generally arrange the arguments under three
headings.[1] The most common explanation is that these schools
are simply the outgrowth of the traditional interest of the
Church in Christian education. Thus, the argument proceeds
from the early origin of parish and chantry schools and traces
the development of these schools through the universities
and into the sphere of more widespread popular education.
Underlying the reasoning is the basic interest which Christianity has always shown for the education of its members.
The explanation may be further developed and extended by
more immediate application. Power, for example, in his analysis of Catholic higher education, discusses the difference in origin between boys' schools and girls' schools.
Schools for boys originated at the higher levels of education and gradually extended their training downward; whereas
the training of girls began at the bottom level and traced

---

[1]The presentation of these three groupings is given
in the article: Sr. M. Carolyn Klinkhamer, "Historical Reason for Inception of Parochial School System," Catholic
Educational Review, LII (February, 1954), 73-94.

upward.[1] Perhaps implicit in the argument is the fact that
boys were trained in schools in large measure staffed by
priests who had the training of boys for the priesthood always as an end in view; girls on the other hand were trained
by religious women, who oftentimes turned to teaching as their
most logical means of support. By training they were ill-
equipped to offer more than an elementary training, while
the priests had been prepared by their course of studies in
the seminary training program to offer instruction of a higher level. Certainly this explanation of the parochial school
system is a truly coherent and convincing argument. The general concept that schools were religious in origin has never
been seriously challenged. Even the most ardent advocates
of public schools pay homage to the great work done by the
representatives of Christianity in preparing the way for
universal education and the era of public schools. Dr. Henry
Browne has rightly assessed the role of religion in early
American society:

> It was of the nature of religious
> groups in American society that they should
> remain in a certain kind of isolation from
> one another. The process of growth of Catho-
> lic parochial education was a clear example.
> At first, it was the churches and not the
> common school societies that gathered to-
> gether the children of the cities for the
> purposes of education. By mid-century,
> however, it had become increasingly diffi-

---

[1]Edward J. Power, A History of Catholic Higher Education in the United States (Milwaukee: Bruce, 1958), pp.
33-39.

cult to maintain church schools because state
funds in aid of this work were going only to
public schools.[1]

If one were to follow this line of thought to its conclusion,
then the concept of parochial as opposed to public education
is peculiarly inappropriate because these schools in attempting to educate all their constituents were truly public and
common. The early debates over state support for religious
schools always bore the strong stamp of the public nature of
the work which the religious schools were doing.[2]

From this short survey, we can see that the explanation as expressed above of the origin and rise of parochial
schools is a true one but it does not offer the needed fuller
explanation of the unique nature of the parochial system in
America where all parishes are commanded by ecclesiastical
law to build and support parish schools.

A second hypothesis suggested by Klinkhamer[3] sees
in the various religious communities which sprang up in the
United States the impetus for the establishment of schools.

---

[1]Henry J. Browne, "Catholicism in the United States,"
The Shaping of American Religion, Vol. I of Religion in American
Life, eds. James Ward Smith and A. Leland Jamison (Princeton:
Princeton University Press, 1961), pp. 85-86. Cf. also: Henry
J. Browne, "Public Support of Catholic Education in New York,
1825-1842: Some New Aspects," Catholic Historical Review, XXXIX
(April, 1953), p. 1.

[2]Bernard J. Kohlbrenner, "The Controversy over Public
Support to Parochial Schools," Religion, Government and Educa-
tion, eds. William Brickman and Stanley Lehrer (New York:
Society for the Advancement of Education, 1961), pp. 65-66.

[3]Klinkhamer, Catholic Educational Review, LII, p. 74.

This is a more pertinent suggestion than appears at first
glance. We have already alluded to the general pattern of
development for male and female institutions. The presence
of religious orders within the ranks of the Catholic Church
may well have been an impelling factor in the decision to
establish a parochial system. Faced with the question of
the implementation of their decisions, the Bishops could see
in the ranks of the sister religious the practical solution
to their need. Protestant Churches, faced with the same
decision, had no religious orders, no teaching brothers and
sisters; and, hence, no real alternative to a system of public
education. In addition to the practical help offered to the
hierarchy in the fulfillment of the decrees of the councils,
religious orders were a stimulus to education in that they
were willing and eager to found and finance their own schools.
Each community had its own purposes and traditions and they
were eager to apply their particular skills and methods in
their own institutions.[1] This hypothesis, however, while
accounting for many of the early educational ventures of the
Catholic Church in this country, fails to make the necessary
distinction between the general pattern of Christian education and the specific program of parochial education as

---

[1]As an example, cf. the study of the development of
the first American community: Annabelle Melville, Elizabeth
Bayley Seton, 1774-1821 (New York: Charles Scribner's Sons,
1951).

found chiefly in this country. Certainly both the factors mentioned above played a significant role but the complete solution goes deeper into the fabric of the American educational scene. Perhaps it might be accurate to say that had American public education developed along different lines, there might never have been the system of parochial education as we know it today. Stated briefly, then, the hypothesis is simply that peculiar pressures and forces resulting from the emergence of the American common school forced a full-blown system of private education upon the Catholic American scene. Since the Church is organized with the parish as the basic unit of worship, it was natural that the parish should become the unit of education also. It was the very commonness of the public school which put it and many of its principles in direct conflict with the philosophy and tradition of the Catholic Church.[1] Perhaps also much of the distrust of contemporary Catholics of the public schools lies in previous experience. American Catholics had little reason to expect a fair hearing in the early public schools, controlled as they were by Protestant influences. The early bias of Horace Mann against papists was well known and he did not hesitate to underscore his contempt for the Catholic religion. During his trip to Europe in 1843, Mann was brought into first hand

---

[1]Cf. Lawrence A. Cremin, The American Common School: An Historic Conception (New York: Bureau of Publications, Columbia Teachers College, 1951).

contact with many Catholic institutions and he kept his re-
collections in a special diary. He wrote regarding his visit
to Brussels:

> Here I see many Catholics worshipping
> in the churches; and everything which I have
> seen of them, here and elsewhere, impresses
> me more and more deeply with the baneful in-
> fluence of the Catholic religion upon the
> human mind.[1]

More influential upon the thinking of the members of
hierarchy were the traditions of the colonial period, carried
over into the young republic. The genesis of religious
prejudice and controversy is discussed by Sr. M. Augustine
Ray in the following terms:

> The sixteenth century notion of contro-
> versy, whatever the subject was summed up in
> the maxim, "Know your enemy in the wrong."
> Convinced of their own rectitude, the Protes-
> tant Reformers adopted the slogan, and aided
> in no small measure by political events, domes-
> tic and foreign, built up a conception of
> "Popery" as a composite monster reaching out
> its tentacles to draw all good Protestants to
> destruction. This travesty of Roman Catholi-
> cism was brought to America by the early im-
> migrants as part of their intellectual and re-
> ligious equipment. Its vitality was insured
> by new-world conditions; by the dominant in-
> fluence for several generations of a clergy
> almost uniformly hostile to the Church of Rome;
> by an educational system, equally antagonistic,
> from which Catholics were excluded except at
> the price of apostasy; by a press which catered
> to political, social and religious antipa-
> thies; by colonial governments which, with
> few exceptions, would exclude the Catholic
> from the province or penalize him after he
> had entered; by non-English immigration with

---

[1] Horace Mann, *European Journal*, Sept. 12, 1843,
quoted in McCloskey, *Public Schools and Moral Education*,
pp. 48-49.

a European experience that had been for the
most part an education in intolerance.
　　To these factors were added two that were
peculiarly American. There were generations
of colonists who had no contact whatever with
a Catholic in the flesh. Naturalization and
immigration laws, land regulations, penal
statutes had seen to that. There was no
opportunity therefore for the amenities of
social relationships to soften the harsh
outlines of their mental picture. Where contact did exist, as in Maryland, Virginia, in
early New York, or on the Indian frontier,
relationships were so complicated by political,
economic or international rivalry that religious
partisanship was strengthened rather than
weakened. Religion was the scapegoat which
bore the onus of many a selfish or sordid
policy that could not bear the light. This
applies especially to the Indian question
whether on the northern, western or southern
frontiers.[1]

When one views the question of the Catholic paro-

chial system in the framework of its historical development,

some of the situations which today seem inexplicable become

more understandable. Thus we no longer expect to see a

tremendous difference between the common school and its rival

parochial system. Both were designed to fulfill the same

function; both offer a similar remedy for ignorance, the

only difference being that parochial education insists upon

the inclusion of religious elements in this program of en-

lightenment. Both borrowed from a common ancestry and both

used identical methods and techniques. Perhaps in point of

fact the major difference between them in the nineteenth and

in the twentieth century is the method of support. For some

_____

[1]Sr. Mary A. Ray, American Opinion of Roman Catholicism in the Eighteenth Century (New York: Columbia University
Press, 1936), pp. 394-395.

portion of the earlier century at least, Church schools received support from the state, whereas in the present situation, state support is scrupulously avoided. This final hypothesis as to the origin of parochial schools has the flexibility needed to explain why many early prelates of the Catholic Church were enthusiastic supporters of the common schools.[1] Roughly, therefore, up to the point of the vigorous debates in the forties, there seems to be justification for viewing the simple desire to eliminate ignorance as the main drive in all educational ventures, Protestant, Catholic or civil. It is not denied that religious groups recognized the proselytizing value of the classroom. The Society for the Propagation of the Gospel in Foreign Parts is ample proof of this. Yet it cannot be denied that the bitterness of sectarian dispute arose only later. When immigration led nativist parties to the highly volatile propaganda of their sect, all groups concerned oftentimes forgot that the major purpose of education was the eliminating of ignorance and concentrated almost entirely upon its propagandist value. The question as posed in these formative years of the public schools was a basic one: should schools be conducted in such a way that all students, regardless of the creed professed by them or by their parents, be given some religious instruction? Or should the schools be charged with the responsi-

---

[1]Edward Connaughton, A History of Educational Legislation and Administration in the Archdiocese of Cincinnati (Washington: Catholic University of America Press, 1946), passim.

bility of secular education alone, leaving the total sphere
of religious education to the Church? Although these issues
became clearly defined by the controversies of Bishop Hughes,
Father John Bapst, the Blaine amendment, and others, the
implications of the various positions were not so clearly
understood in the earlier decades. Catholics, in general,
at the end of the Revolution had no precedent to guide them
in the matter of schools. Throughout the colonial period
Catholics had been forbidden to maintain their own schools
and they entered the national period without a single major
educational institution.[1] Moreover, because many of the
Catholics were poor immigrants, there was almost no tradition of education among them. The educated Catholics had
received their training abroad at great expense but these
represented a small, if highly influential, portion of Catholics. Their lack of education, however, was not unusual.
In studying the development of the Catholic minority Thomas
T. McAvoy points out that during the pre-immigration period
the cultural and social position of English-speaking Catholics
was higher than it has ever been since. Because the Catholic
body achieved national importance only during the middle
period of the nineteenth century, Catholicism has been identified with the foreign element which at that time made up
a large portion of its membership. In point of fact, since

[1]John Tracy Ellis, American Catholicism (Chicago:
University of Chicago Press, 1956), pp. 52-53.

1636, there was always an English Catholic minority. They
were never numerous, 30,000 being the most generally accepted
estimate in 1790, but their position on the American scene
was secure. As McAvoy continued: ". . . they were accepted
as fully American, even though their faith was not fully approved."[1] We may continue the story by demonstrating that
all cultural ideas in America are compounded of two elements,
the European tradition brought by the immigrant and the effects of the American frontier -- in the broad sense of that
term -- upon the immigrant. Catholic culture was no exception
to the process but the Catholic minority differs from the
Protestant majority in that the Catholic immigrants have
been overwhelmingly non-English. American Catholic culture
has undergone a series of rises and declines under the effect
of the huge influx of non-English immigration and has not
solved the problems of its later immigrant groups even
at the present time. Yet the essential characteristics
of American Catholic culture were determined by the generation
of Catholics in America during the great immigration from
1830 to the Civil War. Unwittingly, perhaps, the nativistic
and anti-Catholic reaction of the 40's and 50's furnished
the hammer and anvil by which such diverse elements as Polish,
Irish and German Americans were welded into a solid unified
Church which was able to withstand these same attacks.[2]

---

[1]McAvoy, Review of Politics, X, p. 15.

[2]McAvoy, Review of Politics, X, pp. 13-14.

Just as there was a difference in the physical body
of Catholics before and after the immigration period, so too
there was a difference in their educational activity. Before the period of intensive immigration and the simultaneous
public school movement, the educational processes of the
Catholic and Protestant Churches moved hand in hand. There
was no need for one to compete with the other because there
never were enough of these facilities to meet the demand.
When education become more universal, competition also became prevalent and Catholics, Protestants and public school
people began to compete for the same minds.

As already mentioned, early Catholic education was
extremely limited in the colonial period because of the pro-
scription against Catholics. Only one instance is known of
state aid to Catholic education before 1800 and that was
given to a Catholic priest, Juniper Berthiaume, by the State
of Massachusetts to support his efforts at educating the
Indians.[1] John Carroll, who was appointed Vicar-Apostolic
of the Church in the United States June 9, 1774 and Bishop
by the Bull Ex Hac Apostolicae on November 6, 1789, had himself left the American colonies in his early youth in order
to obtain a Catholic education abroad at the famous Jesuit
school, St. Omer's in Flanders. Here he was deeply imbued

[1]Richard J. Gabel, Public Funds for Church and Private
Schools (Washington: Catholic University of America Press,
1937), p. 189.

with the spirit and temper of a continental education and
it was not in the least surprising that as Bishop his thoughts
often turned to Catholic education in his own vast diocese.[1]
Carroll had many difficulties to face in establishing his
administration on a sound basis in this country, and he
could not devote the energy to education that he would have
desired. The prospect of freedom in the United States had
attracted clergy from abroad who were eager to leave their
local episcopal problems and have their say in the new country. As Catholic hierarchies were different in the various
countries as to their manner of government it was to be expected that each of these groups of immigrant clergy should
insist upon the type of control to which they were used in
their old country. It was only with the utmost diligence
and care that Carroll was able to hold a semblance of balance and unity among his clergy.[2] Carroll at once recognized
that his only hope for a strong and solid Church was to establish a native clergy. For a native clergy he needed educational institutions in which to train them. Here then is
the hub around which Carroll's interest in education constantly

---

[1]Mother Peter Carthy, English Influences on Early
American Catholicism (Washington: Catholic University of
America Press, 1959), pp. 61-64.

[2]Cf. the series of articles: John Tracy Ellis,
"Catholics in Colonial America," American Ecclesiastical Review, 136 (January-May, 1957), pp. 11-27, 100-119, 184-196,
265-274, 304-321.

revolved. During his own life he seems to have originally
had great hope in working harmoniously with the existing
public institutions. Early in his career he had been cheered
by a heartwarming response to his address to Pres. George
Washington. Speaking in the name of the American Catholics,
he testified to the joy and unbounded confidence that American Catholics had in his election to lead the new nation.
Washington, in turn, responded with a letter of generous
thanks and pledged his efforts at aiding Catholics to gain
their rightful part in the Republic.[1] Five years earlier,
Father Carroll had written to the officers of the Propaganda,
which directed missionary activity throughout the world:

> There is a college in Philadelphia, and
> it is proposed to establish two in Maryland,
> in which Catholics can be admitted, as well
> as others, as presidents, professors, and
> pupils. We hope that some educated there
> will embrace the ecclesiastical state. We
> think accordingly of establishing a seminary,
> in which they can be trained to the life
> and learning suited to that state.[2]

Not only was Carroll enthusiastic about the prospects
of this college, but he even wrote his friend, Fr. Charles
Plowden, concerning the possibility of Plowden's sending
him a few young men who would seek posts as professors in
the colleges of Pennsylvania and Maryland. He recognized
the danger inherent in these mixed schools but he asked

---

[1]Both letters are reprinted in Peter K. Guilday,
The Life and Times of John Carroll (Westminster, Maryland:
The Newman Press, reprint, 1954), pp. 365-366.

[2]John Gilmary Shea, History of the Catholic Church
in the United States (New York: John G. Shea, 1888) Vol. II,
p. 260.

somewhat plaintively: "Are we able to do anything better?"[1]
Carroll obviously was thinking of these schools as the training grounds for his future ecclesiastics. In his own seminary they could receive the further training required. By
the next year, though, Carroll had thought better of the
whole scheme and confided to Plowden again that only the
establishment of a college and subsequently a seminary could
solve the question of ecclesiastical training.[2] His plan
eventually flowered and Georgetown University became the
first Catholic college in the United States. In addition,
Carroll continued to give Georgetown generous physical and
moral support during the first tenuous years of its existence.

During the five years that Carroll had served as
Vicar-Apostolic (1784-1789) he had studied the American scene
and was well-equipped to handle his episcopal authority.
Once consecrated Bishop, one of his earliest acts was to
convoke a national synod of the priests in America. Primary
among the reasons for convoking the synod was the establishment of the American Church upon a firm foundation. During
the war years America had been under the jurisdiction of
the aged Bishop Challoner of London. Both because of dis-

[1]Carroll to (N. N.), December, 1784, Georgetown
University Archives, Shea Transcripts.

[2]The saga of Georgetown is retold in: John M. Daley,
Georgetown University: Origin and Early Years (Washington:
Georgetown University Press, 1957). Cf. especially pp. 30-
34.

tance and of the political implications, Challoner did little
in regard to the direction of the Catholic Church in America.
Carroll himself did not consider his position as Vicar-Apostolic
strong enough to carry the burden of a national meeting.
When Carroll began to notice that French ecclesiastics were
eager to take over control or at least to influence the American Church, he was pushed into action. Guilday lists among
the reasons for convoking this synod the uniformity of Church
discipline throughout the United States and the establishment of stronger bonds with the Holy See.[1] The Roman authorities always had a fear that the American Church was striving
for too much independence and thus the efforts of Carroll
to reassure the Holy Father of the love and obedience of his
American subjects were most important.

The official letter of convocation was sent out on
October 27, 1791. It was a simple letter and in it Carroll
dwelt especially upon the mode of preserving the succession
of the episcopacy.[2] The meeting itself was held November
7 - 10th. On the final day twenty-four decrees were passed,
none of which concerned the question of education or schools.
In addition to the Bishop, twenty priests were present for

---

[1] Guilday, Councils, p. 64.

[2] John Carroll Brent, Biographical Sketch of the Most
Reverend John Carroll (Baltimore: John Murphy and Associates,
1843), pp. 153-154.

the opening sessions and two more arrived later.[1] The approval of the decrees by Roman authorities was given the next year. According to Guilday, the _Acta_ were submitted for approval shortly after the Synod and in April of 1792, Carroll submitted a supplementary report. These were discussed by Propaganda in August, 1792, and Cardinal Antonelli gave final approval pursuant to several changes in the Acta.[2]

If the Synod of 1791 had included only the Acta its significance for American Catholic education would be extremely limited since none of the decrees dealt with education and no minutes are extant to show that the topic of education had been discussed. Fortunately, after the conclusion of the synod, Bishop Carroll began work immediately on a pastoral letter by which the work of the synod was announced to the laity. The letter was published on May 28, 1792 and a large portion of this letter deals with the subject of education. In this letter the Bishop points to the necessity of a Christian education in no uncertain terms. He announced that he considered the virtuous and Christian education of youth as a principal object of pastoral solicitude.

---

[1] Guilday, _Carroll_, pp. 443-446. Cf. also Annabelle Melville, _John Carroll of Baltimore: Founder of the American Catholic Hierarchy_ (New York: Charles Scribner's Sons, 1955).

[2] Guilday, _Carroll_, pp. 443-446.

Knowing, therefore, that the principles
instilled in the course of a Christian education, are generally preserved through life,
and that a young man according to his way,
even when he is old, he will not depart from
it (Prov. xxii. 6), I have considered the
virtuous and Christian instruction of youth
as a principal object of pastoral solicitude.
Now who can contribute so much to lighten
this burthen, which weighs so heavy on the
shoulders of the pastors of souls and who
can have so great an interest and special
duty in the forming of youthful minds to
habits of virtue and religion, as their parents themselves? Especially while their
children retain their native docility, and
their hearts are uncorrupted by vice. How
many motives of reason and religion require,
that parents should be unwearied in their
endeavors, to inspire in them the love and
fear of God; docility and submission to His
doctrines, and a careful attention to fulfill
His commandments? Fathers -- bring up your
children in the discipline and correction of
the Lord (Ephes. vi. 4). If all, to whom God
has given sons and daughters, were assiduous
in the discharge of this important obligation,
a foundation would be laid for, and great progress made in, the work of establishing a prevailing purity of manners. The same habits of
obedience to the will of God; the same principles of a reverential love and fear of Him;
and of continual respect for His Holy Name;
the same practices of morning and evening
prayer; and of the frequentation of the sacraments; the same dread of cursing and swearing;
of fraud and duplicity; of lewdness and drunk-
enness; the same respectful and dutiful behaviour
to their fathers and mothers; in a word, the
remembrance and influence of the parental
counsels and examples received in their youth,
would continue with them during life. And if
ever the fraility of nature, or worldly seduction, should cause them to offend God,
they would be brought back again to His service and to true repentance by the efficacy
of the religious instruction received in
their early age. Wherefore, fathers and mothers,
be mindful of the words of the Apostles,

and bring up your children in the discipline
and correction of the Lord. In doing this,
you not only render an acceptable service to
God, and acquit yourselves of a most important duty, but you labour for the preservation
and increase of true religion, for the benefit
of our common country, whose welfare depends
on the morals of its citizens, and for your
own happiness here as well as hereafter; since
you may be assured of finding, in those sons
and daughters whom you shall train up to virtue and piety, by your instructions and examples, support and consolation in sickness
and old age. They will remember with gratitude, and repay with religious duty, your
solicitude for them in their infancy and youth.
    These being the advantages of a religious
education, I was solicitous for the attainment
of a blessing so desirable to that precious
portion of my flock, the growing generation.
A school has been instituted at George-Town,
which will continue to be under the superintendence and government of some of my reverend
brethren, that is, of men devoted by principle
and profession to instruct all, who resort to
them, in useful learning, and those of our own religion, in its principles and duties. I earnestly wish, dear brethren, that as many of
you, as are able, would send your sons to this
school of letters and virtue. I know and
lament, that the expense will be too great for
many families, and that their children must
be deprived of the immediate benefit of this
institution; but, indirectly, they will receive it; at least, it may be reasonably
expected, that some after being educated at
George-Town, and having returned into their
own neighborhood, will become, in their turn,
the instructors of the youths who cannot be
sent from home; and, by pursuing the same
system of uniting much attention to religion,
with a solicitude for other improvements,
the general result will be a great increase
of piety, the necessary consequence of a
careful instruction in the principles of faith,
and Christian morality.
    The school, dear brethren, if aided by
your benevolence, and favoured with your
confidence, will be the foundation of an addi-

tional advantage to true religion in this our
country. Many amongst us you have experienced inconvenience and disadvantage from
the want of spiritual assistance in your
greatest necessities, in sickness, in trou-
bles of conscience, and counsels and offices of the ministers of religion. It is
notorious to you all, that the present clergymen are insufficient for the exigencies of
the faithful; and that they will be more and
more so, as the population of our country
increases so rapidly; unless, by the providence of our good and merciful God, a constant
supply of zealous and able pastors can be
formed amongst ourselves; that is, of men accustomed to our climate, and acquainted with
the tempers, manners, and government of the
people, to whom they are to dispense the
ministry of salvation. Now, may we not reasonably hope, that one of the effects of a
virtuous course of education will be the preparing of the minds of some, whom providence
may select, to receive and cherish a call
from God to an ecclesiastical state?[1]

A simple analysis of this portion of the Pastoral
reveals that Carroll was concerned immediately and directly
with the preservation of the faith and the sanctification
of souls. His solicitude for the increase of the clergy
is also apparent. To view this instruction as an appeal
for a Catholic system of education, however, seems to go
beyond the text. The general terms of the exhortation indicate that Carroll meant this portion of the Pastoral as
a reinforcement of the traditional care that parents in all
ages and generations have exercised over their children.
The appeal for support for Georgetown may be rightly viewed

---

[1] Peter Guilday (ed.), The National Pastorals of the
American Hierarchy, 1792-1919 (Washington, D. C.: National
Catholic Welfare Council, 1929), pp. 3-5.

as springing from Carroll's intense hope that this institution would function as a training institution for his sem-
inarians. The following summary of the educational efforts
of the first Bishop of the Catholic Church in the United
States has been given by Power:

> . . . the Prefect finally arrived at the con-
> clusion that nonsectarian lower schools were
> not satisfactory and he expanded the plan he
> was then formulating to include Catholic
> education for those who were not preparing
> for the priesthood as well as for those who
> were. In his first evaluation of the lower
> schools of the country Carroll saw neither
> prejudice nor hostility to Catholicism, but
> a closer examination of the actual condi-
> tions required him to alter his stand, for
> he found them to be militantly anti-Catholic
> in their books, teaching and general attitude.[1]

This interpretation of the work of John Carroll has
been rightly challenged by Diffley who claims that inser-
tion of the "non-sectarian" emphasis is far in advance of
the actual dispute over sectarianism which came with the
Dedham Act of 1827. Diffley maintains that Carroll almost
certainly had no intention of a parochial or separate school
program.[2] Had he, in fact, such an intention he had but
to look to the woes of Georgetown to convince him that there
was little hope of fulfillment in the immediate future.

During the years that followed the Synod of 1791
the Catholic Church in America gradually began to take on
many of the characteristics of the new republic in which it

---

[1]Power, Catholic Higher Education, p. 39.

[2]Diffley, American Catholic Reaction, p. 229.

thrived. By extraordinary privilege the American clergy
had been allowed to choose by election their first Bishop,
a concession by the Roman authorities to the touchiness of
Protestant Americans on the danger of foreign influence.
Likewise crucial to the new Church was the problem of the
management of the temporal affairs of the Church. In American law the Church was not recognized as such and while this
fact freed the members of the hierarchy from political inter-
ference, it also complicated the means of registering Church
deeds. Since buildings were being built largely through the
energies of congregations, it was but natural that the congregations should demand an element of control over the Church.
Carroll, beseiged with problems and hampered by the lack of
an adequate clergy, was content to let these laymen participate more fully in the incorporation and management processes of the Churches than was normally desired or tolerated.
The most bitter conflicts of the American Church were waged
in the next fifty years over this issue of lay control.
Bitter, however, as this struggle was, an element of good
was found in the system in that it allowed the parish members to become more aware of their unity as a parish and
forced them to act as a corporation. When the parish was
later chosen as the school unit, the people were ready to
act in unison in the face of a common cause.

Baltimore remained the sole ecclesiastical province
in the United States until the year 1808. The Pontifical
Briefs making Baltimore a metropolitan see with the four
suffragan sees of Boston, New York, Philadelphia and Bardstown, were issued by Pope Pius VII on April 8, 1808. They
were entrusted to Bishop Concanen but were delayed in transmission because the newly-designated Bishop of Philadelphia
was caught in Italy by the Napoleonic embargo upon American
ships in Italian harbors. The Bulls finally reached the
United States in 1810 through Flaget, bishop-elect of Bardstown, who had gone to Paris in order to plead his case for
release from the onus. The three designates already in
America were quickly consecrated; Egan of Philadelphia on
October 28; Cheverus of Boston on November 1; and Flaget,
on November 4. During the next two weeks the three newly
consecrated Bishops conferred together with Carroll and his
co-adjutor, Leonard Neale, on the state of Church affairs.
These conferences have come to be designated as the Meeting
of the American Hierarchy in 1810. Little of their deliberations has come down to us but the series of resolutions
which they passed are illustrative of the probable nature
of their discourses. Although the points discussed seem
in some cases to be trivial, there is no mention of educational matters and problems; hence it seems safe to conclude
that at least during this period education was not viewed

as an outstanding problem. Towering over all other concerns
were the scarcity of priests and the lack of material resources.[1] The pinch of economic necessity may be gathered
from the bitterness of the disputes between the restored
Jesuits and the metropolitan of Baltimore regarding the
disposition of Jesuit properties and the emoluments due to
the Bishop from these properties. In spite of the meagre
resources, however, Bishop Carroll and his coworkers strove
mightily to advance the Church on all fronts. Of prime
importance in the story of the educational movement was the
foundation of the Sisters of Charity by Elizabeth Bayley Seton.[2] The impetus which these early religious orders gave
to the cause of Catholic education can hardly be over-
estimated.

---

[1]J. A. Baisnee, "The Catholic Church in the United
States," Records of the American Catholic Historical Society
of Philadelphia, LVI (September, 1945; December, 1945), pp.
134-162; 254-292.

[2]The story of the work of Mrs. Seton has been told
many times. The most authentic is probably that done by
Annabelle Melville. This remarkable woman has written a
trilogy on the lives of the three great figures in early
American Catholicism, John Carroll, Mrs. Seton, and Cheverus of Botson. Jean Le Febvre de Cheverus, 1768-1836
(Milwaukee: Bruce, 1958).

Chapter III
Early Provincial Councils

While it is true that the affairs of the Catholic Church moved slowly during the first two decades of the nineteenth century, the third ten year period saw much progress. Catholic education had begun to take a firm root. In Cincinnati Bishop Edward Fenwick was eager and able to establish solid educational foundations.[1] Bishop's Flaget's communication with Propaganda in 1820 has been widely reported and in it he was urged by them to establish schools for children, and to place them under the supervision of clergymen.[2]

More significant perhaps than any movements within the Church itself were the changes taking place in American society in general. During the previous years the Catholic minority had been left quite in peace because no one saw in them any threat to themselves or to American institutions. Probably the onrush of immigration following the Napoleonic Wars was the greatest factor in this changed and charged atmosphere. Post-war depressions struck the masses, especially in England and Ireland.[3] It was the immigration of the latter

---

[1]Connaughton, Education in Cincinnati, pp. 8-9.

[2]Spalding, Life of Spalding, p. 154.

[3]Ray Allen Billington, The Protestant Crusade, 1800-1860. A Study of the Origins of American Nativism. (New York: Macmillan, 1938), pp. 32-52.

which set the stage for revitalized religious antagonism.
Probably they were resented largely because they represented
an economic challenge to the native laborer, but the concen-
tration of the Irish in the seaboard cities did much to
intensify the fear that Papism was indeed about to take over
the country. The Irish were never reluctant to proclaim
their belief in God and His Blessed Mother, and when God-
fearing Protestants heard these doctrines proclaimed at the
top of whiskey-fortified tenors, there were whispered rumors
that the Pope himself would soon become an immigrant.

It was during these years that the first of many
anti-Catholic and nativistic publications began to appear.
According to Billington, the first newspaper of this type
was the Boston Recorder, founded in 1816. The Christian
Watchman followed shortly after in 1819; and the Morse Brothers founded the New Observer in 1823.[1] By 1827 the total
of these newspapers had reached thirty, all of which were
distinctly anti-Catholic in tendency. With the passage of
the English Catholic Emancipation Act in 1829, all these
newspapers intensified their campaign against the Church.
The Catholic Press in turn probably owes its origin to the
flurry of attacks which were aimed at her during this out-
burst. The first stable Catholic newspaper was the U. S.
Catholic Miscellany of Charleston, launched by Bishop John

---

[1]Billington, Protestant Crusade, pp. 43-44.

England of that diocese on June 5, 1822. The paper was poorly
supported and twice England had to suspend publication for
a period of time, but it endured on to 1861. In its first
issue, the Bishop placed a prospectus; in addition to a
promise to report Catholic news from all areas and regions
for its readers, he pledged:

> The principles of the publication will
> be candour, moderation, fidelity, charity and
> diligence. Not that its conductors presume
> to attain the perfection of all or any of those
> qualities; but they will constantly keep them
> in view.
> The topics it will embrace are,
> 1. The simple explanation and temperate
> maintenance of the doctrines of the Roman
> Catholic Church; in exhibiting which, its
> conductors are led to hope, that many sensi-
> ble persons will be astonished at finding
> they have imputed to Catholics doctrines
> which the Catholic Church has formally con-
> demned, and imagined they were contradicting
> Catholics, when they held Catholic doctrines
> themselves.
> 11. The examination of history for the
> purpose of investigating the truth of many
> assertions which have been, perhaps, too lightly
> hazarded, and which have obtained too ready
> and general credence; and which have excited
> unfounded prejudices in the minds of many
> well-disposed individuals.
> 111. The correct statement of occur-
> rences regarding the Catholic religion: for
> the purpose of better discharging which duty,
> communications and periodical publications
> from Rome, Paris, London, Dublin, Canada,
> South-America, the various parts of the United
> States, and other portions of the world will
> be obtained, and are solicited. . . .[1]

Quite naturally, John England, the immigrant from Ireland,
who had so boldly and generously adopted America as his

[1] John Tracy Ellis (ed.), Documents of American
Catholic History (Milwaukee: Bruce, 1956), pp. 232-234.

own, was deeply grieved to see his Catholic countrymen challenged and abused. Throughout his careet he fought boldly
and successfully to show that there was nothing against the
American way of life in the beliefs of Catholicism. More
than any other person he gained for the Catholic Church a
fair hearing in the American forum. The Truth Teller, another aggressive publication, was founded in New York in
1825, and The Jesuit, later to become The Pilot, began publication in Boston on September 5, 1829.[1]

It was within this atmosphere that the clergy of
America were called together in the First Provincial Council
of Baltimore. After the Meeting of the Hierarchy in 1810,
it had been decided that the Bishops would meet again in
1812, but Cheverus of Boston was reluctant to attend and
to spend time discussing problems which he felt were of
minor consequence and could be settled without the costly
meetings.[2] After the death of Carroll and the ascension
of Ambrose Marechal to the See of Baltimore, there was
even less chance of a meeting. England was especially per-
sistent in demanding that a council be called, but Marechal
turned a deaf ear to the appeals of the Bishop of Charleston,
and it was only after the former's death and the elevation of
Whitfield as Archbishop of Baltimore that the meeting was

---

[1] The best general study of early Catholic journalism
is that by Paul J. Foik, Pioneer Catholic Journalism (New
York: United States Catholic Historical Society, 1930). A
current bibliography of Catholic publications is being edited
by Eugene Willging and Herta Hatzfield in Records of the
American Catholic Historical Society of Philadelphia.

[2] Cf. Melville, Cheverus, for a competent study
of this phase of conciliar activity.

finally held.[1]

Although Burns and Kohlbrenner remark at the rapid
spread of Catholic education during this period, closer examination reveals that the schools and institutions which existed
had arisen as the result of the specific endeavor of one person
or, in some cases, of a single community. There is no evidence
available to support the conclusions that these ventures were
viewed as part of a larger pattern.[2] Each seemed to be working
independently of the other. In point of fact, so many other
serious problems were facing the Church that even had they intended such efforts as a coordinated movement they could not
have helped each other in an effective fashion. In discussing
the internal problems of the Catholic minority group, McAvoy[3]
emphasizes the structure of the Catholic group. He contends
that the Catholic body was rigid, mainly because of the total
absence of internal strifes which might destroy unity. Within
its own ranks, however, the Catholic Church has suffered
many discomforts. The huge disparities among Irish, French
and German Catholics were much too large to be hidden under
the cloak of a common Latin liturgy. The bond of religion was
often threatened and strained to the breaking point, as these

---

[1]Peter Guilday, The Life and Times of John England
(New York: The America Press, 1927), Vol. II, 68-72.

[2]James A. Burns and Bernard Kohlbrenner, A History
of Catholic Education in the United States (New York: Benziger, 1937), pp. 59-95.

[3]McAvoy, Review of Politics, X, pp. 13-20.

groups strove to live within the same congregation. Irish
Catholics who expected fiery and demanding leadership from
clergy of their own kind were restive under the control
of a German or French emigre. An interesting example of the
way in which national jealousies penetrated into the ranks
of the Catholic hierarchy is shown by Guilday in a quotation
from the Propaganda archives. This is a document probably
written by Marechal in 1821; after giving a general picture
of the Church in the United States the author goes on to
describe the state of the various dioceses in the country.
Judging from this report, the French Marechal was eager
to convey the impression that the dioceses ruled by Irish
Bishops were ruled ineptly while under the French Bishops
the opposite was the case. His succinct descriptions:

Baltimore:	Peace and great prosperity
Boston:	Everything prospering
New York:	Grave disorders
Philadelphia:	Complete confusion
Richmond:	Confusion
Bardstown:	Peace and religious growth
Charleston:	Peace and hopes for future prosperity
Cincinnati:	Situation unknown.[1]

The problem of the national origin of Bishops may
indeed have been one of the reasons for the delay in calling
the First Provincial Council. Constantly irritated by the
importunate demands of England for a council, Marechal perhaps rightly felt that this choleric Irishman would dominate
the discussions and wrest leadership of the American Church

[1]Guilday, England, Vol. II, p. 74.

from the hands of the French. When the meetings were finally
held it was England who rallied the prelates with his impres-
sive discourses and he in turn presented the deliberations
of the council to the Catholics of the nation in the Pastoral
issued at its conclusion.[1] The seven Bishops who participated
in this first council were: Archbishop James Whitfield of
Baltimore; Bishop Benedict Joseph Flaget of Bardstown; Bishop
John England of Charleston; Bishop Edward Fenwick of Cincinnati;
Bishop Joseph Rosati of St. Louis; Bishop Benedict Joseph
Fenwick of Boston; and William Matthews, the Administrator
of the terribly disturbed see of Philadelphia, who was repre-
senting Bishop Conwell. Even a glance at the geographical
spread of the dioceses indicates that these men had a fair
estimate of the range and temper of the country. Living and
ministering immediately to their people, they probably were
acutely aware of the trend of religious opposition; the needs
and poverty of the immigrant groups likewise were too pronounced to be overlooked.

The preparation for the council had been as thorough
as one could expect for the times. Archbishop Marechal had
died on January 29, 1828 and James Whitfield succeeded him.
One of his early moves was the convocation of this council.
Consecrated on May 25, 1828, he sent the general letter of
convocation to his suffragans seven months later on December
18th, indicating that the council would convene on October

---

[1]McAvoy, Review of Politics, X, p. 21.

1st of the following year. At the time of the meeting there
were nine suffragan Bishops. John Dubois of New York and
Michael Portier of Mobile were on the continent; Bishop
David was too old and feeble to make the trip (although he
did attend the next council, four years later). Conwell of
Philadelphia had been relieved of jurisdiction; Richmond
was vacant at the time of the council. De Neckere had already
been newly appointed to the See of New Orleans but the members of the council were not aware of this appointment. The
preparation for the council included a certain amount of
correspondence between the suffragans and their superior.
The Archbishop had called for suggestions and two of these
responses are pertinent to the theme of this study. Fenwick
of Boston wrote to Whitfield in September in 1828, even before plans for a general meeting had been announced, concerning the advisability of establishing an organization
for the printing and dissemination of Catholic books. After
alluding to the advantages to be gathered from a general
meeting of the Bishops, he includes as agenda for discussion:

> 1st the forming & adopting a plan for
> the compiling & printing Cath. school books
> for the whole U. States, such as: Spelling
> books, Reading Do Geography Do Histories
> etc. etc. As matters stand, all the children
> educated in the common schools of the country
> are obliged to use books compiled by Protes-
> tants by which their minds are poisoned as it
> were from their infancy. Is there a single
> geography or history or reading book in which
> the Cath. religion is not aspersed? A plan

can be formed which if encouraged by the
body of Bps. will & must succeed.[1]

John England who had for so long championed the cause of an
Episcopal meeting had many suggestions to make as to the
matter for discussion and among his suggestions two are
most important:

> 2. The best mode of counteracting the
> pernicious influence of our adversaries, in
> their publications, schools, and societies
> all directed against us.
> 3. The best mode of regulating the in-
> struction of our youth and determining how
> we could best procure for them the most ex-
> tended course of solid religious instruction.[2]

Although the specific study of Catholic publications
is outside the scope of this research, it seems that the letter from Fenwick quoted above is important because it demonstrates that the Church Fathers when talking about these
Catholic books intended them for use in the common schools
as well as in Catholic schools, otherwise how could Fenwick
hope to help these youngsters avoid the poison of the biased
texts? Because of the importance of this aspect, I would
like to quote another letter, this time from Bp. Dubois in
New York. Writing in reference to the proposed discussions
of this first council, he says:

---

[1] Archives University of Notre Dame: Fenwick to Whitfield: Sept. 10th, 1828.

[2] Baltimore Cathedral Archives, 23 G 2 England to
Whitfield, Dec. 26, 1828. Cf. also Guilday, England, p.
117.

[Referring to the quality of state texts]
. . . . There is not one good compilation to be
had even by the Protestants. Pure compositions
including elegant extracts of all kinds of elo-
cution would answer our purpose and would not
be objectionable even to Protestants. Historical style, /a/ familiar one, dialogues,
forensics, & very little poetry -- sublime,
simple style, excluding all panegyrics of mere
politicians, all affected declamations on
liberty &c.[1]

In addition to these appeals, there is extant a petulant
letter of Father Stephan Badin, written to Bishop Rosati
at about this same time. Badin was an active missionary
in the middle west and had given his life to the service
of the Church in that area. The importance he attached to
sound education is evident from the following:

. . . . We are here in great distress for want
of a Bishop and of ten or twelve priests;
of schools, of a college and a convent.
Infidels in general, and a certain proud
aspiring sect in particular, are massing
great efforts to make proselytes of our
poor ignorant Catholics. Nous "Richard"
has spent money for his Cathedral sufficient
to have founded free schools in every part
of the country where they are wanted, and
to have built, besides, a sufficient Church
for Detroit.

. . . . I feel distressed as often as I
ruminate upon this subject, and regret that
"Nous" Richard made himself, by his expensive
and unnecessary edifice, incapable of founding
ten free schools, which would have been
encouraged by the Legislature, endowed with
lands, and would offer salutary instruction
even to Protestant children, whereas our

[1]BCA, 24 R 13 Dubois to /?/. Although found
among papers of the 1837 council, these notes of Dubois
probably belong to this time period. Cf. Henry J. Browne,
"Public Support of Catholic Education in New York: 1825-
1842: Some New Aspects," Catholic Historical Review, vol. 39
(April, 1953), p. 9, ft. 24.

> Catholic youth are enticed and almost com-
> pelled into heretical Sunday Schools!!!
> <u>Quis talia fando temperet a lacrymis?</u>[1]

Prior to the council itself, the Archbishop held a
series of meetings with the professors of St. Mary's Seminary.
A program for the conduct of the meeting was worked out and
among the notes which are preserved there is a list of the
general things to be discussed in the deliberations. The
following item is pertinent:

> Tractanda in Concilio
> De Fide et Disciplina
>
> no. 10 It is very desirable that a religious
> Society of men for the education of Boys should
> be instituted.[2]

The prelates gathered in Baltimore during the last week of
September and on the evening of September 30th, they gathered
in the episcopal residence and laid down general regulations
for their discussions. The first two of these rules are of
import, because they reflect the concern of the participants
to enact legislation which would be functional and practical.
These rules read as follows:

> 1. Nothing would be sanctioned by the Coun-
> cil which could not be easily carried into
> execution.
> 2. No decree would be binding upon the
> faithful until the Holy See had given its
> approval.[3]

---

[1] St. Louis Archives, Badin to Rosati, Feb. 6, 1829.

[2] BCA, 23A T 3, p. 4.

[3] Guilday, <u>Councils</u>, pp. 88-89.

The issues to be discussed in the council have been succinctly listed by Guilday in several places. Since these same issues came into play at succeeding councils, it may be well to list them here:

> . . . Among these [problems faced in 1829] were:
> 1. the best means of educating candidates for the priesthood; 2. the best method of counter-acting the pernicious influence of the anti-Catholic politico-religious groups in the country; 3. the best method of providing instruction for Catholic youth; 4. the encouragement and support of religious communities, especially of women, devoted to educational work; 5. the best method of publishing and distributing Catholic books on doctrinal questions; 6. the best legal method of safe-guarding Catholic property; and finally 7. the laying down of general principles of discipline upon which we might enact our respective statutes with as much an approach to uniformity as possible.

Within the council deliberations, three decrees were passed which had a bearing on educational concerns. The seventeenth decree was a simple statement to the effect that the children of non-Catholics whose parents brought them for baptism should be baptized as long as there was hope of their probable Catholic upbringing. The thirty-fourth and thirty-fifth decrees are more intimately concerned with the subject of this study:

---

[1]Peter Guilday, "Les Conciles de Baltimore (1791-1884)," _Miscellanea Historica in Honorem Alberti de Meyer, Universitatis Catholicae in Oppido Louvaniensi Iam Annos XXV Professoris Louvain_ (Louvain: Bibliotheque de l'universite, 1946), vol. II, p. 1206; authorized translation. Much the same information is given in Guilday, _England_, p. 118.

XXXIV Quoniam quamplurimos adolescentes ex
Catholicis parentibus, praesertim pauperibus,
ortos, in multis Provinciae hujus locis exposi-
tos esse, et adhuc exponi constat magno fidei
amittendae periculo, vel morum corruptelae, ob
inopiam talium magistrorum quibus tantum munus
tuto committi possit; necessarium omnino censemus
ut Scholae instituantur, in quibus juvenes edoceantur fidei morumque principia, dum litteris
imbuuntur.

XXXV Cum non raro plura reperiantur in libris
qui in scholis plerumque adhibentur, quibus
principia fidei nostrae impugnantur, dogmata
nostra perperam exponuntur, et ipsa historia
pervertitur, qua ratione puerorum animi erroribus imbuuntur, in animarum damnum gravissimum; postulat tum Religionis studium, tum
juventutis recta educatio, et ipsum Foederatae
Americae decus, remedium aliquod tanto malo
afferri. Ea de causa statuimus quamprimum
edendos in scholarum usum, erroribus omnino
expurgatos, quibus nihil contineatur quod
Catholicae fidei odium vel invidiam parere
possit.[1]

___

[1]Text of decrees taken from Concilia Provincilia,
Baltimori Habita Ab Anno 1829 usque ad annum 1849. Editio
Altera (Baltimori: Apud Joannem Murphy et Socium, 1851), p.
84. The thirty-fifth decree is amended to read as it was
sent to Rome for approval. A private translation of the
decrees:
    34. Since it is evident that very many of the young,
the children of Catholic parents, especially the poor, have
been exposed and are still exposed in many places of this
Province, to great danger of the loss of faith or the corruption of morals, on account of the lack of such teachers
as could safely be entrusted with so great an office, we
judge it absolutely necessary that schools should be established in which the young may be taught the principles of
faith and morality, while being instructed in letters.
    35. Since it frequently happens that many things are
found in the books used in most schools by which the principles of our faith are attacked, our dogmas explained falsely and even history perverted, the minds of youth are imbued
with errors and very grave harm done to their souls, the
zeal for religion, the proper education of youth and even the
glory of the United States demand that some remedy be offered
for such an evil. For this reason we decree that, as soon
as possible, books, completely cleansed of error, in which
nothing is contained which could bring forth hatred of the
faith or ill-feeling, be edited.

There can be little doubt that the Bishops were much
concerned with the state of education in the larger cities.
The situation in New York with the Public School Society
had already begun to worsen and the need there for Catholic
education was acute. However, if one is looking to these
decrees to find a beginning point for the parochial school
system, then one is surprised at the lack of specificity
which this decree displays. Burns in his commentary on this
decree states:

> . . . This rather mild decree was viewed by many
> members of the hierarchy, in the course of
> time, as leaving much to be desired, and later
> councils attempted to provide more stringent
> legislation in the matter.[1]

As demonstrated by Gabel and Dunn the tradition of education
up to the period under discussion had been that of state
aid for church and private schools.[2] Even Evarts Greene
who has a somewhat rigid interpretation of the interaction
of Church and State admits that the American tradition of
separation of Church and State was far from being universally accepted at the close of the Revolutionary War. According to him, that result was the outcome of another half century of experience and public discussion.[3] This state co-

---

[1]James A. Burns and Bernard Kohlbrenner, A History
of Catholic Education in the United States (New York: Benziger, 1937), p. 137.

[2]This is the major thesis of the ponderous volume
by Gabel.

[3]Evarts Greene, Religion and the State: The Making
and Testing of an American Tradition (Ithaca, New York:
Great Seal Books, 1941, reprint, 1959), p. 85.

operation in education was commonly accepted and had been the
colonial tradition. Consequently, it seems quite likely that
these decrees are a reflection of the American Bishops' hope
that the state would cooperate with Catholic educational
agencies. The letters quoted earlier in reference to textbooks for the children in public schools seem to bear out
this point.[1] The 34th decree can be viewed in this light if
we see it as a general appeal for the construction of schools
which would at least not be inimical to the Catholic tradition. Admittedly, the common view of this decree is to see
in it an appeal to Catholics to set up and maintain their
own schools. Burns considered it as such when he commented
upon its mildness. No one goes so far as to maintain that
a parochial system was commanded here, but it is assumed by
many that the Bishops were envisioning a rather widespread
program of Catholic education. It seems, however, that since
conflict with the nature of public education looms so promi-
nently in future legislation, we can argue from the lack of
it here.[2] The pattern of public support for private education was not legally decided until much later after prolonged
disputes in several states, even though public schools of a
sort had begun to emerge at this early period. The New

---

[1]Daniel F. Reilly, The School Controversy (1891-1893),
(Washington: Catholic University of America Press, 1943),
p. 7.

[2]Diffley, American Catholic Reaction, pp. 236-240.

England schools, as usual, were taking the lead. Nevertheless, we would be mistaken if we underestimate the resolution
of the participants in this first council. They recognized
the dangers which threatened their people and their 35th
decree was a forthright plea and likewise a pledge that they
would act to the best of their ability when their people were
being challenged. Guilday maintains[1] that the decree referred
only to the teachers and the textbooks being used in Catholic
schools, since Church decrees could have no binding force
upon others outside the Church. Conversely, it seems reasonable to assume that the Bishops had in mind the larger plan
of modifying and improving the texts that were then being
used not only in the Catholic schools but in the Protestant
ones as well. Only in the light of such thinking does the
letter of Dubois quoted above make sense. The number of
Catholics at this time was so small that the market for books
would have been prohibitively small had the circulation been
intended only for that small portion of these Catholics being trained in schools under Catholic auspices. Shaughnessy
estimates that in 1829 there were 318,000 Catholics in the
United States, a substantial increase from the 24,500 in
1790 but still a very limited market for publications.[2]

---

[1]Guilday, Councils, p. 95. Guilday assumes throughout that whatever legislation was enacted by Catholic Bishops
was intended solely for their private schools. As indicated,
this view may, perhaps, be too limiting.

[2]Gerald Shaughnessy, Has the Immigrant Kept the Faith?
(New York: Macmillan, 1925), appendix viii.

Bishop England's presence and influence in the council would also seem to justify the conclusion that the prelates intended the wider dissemination of their materials, since England himself had expressed this as one of the purposes of his newspaper. Perhaps the strongest argument that can be adduced for a broader interpretation of this decree is that fact that in their preliminary session, the Bishops had agreed not to enact anything that would be difficult to execute. Considering the lack of available funds and manpower, a studied program of private education was certainly far beyond even the scope of intelligent idealism.[1]

Following the pattern used by Bishop Carroll in his synod, the Fathers of the council prepared a Pastoral Letter in which the deliberations of the council were related to the laity. If the consideration of education was disappointingly brief in the Acta, such is not the case in the letter, which was written in the name of the Bishops by John England. In the space devoted to Christian education, Bishop England exposes in detail the teaching of the Church regarding parents and their duty to provide for and insist upon the children's attendance at schools where they could receive a Christian education. As a study of the text will reveal, England has no intention of demanding of each and every parent that they place their children in schools directly under the auspices

---

[1] Diffley, American Catholic Reaction, pp. 237-238.

of religious teachers. In fact he holds this only as an
ideal for those whose means and opportunities allow this
procedure. The full text of this section of the Pastoral
follows:

> From this topic [the need for priests]
> we naturally pass to that of the education of
> your children. How important, how interesting,
> how awful, how responsible a charge! "Suffer
> little children to come unto me, and forbid
> them not" says the amiable Jesus, "for of such
> is the kingdom of Heaven." Yes! the char-
> acteristic of the child, as St. John Chrysos-
> tom well observes, is the characteristic of
> the saint. Genuine simplicity, without guile,
> uncalculating ardent devotion to the loving
> parent, preferring an humble mother in her
> homely garb, to a queen in her variegated dec-
> oration; exercising an irresistible power
> over the parental heart by the bewitching con-
> fidence of helplessness itself. Those chil-
> dren, the dear pledges of your elevated and
> sanctified affection, deserve and demand your
> utmost solicitude. For them you brave danger,
> on their account you endure toil; you weep
> over their afflictions, you rejoice at their
> gratification, you look forward to their
> prosperity, you anticipate their gratitude,
> your souls are knit to theirs, your happi-
> ness is centered in their good conduct; and
> you cherish the enlightening hope that when
> you and they shall have passed through this
> vale of tears, you will be reunited in the
> kingdom of a common father. How would your
> hearts be torn with grief did you foresee,
> that through eternity those objects of all
> your best feelings should be cast into outward
> darkness, where there is weeping and gnashing
> of teeth! May God in His infinite mercy pre-
> serve you and them from the just anticipation
> of any such result! But, dearly beloved, this
> is too frequently the necessary consequence
> of a neglected or an improper education. God
> has made you the guardians of those children
> to lead them to His service upon earth, that
> they might become saints in Heaven. "What

will it avail them to gain the whole world
if they lose their souls?" Or could it con-
sole you in the progress of eternity, to
recollect that you had for a time beheld them
elevated to power, applauded by fame, entrusted with command, swaying nations, dis-
pensing wealth and honours; but misled by
vice and now tortured in disgrace; and, thus
to be tortured for eternity? If you would
avert this dreadful calamity, attend to the
education of your child; teaching him first to
seek the kingdom of God and His justice, and
having food and raiment, to be therewith content. Teach him to be industrious, to be
frugal, to be humble and fully resigned to the
will of that God who feeds the birds of the
air, clothes the lily of the field; and who
so loved the children of men that when they
were His enemies they were reconciled to him
by the death of His Son, that being reconciled
they might be saved from eternal death by His
life being justified now by His blood.

Alas! beloved children, how many are
there, who, yielding to the pride of life, and
ashamed of Him who was not ashamed for our
sakes to die upon an ignominious cross, "being
made the reproach of men and the outcast of
the people," how many such wretched parents
have trained up their children to be themselves the victims of passions in time, and
of that death from which there is no resur-
rection in eternity!

How frequently have their brightest hopes
faded away into a settled gloom? How often has
the foot which they elevated, spurned them? How
often whilst the children of revelry occupied
the hall of mirth, has the drink of the wretched
parent been mingled with his tears, and whilst
his ungrateful offspring, regardless of his
admonition, rose in the careless triumph of
enjoyment, have his gray hairs been brought
with sorrow to the grave? Believe us; it is
only by the religious education of your children that you can so train them up, as to
ensure that, by their filial piety and their
steady virtue, they may be to you the staff
of your old age, the source of your consolation, and reward in a better world. Begin
with them in their earliest childhood, whilst

the mind is yet pure and docile, and their
baptismal innocence uncontaminated; let
their unfolding perceptions be imbued with
the mild and lovely tints of religious
truth and pure devotion; allure them to the
service of their creator who delights in
the homage of innocence; and give to their
reason, as it becomes developed, that substantial nutriment which it requires, and
which our holy religion so abundantly affords;
shew your children by your conduct, that you
believe what you inculcate; natural affection
disposes them to imitate your example, you
should, therefore, be awfully impressed by
that solemn admonition of the Saviour: "Woe
to him that shall scandalize one of these
little ones that believe in me, it were better for him that a millstone were tied round
his neck, and that he were drowned in the
depths of the sea." In placing them at school,
seek for those teachers who will cultivate the
seed which you have sown; for of what avail
will it be, that you have done so much, if the
germs which begin to put forth, shall now be
stifled or eradicated; and should tares be
sown where you have prepared the soil? Again,
and again, would we impress upon your minds the
extreme importance of this great duty, and
your responsibility to the God of truth, in
its regard. How well would it be, if your
means and opportunities permitted, were you
at this period to commit your children to the
care of those whom we have for their special
fitness, placed over our seminaries and our
female religious institutions? It would be
at once the best mode of discharging your
obligations to your children, and of aiding
us in promoting the great object which we
have already endeavored to impress upon your
minds. Remember also, that not only affection, but, duty requires of you to be vigilant in securing the spiritual concerns of
your offspring, during the period of their
preparation for business or for professions;
that this security can, in general, be far
better attained under the parent's roof; or
if it be necessary to entrust the sacred
deposit of your child's soul to another, it

ought to be one of tried virtue, and surrounded by favourable circumstances.
Should your family be thus educated, you
may naturally expect that they will freely
allow your just influence in that most important of all temporal concerns, the selection of a wife or husband; and it becomes
you, whilst you pay a proper respect to
the affections of those most deeply interested, to be careful that you have more
regard to those things which belong to
eternity, than to those of a mere tran-
sient nature. What we have written might
appear importunate. But remember we watch
over you in order to render unto God an
account of your souls; therefore, it is
that we write these things to you to admonish you as our dearest children, "to
confirm your hearts without blame, in holiness, before God and our father," because
you are our joy and our crown, and therefore,
we labour, whether absent or present, for
your advantage, in the word of truth, in
the power of God; through honour and dis-
honour, through infamy and good name, our
mouth is open to you, our heart is enlarged;
great is our confidence in you, we are con-
soled by your joy, we are saddened by your
sorrow, we write, not as commanding, but as
entreating our children in whom we confide.[1]

No efforts were made in this report to influence the
Catholics in general into an organized pattern of support
for religious schools. The major import of the section
is that the clergy are properly concerned about the religious
education of their flock. The First Provincial Council is
unique in the sense that two Pastorals were issued at the
conclusion of this council; the one to the laity, quoted
above; and another, to the clergy. The passage in this
latter letter dealing with education points more directly
at the priest's duty of religious education.

---

[1]Guilday, Councils, pp. 24-27.

Of one other duty, brethren, we would
affectionately but earnestly remind you.--
The solicitude for the insturction of youth.
Continue your efforts in this most useful and
indespensable line of duty. Thus will you
render comparatively light and incalculably
more beneficial, the labours of yourselves
and of your successors. If the great truths
of religion be not deeply inculcated upon the
youthful mind, your discourses will be scarcely intelligible to those who will have been
left untaught; they know not the facts to
which you allude; they do not appreciate the
principles from which you reason; they do
not feel the obligations which you enforce;
your assertions appear to be unfounded, and
they grow weary of hearing what they cannot
understand; you beat the air and spend your-
self without advantage. Unless you watch over
them when they are first exposed to temptation,
they will be robbed of their innocence, they will
lose their horror for vice, they will be famil-
iarised with crime, and when their habits are
thus formed in early life, what prospect can
you have of successfully engrafting virtue
upon this stock of evil which has been deeply
rooted in a soil of sin? What a task do you
leave for your successors! What an account have
you to render to the Great Father of those children entrusted to your care! Beloved, we rejoice to behold you assiduous in the instruction
of youth. O! it is a godlike, though to a
man a laborious occupation; it is indeed re-
deeming a world, or rather, it is creating a
new earth as the preparation for a new Heaven.
How we do rejoice and bless God at beholding
the venerable institutions of our Church
springing up to your aid! Do, we entreat of
you, encourage and cherish those pious souls
that so meritoriously devote themselves to the
instruction of children in the way of the God
of truth.[1]

Because of the importance of this pastoral in demon-

strating the attitude of the clergy during this period,

---

[1] Guilday, _Pastorals_, pp. 57-58.

the following paragraphs in regard to the attacks upon the
Catholic religion are pertinent:

Amongst the various misfortunes to which
we have been exposed, one of the greatest is
misrepresentation of the tenets, the principles
and the practices of our church. This is not
the place to account for the origin and contin-
uance of this evil; we merely remind you of the
melancholy fact. Good men, --men, otherwise
well informed, deeply versed in science, in history, in politics; men who have improved their
education by their travels abroad as well as
they who have merely acquired the very rudiments of knowledge at home; the virtuous women
who influence that society which they decorate,
and yielding to the benevolence of their hearts
desire to extend useful knowledge; the public
press, the very bench of public justice, have
been all influenced by extraordinary efforts
directed against us; so that from the very
highest place in our land to all its remotest
borders, we are exhibited as what we are not,
and charged with maintaining what we detest.
Repetition has given to those statements a
semblance of evidence; and groundless assertions remaining almost uncontradicted, wear the
appearance of admitted and irrefragable truth.
It is true, that during some years past, an
effort has been made to uphold a periodical
publication in the south, which has refuted
some of these allegations; but we say with regret that it has been permitted to languish for
want of ordinary support, and must, we are informed,
be discontinued, unless it receives your more
extended patronage. Other publications for similar objects have lately been established in
Boston and Hartford. We would advise you to
encourage well-conducted works of this description. If you look around and see how many such
are maintained, for their own purposes, by our
separated brethren, it will indeed be a matter
of reproach should we not uphold at least a few
of our own.
But not only are the misrepresentations of
which we complain, propagated so as to affect
the mature; but with zeal worthy of a better
cause, and which some persons have exhibited in

contrast with our seeming apathy, the mind
of the very infant is predisposed against us
by the recitals of the nursery; and the school-
boy can scarcely find a book in which
some one or more of our institutions or practices is not exhibited far otherwise than it
really is, and greatly to our disadvantage:
the entire system of education is thus tinged
throughout its whole course; and history itself has been distorted to our serious injury.
We have during a long time been oppressed by
this evil, and from a variety of causes, have
found it almost impossible to apply any remedy;
but we have deemed it expedient now to make
some effort towards a beginning. We have
therefore associated ourselves and some others,
whom we deem well qualified for that object,
to encourage the publication of elementary
books free from any of those false colourings,
and in which whilst our own feelings are protected, those of our fellow-citizens of other
religious denominations shall be respected.
We should desire also to see other histories
corrected, as that of England has been by
the judicious and erudite Doctor Lingard;
that our standard books should be carefully and
faithfully printed under proper supervision,
and even that temperate and useful explanatory
essays to exhibit and vindicate truth, should
be written without harsh or unkind expressions,
and published, so that our brethren might have
better opportunities of knowing us as we really
are, and not imagine us to be what in bad times,
unprincipled and interested men have exhibited
as our picture.[1]

Fifty years after the council, a reported writing
in the Catholic Mirror just prior to the convocation of the
Third Plenary Council made these remarks concerning the
educational legislation enacted by this first council:

---

[1]Guilday, Pastorals, pp. 27-28.

. . . . It has been charged that the Church's
policy has greatly changed on the subject
of the danger to Catholic youth from education in mixed schools. Certainly the evil
is aggravated now by the vast expansion of
the system, but as far back as 1829 we see
no difference in the tone of the prelates
-- that is, measured by the lesser danger
at that day. The thirty-third, thirty-
fourth and thirty-fifth decree deal with
the matter in no honied tones. Wherever
parochial schools are possible, they are
ordered to be opened, and Sunday-Schools
are insisted upon as an absolute necessity;
when a school is found in which Catholic
doctrines or moral principles are attacked
it is the duty of the pastor in its neighborhood to prohibit its attendance by the
children of his flock.[1]

Much of the above comment is really an anticipation
of later legislation; and the reporter, eager to show the
age of the parochial system, goes far beyond the words of
the decrees. There is no mention of parochial schools any-
where in the actions of the provincial councils, and nearly
all of the legislation enacted can be understood in reference to contemporary educational programs, without the
substantial modifications that a separate system of
training would have called for.

One of the important issues to be settled in this
first council was the relationship of the American Bishops
to the Holy See. It was, therefore, important that the
Council Fathers should exercise extreme care in remitting
their decisions and decrees to the approval of the Holy See.
On October 24, the decrees and minutes were sent to Pope

[1]The *Catholic Mirror*, November 8, 1884.

Pius VIII. Included with the _Acta_ was a letter from the
prelates, attesting their love and devotion to the Holy
Father. In speaking of the great progress which had been
made by the Church in this country, they include a description of the educational program in the country. Among
other items, they mention that the country at that time
boasted six ecclesiastical seminaries, nine colleges under
ecclesiastical control, thirty-three monasteries and houses
of religious women, and many schools where the poor of both
sexes were taught gratuitously.[1]

The usual procedure of the Propaganda was to prepare
an analysis of the decrees and to present them in printed
form before the officials of the Sacred Congregation. They
in turn spent a great deal of effort in discussing and comparing the various decrees before they finally gave their
approval. In the case of this First Provincial Council of
the United States, the Propaganda had called upon Father
Bernard Kohlmann of the Society of Jesus, a former president of Georgetown, and Bishop John Dubois of New York for
their advice. Of the decrees with which we are concerned
only the thirty-fifth underwent any change. At the insistence of Cardinal Caprano, it was suggested that the proposed
books should be submitted to the approval of the ordinary.
His reason for so insisting was the standard practice of
the Church in demanding that books meant to be free of error

---

[1]Murphy, _Concilia_, pp. 56-57.

should be approved by the Bishop before being printed.[1] The decrees with the suggested changes were approved and on October 16th the letter of approval was sent from the Sacred Congregation of Propaganda and the <u>Acta</u> of the First Provincial Council became the law of the Church in America.[2] In order to understand how in point of fact the decrees were put into effect it is necessary to turn to the synods and meetings which were held in the smaller jurisdictional areas after the major council. In addition, also, we can look to the actions of the Bishops upon their return from the council. The <u>United States Catholic Miscellany</u> carried this notice of a talk by Bishop England:

> . . . . One of our most interesting concerns,
> is to provide for the proper education of
> the children of our flocks. This is the
> parents' special obligation, and the Pas-
> tors' most pressing and elevated duty, as
> it is also the patriot's and the charitable
> man's field of active and useful benevolence.
> As yet we have not been able to do much in
> its regard: our children are scarcely pro-
> vided in the city with sufficient oppor-
> tunities of proper religious instruction,
> in the country and in remote towns they are
> still more destitute; our orphans have fal-
> len into the power of those by whom they are
> estranged from the creed of their fathers,

---

[1] The entire story of the approval of the actions of the First Provincial Council has been studied and reported: Thomas F. Casey, <u>The Sacred Congregation de Propaganda Fide and the Revision of the First Provincial Council of Baltimore, 1829-1830</u> (Romae: Apud Aedes Universitatis Gregorianae, 1957). The filmed letters of the Roman archives were consulted at the University of Notre Dame, through the courtesy of Rev. Thomas McAvoy, C.S.C.

[2] Cf. Shearer, <u>Pontificia</u>, for a reprint of these letters and documents. Pp. 170-171 are especially pertinent.

and our little females are especially exposed.
It is true that more urgent wants must be
first supplied; but these concerns ought not
to be forgotten.[1]

Two years later, the same newspaper reports England as say-

ing:

And I know now that I have ever been placed
in a station which created in me a stronger
conviction of the necessity of calling upon
you, that we may take counsel for the purpose
of devising some mode by which this great
duty might be discharged upon a better system than has hitherto been pursued amongst
us.[2]

In the interval between the first and the second

council, three of the dioceses held their own synods but

in none of them was education an important topic. The Acta

of the first diocesean synod of Philadelphia, held in 1832

under the direction of Francis P. Kenrick, mentioned schools

only to the extent that previous permission of the Bishop

was required to build them.[3] The diocese of Charleston had

---

[1]U.S. Catholic Miscellany, Vol. IX, no. 23, Dec. 5,
1829. By citing this example, I do not pretend that this is
the only comment available. The opinions selected throughout this study are meant to convey an impression of the general trend at the particular moment. Composed as the hierarchy was of highly different and individualistic members,
it is nearly impossible to obtain a consensus on any given
point.

[2]U.S. Catholic Miscellany, November 19, 1831.

[3]Acta Synodi Dioecesanae Philadelphiensis Primae,
habitae in Ecclesia Cathedrali S. Mariae, Philadelphiae,
Anno Domini MDCCCXXXII, Mense Maji. A reverendissimo Francisco Patricio Kenrick, Episcopo Arathensi et Coadjutore
Episcopi Philadelphiensis, (Philadelphiae: Cummiskey, edidit
-- ex typis F. Pierson, 1832). These volumes were consulted
at Woodstock College where they are preserved on microfilm.

met the previous year and under the sponsorship of England
had discussed the local application of the decrees of Baltimore. The report of that meeting as given in the U. S.
Catholic Miscellany follows:

> Deep and lively interest was felt and
> expressed upon the subjects of canons xxxiv,
> xxxv and xxxvi and some propositions sug-
> gested for carrying the canons into execu-
> tion, but it was thought more prudent to
> defer taking any immediate steps, in the
> hope that the provincial council of 1832
> would combine the energies and means of the
> whole province for some one if not all the
> designated purposes, of proper schools for
> the young, and books for the adolescent
> and the ripe.[1]

Thus, in concluding the discussion of the first
council, it is evident that from this time onward the necessity of Christian education of youth became an intimate part
of the thinking of the council members. The dominant force
compelling the Fathers to found schools was given at this
time as the unfortunate lot of poor children who were in
danger of losing their faith. The tracing of the legislation
from this simple iteration of purpose to the complex legislation of the Third Plenary Council which spelled out the
parochial pattern of education is the major purpose of this
study. The program of development, however, is complicated
by the fact that forces other than the mind and will of the
Church Fathers played important roles. Two of these inter-
vening forces are immigration and nativism. The period of

---

[1] U. S. Catholic Miscellany, November 26, 1831.

history covering the next two councils of 1833 and 1837 represents a particularly difficult era in the story of American Catholicism, for it was during these years that the
volume of anti-Catholic propaganda became most intense; it
has been a tradition in Catholic church history to speak of
nativism and the anti-Catholic riots in the same breath, as
if stemming from the same forces. The studies of Billington
have added to this trend, but John Higham in his work on
later nativism has applied a gentle corrective to this concept. Higham rightly sees the nativist movement as composed
of two facets. The first is an anti-foreign tradition which
came from the shock of the Reformation. This hatred did,
indeed, play a large role in the early nativist movements
of this period. However, to identify the anti-foreign and
anti-Catholic forces seems to over-simplify the case. Factors
other than nativist feelings have been responsible for anti-
Catholic feelings, and even native Catholics feared the force
and influence of immigrant groups. Anti-Catholicism became
truly nativistic and reached dangerous intensity, when the
Church's adherents seemed to be dangerous foreign agents in
the national life of America.[1] A second nativist tradition,
according to Higham, was the fear of radicalism, espoused
by many foreigners. While agitated Protestants regarded

[1]John Higham, Strangers in the Land (New Brunswick;
New Jersey: Rutgers University Press, 1955), p. 5.

the immigrant as yoked to religious despotism, timid conservatives sometimes found him prone to political revolutions.[1]

The nativistic outrages of this period have been thoroughly and adequately studied in other works. They are mentioned here because of the bearing which they have upon the educational thinking of the period. The most noticeable of the movements was in the founding of the American Protestant Association in New York in 1830. This organization spearheaded many drives against Catholics and was active in nearly all parts of the country. As Billington points out, the bias of the people had many angles but, stirred by the Maria Monk variety of stories and the sermons of preachers like Rev. Lyman Beecher, the most detached and sincere Protestant was caught up in the popular hatred of Romism. The violence displayed in the attack upon the Ursuline convent in Charlestown, Massachusetts, was tragic enough, but the failure of civil officials to make any attempts to repair the damages of the mob action or to take the necessary protective action to insure that such outrages would not happen again was totally inexcusable. The refusal of the legislature to provide for damages and to recognize the rights of Catholic citizens became a major point in the Pastoral Letter which England composed for the third provincial meeting.[2]

---

[1] Higham, Strangers, p. 7.

[2] A series of dissertations was done at Catholic University of America under the direction of Richard J. Purcell, dealing with the force of nativism in several separate states.

This time span also saw the flowering of the inter-
denominational debate. In the absence of other effective
news media, these highly publicized debates drew large crowds;
and, often to the chagrin and expense of the sponsors, the
audiences did not always display the same self-control and
urbanity which the speakers so laboriously demonstrated on
stage. Subtle differences of theology and dogma were more
often settled by fisticuffs than by logic.

In defense of the more reasonable Americans, it must
be pointed out that not all Protestant groups were involved
in the movement. Many moderate Protestants decried the ex-
cesses and the lack of Christian spirit. Many Protestant
clergymen, too, deplored the methods employed by The Protestant, the anti-Catholic journal which first appeared in New
York on January 2, 1830.[1] Horace Mann himself is said to
have served as legal counsel for the public committee of
protest against the burning of the Charlestown convent.[2]
The Catholic people also, even while undergoing these severe
trials, were making progress of their own. Owing somewhat
perhaps to the pressure of the nativists, more and more native born Americans were being advanced to posts of importance in the Church; with the death of Whitfield, Samuel
Eccleston became the Archbishop of Baltimore, and, aided by

[1]Billington, Protestant Crusade, pp. 62-73.

[2]McCluskey, Public Schools, p. 50. Cf. also Anson
Stokes, Church and State in the United States, 3 vols. (New
York: Harper & Bros., 1950).

other far-seeing leaders, insisted upon a policy of advancing
native-born clergy in preference to those of foreign origin.
As attention was focused on the traditions of the Church
by the attackers, it became necessary for the Catholics to
publicize and defend their own policies; the consequent iden-
tification as a Catholic body also helped the nationalist
groups within the Church to forget their differences and
to work together in the common cause. It was during this
period that the European observers Alexis de Tocqueville,
Gustave de Beaumont and Harriet Martineau made their observations on the American scene.[1] All three remarked on the
unity of American Catholics and de Tocqueville's companion
wrote enthusiastically of the work which the American Catholic
clergy were doing among the poor.

At the same time as these movements were taking place
on the religious scene, the development of the common school
was proceeding apace. The influence of Horace Mann was beginning to be felt; the early journals of education were
gathering readers and associations for the advancement of
education amassed funds. They were able shortly to offer a
realistic alternative to the Church-dominated system that
had hitherto been the sole functional program of education
for the masses.[2]

_____

[1]Ellis, American Catholicism, pp. 59-61.

[2]Edward Reisner, The Evolution of the Common School
(New York: Macmillan, 1930), pp. 321-323.

At the conclusion of the sessions of the 1829 congress, the Bishops had resolved to meet again after three years. Dr. Whitfield, however, saw no reason to convoke the second council at that time and only upon urgent command from the Holy See was he led to call the sessions the next year. Prior to the council Kenrick and Purcell had exchanged letters regarding a proposal for an Association of Clergymen who would devote their lives to the instruction of youth. This letter was an indication of the interest which Purcell had in the problems of education and during his fifty year reign Cincinnati became the leading (arch)diocese in this regard. It was likewise indicative of the awareness these men had regarding the problem of school personnel.[1]

The meeting began on the 20th of October, 1833, and ten prelates and twenty priests were present. No minutes of the private or public meetings were located and our information concerning the dealings of this council is drawn from the Acta and from a few scattered papers left by the participants. In their request to Whitfield on April 3, 1833, Propaganda officials had indicated that one of their reasons for wishing a council held was the need for a more accurate determination of the boundaries of dioceses. The province of Baltimore had at that time twelve suffragan

[1]Archives University of Notre Dame, Kenrick to Purcell, 14th September, 1832.

sees, which were well situated in the twenty-five states and territories.[1] Present at the deliberations were Bishops David, England, Rosati, Fenwick of Boston, Dubois, Portier, Francis Kenrick, Rese, and Purcell. This time Flaget pleaded feebleness, although his good friend Bisnop David overcame his weariness sufficiently to make the long journey.[2] The actions of this council were marked by a spirit of controversy among the participants themselves. One of the major reasons for this was Whitfield's ill-concealed distrust of the Irish Bishops. One of the chief factors in his reluctance in calling the council was his fear that the Irish members of the hierarchy were becoming too powerful. Consequently, he had written to Cardinal Pedini of Propaganda: "Pax, qua in suis Diocesibus non omnes gaudent, apud nos, dante Deo, viget: sacerdotes et populi obsequentes sunt: pietas colitur; multi fidem Catholicam quotannis amplectuntur, . . ."[3] In the sittings of the council he displayed open hostility to England, and this prelate was deeply grieved by the action. This uneasiness among the members may be one of the reasons why

---

[1] Guilday, Pastorals, pp. 60-61.

[2] Murphy, Acta et Decreta, pp. 95-99.

[3] Whitfield to Cardinal Pedini, June 14, 1832. Translation: Tranquillity, which not all enjoy in their dioceses, flourishes here, thanks be to God: the priests and people are docile: piety is fostered; many embrace the Catholic faith every year, . . .

this council produced such meagre results. England, stunned,
was strangely silent and the other Bishops, deprived of their
usual spokesman, left things unsaid.[1]

The ninth decree of the council was specifically
directed to the quality of textbooks, indicating that not
much progress had been made on the scheme to publish expur-
gated texts:

> IX. Visum est Patribus munus seligendi, com-
> ponendi vel corrigendi libros in Catholicorum
> collegiorum et scholarum praesertim usum, et
> ut ab omni errore contra fidem expurgati in
> lucem edantur curandi, committere Praesidibus,
> pro tempore existentibus, trium Collegiorum
> in Archidioecesi Baltimorensi, nempe S.
> Mariae Baltimorensis, S. Mariae apud Montes,
> et Collegii Georgiopolitani. Sanxerunt etiam
> Patres ut hi libri cum approbatione duorum
> saltem ex Praesidibus praedictorum Collegiorum,
> atque ex auctoritate Archiepiscopi Baltimoren-
> sis, typis mandentur; operam omnem se adhibi-
> turos pollicentes ut in collegiis, scholis,
> et ubique apud Fideles, recipiantur.[2]

---

[1]Guilday, Councils, pp. 102-105. Cf. also Guilday,
England, p. 261.

[2]Murphy, Concilia, p. 105. Translation: It seems
to the Fathers that the duty of selecting, composing or
correcting books especially for use in Catholic colleges
and schools, and expurgating them of all error against
faith, as well as editing them for public use should, for
the present time, be committed to the Presidents of the
three Colleges in the Archdiocese of Baltimore, Saint Mary's
of Baltimore, Mount Saint Mary's and Georgetown. Likewise
the Fathers decree that these books should be printed with
the approbation of at least two of the Presidents of the
aforementioned Colleges, and by the authority of the Archbishop of Baltimore. They themselves pledge that they will
exert every effort to insure the reception of the publications
in colleges, schools, and everywhere among the Faithful.

Realizing perhaps that their previously enacted legislation had been too general, the Bishops on this occasion speci- fied the men who were to be responsible for the editing and censoring. Heeding the earlier caution of Propaganda, they were careful to indicate the approval of the Arch- bishop of Baltimore. The Pastoral Letter was again written by England, and it contained the following passage on education:

> The education of the rising generation is, beloved brethren, a subject of the first im- portance; and we have accordingly, at all times, used our best efforts to provide, as far as our means would permit, not only ec- clesiastical seminaries to insure a succession in our priesthood and its extension; but we have moreover sought to create colleges and schools in which your children, whether male or female, might have the best opportunities of literature and science, united to a strict protection of their morals and the best safe- guards of their faith. You are aware that the success and the permanence of such institutions rest almost exclusively with you. It will be our most gratifying duty to see that their superiors and professors are worthy of the high trust reposed in them; but it is only by your patronage and zealous cooperation that their existence can be secured, their prosperity and usefulness be increased, and your children's children be made to bless the memory, and to pray for the souls of those who originated and upheld such establishments.[1]

In summary, the proceedings of the 1833 council indicate that the prelates were still viewing the Catholic

---

[1] Guilday, Pastorals, p. 74.

educational program in general terms. The passage from John
England's Pastoral is especially to the point. He is ad-
dressing himself almost directly to the issue of the degree
of inclusion which the Bishops intended for Catholic schools
and yet he is satisfied to appeal for support for the limited
program then in function. His own dilatory tactics in the
diocese of Charleston suggest that at least for him the future
of the Catholic school movement depended in large measure
upon a share in the public school fund. Subsequent appeals
for public funds in support of already established private
schools also indicate that other Bishops were also thinking
of a pattern of privately-controlled but publicly-supported
Catholic schools. Thus, their emphasis frequently pointed
to the service angle of existing Catholic schools.[1]

The decrees of the second council were submitted to
Roman authorities for approval and on April 23, 1834 the
Sacred College of Propaganda announced its approval. The
Roman documents, prepared under the leadership of Cardinal
Guiseppe Antonio Sola, reveal nothing of importance con-
cerning the sole educational decree.[2]

Three years later, in 1837, the Bishops convened
again, with the following prelates in attendance: Eccleston of

---

[1]Klinkhamer, Historical Reasons, p. 83.

[2]The principal Roman document is: Sagra Congregazione
De Propaganda Fide Ponente L Emo. e Rmo. Sig. Cardinale
Guiseppe Antonio Sola. Ristretto Sugli Atti e Decreti del
secondo Sinodo Provinciale di Baltimore negli Stati Uniti
dell' America Settentrionale. March, 1834.

Baltimore; Rosati of St. Louis; Fenwick of Boston; Kenrick
of Philadelphia; Purcell of Cincinnati; Chabrat of Bardstown; Clancy, coadjutor of Charleston, who two weeks before
had been transferred to the diocese of British Guiana in
South America; Brute of Vincennes; and Blanc of New Orleans.
John England arrived only after the opening sessions had
been completed. Absent were the aged Dubois of New York and
David of Bardstown. Flaget was in Europe. A forceful re-
minder of the times was the fact that Portier of Mobile was
en route but by the time he arrived in Baltimore all the
sessions were completed. There is little to indicate that
educational matters played any important role in the debates
of this council either. Brute had written on February 6,
1837 about other matters but expressed no concern about educational affairs.[1] In view of the fact that earlier Brute
had written to Rome concerning his efforts to found and support schools for both boys and girls in Vincennes, we may
wonder why he did not consider the problem important enough
for council deliberation. Brute, like his fellow Bishops,
was interested in gaining candidates for the priesthood and
for this reason he worked at interesting the Jesuits in
founding a college in his diocese.[2] That this desire colored

[1]BCA 27A A 4, Brute to Eccleston, February 6, 1837.

[2]Thomas T. McAvoy, trans. and ed., "Bishop Brute's
Report to Rome in 1836," The Catholic Historical Review,
XXIX (July, 1943), pp. 186-192.

much of his educational purposes is evident in the above
mentioned report. The only proposal relative to educational
matters located in the archives is a note sent by Purcell
of Cincinnati to Eccleston. He suggested for discussion among
other items the following two topics: "1. Should we allow
Catholic youth to frequent schools wherein Protestant bibles
are the text-books?" Later in the same letter he asked about
the general quality of the textbooks used in the schools and
urged that "Provision be made for male and female schools of
our own."[1] In addition to the above correspondence, Fenwick
of Boston had been corresponding regularly with Eccleston
regarding the printing of the proposed catechism.[2] In the
brief published minutes of the sessions no indication is
given that the discussion ever turned to education. It is
only in the Pastoral Letter, again written by England, that
we find mention of educational problems:

> We would also beloved brethren, renew
> the entreaty which we have made to you on
> other occasions, to unite your efforts to
> ours for upholding those institutions which
> we have created for the education of your
> children. It is our most earnest wish to
> make them as perfect as possible, in their
> fitness for the communication and improve-
> ment of science, as well as for the culti-
> vation of pure solid and enlightened piety.
> And if we occasionally experience some
> difficulty and do not advance as rapidly
> as the wishes of our friends, or their

[1] BCA 25 Q 6.
[2] BCA 24 U 4 (5/22/37; 24 U 5 8/7/37; 24 V 6 11/18/37).

too sanguine hopes would look for, some
allowance must be made for the difficulties
by which we are surrounded and the opposition which we experience. Yet, these notwithstanding, we are persuaded, that amongst
those under our superintendence, are to be
found, some of the most scientific and literary houses of education which our nation
possesses; some establishments for the instruction of youth, male and female, in which
there are successfully taught those speculative
and practical lessons which inform the understanding, regulate the imagination, cultivate
the taste, ameliorate the heart, improve the
disposition, impress the importance and obligation of fulfilling every social, civic,
domestic and religious duty, and teach the
best mode of their performance. And we
trust, that by a continuation of that patronage which they have received, we shall
be enabled to behold them take deep root in
our soul, flourish in beauty and vigour,
and furnish an abundant supply of useful
citizens and christians, fitted for con-
ferring blessings upon that country which
protects them and that religion which they
profess.[1]

Earlier in the Pastoral Letter England had again chosen

to write a paragraph decrying the textbook situation:

. . . We do not dwell upon the gross untruths,
the false charges, the notorious perversions,
the ribald abuse which are continually spread
before the eyes of millions of our fellow-
citizens against you and us, and our religion,
by what is called the periodical religious
press; we need not exhibit to you the pages
of several public journals to show the adverse
spirit of a large portion of political editors to truth and justice, where we are concerned. Not only are the public libraries
and the literary institutions formed upon the
same principle, and tracts and pamphlets which
exhale the poison of virulent misrepresentation and obloquy, widely disseminated, but

---

[1] Guilday, Pastorals, pp. 115-116.

the very school-books for even the youngest
learners are infected; so that from the most
tender childhood to the decrepitude of age,
the great portion of the reading public may
be taught to detest and to despise what they
are led to believe is our religion.[1]

Diffley finds in this Pastoral a sign that a policy
to provide Catholic education for Catholic children is implicit. Moreover, he indicates that, as in the 1833 council,
little specific mention is made of unsatisfactory relations
with the public schools.[2] It can certainly be agreed that
a policy of education had begun to take shape. The importance of schools for the training of clergy has been constantly emphasized and this interest by itself was already
a determined policy. To conclude that the execution of the
will of the Bishops implied a set pattern of regular Catholic
education for all seems to be contraindicated by the facts.
It was only with the subsequent dissatisfaction of the program of public education that the ideal of Catholic education
for all Catholic children began to take shape. The dissatisfaction and the consequent broadening of the base of
Catholic education went hand in hand.

The action of the office of Propaganda on the enacted decrees was swift. The decrees were approved on
September 2, and on that same date the new dioceses requested
in the council were created by Gregory XVI. An examination

[1]Guilday, Pastorals, p. 114.
[2]Diffley, American Catholic Reaction, p. 250.

of the materials prepared for the discussions in Rome show
that by this time the pattern of approval had become pretty
well standardized. Once again, no references to the American pattern of education were located.[1]

---

[1]The major paper prepared for this congregational
meeting was: Sagra Congregazione De Propaganda Fide Ponente
L'Emo. e Rmo. Sig. Cardinale Giacomo Filippo Fransoni
Prefetto Ristretto com Sommario Sinodo Terzo Provinciale
degli Stati Uniti dell' America Settentrionale tenuto in
Baltimore nel mese di Aprile, 1837. Luglio, 1837.

Chapter IV

Later Provincial Councils

The council of 1840 represents a decided advance in
the program of Catholic education. By this time the pattern
of public education, especially in the New England area,
had taken firm root. Synods held in Cincinnati and St.
Louis had almost certainly dealt with the educational problems in their specific localities. Purcell, the native-born
Irishman who had become a real champion of a native American
clergy, was especially vigorous in his work for education.
Several of his debates with the Protestant ministers of Cincinnati dwelt heavily on the relationship of Catholics to
the public schools.

One of the most difficult and absorbing problems of
the educational history of this period is the complex task
of explaining the gradual transfer of allegiance from religious schools to secular institutes. Some authors, i.e.,
Curran,[1] maintain that the Protestant ministers allowed
their hatred of Roman Catholicism to lead them into a religious compromise with public schoolmen. Others, like Culver,[2] would have us believe that Horace Mann was a far-
sighted philosopher who foresaw the sectarian morass and

---

[1]Curran, The Churches and the Schools.

[2]Raymond B. Culver, Horace Mann and Religion in the
Massachusetts Public Schools (New Haven: Yale University
Press, 1929).

84

consciously and courageously directed the course of the public
school away from these entanglements. Dunn in his treatment
of Mann brings to light some documents not utilized before
which would tend to place Mann in the light of an acutely
religious man who solved the dilemma thrust upon him only
in a very gradual way. As Dunn sees it,[1] the problem was
to reconcile the tradition of the times that religion did
indeed belong in public life and consequently that religion
belonged in public education. Obviously, the antithesis
to this was the delicate right of conscience in religious
matters with the adjoining need of non-sectarian teaching.
Mann, in this view, really wanted religion in public education, but saw no efficient solution to the dilemma. Once
again, according to Dunn:

> Horace Mann was a religious person.
> Horace Mann wanted religion in public education.
> Fervent declarations of this, and violent pro-
> tests when he was contrarily accused, rolled
> from his lips and his pen all through his ca-
> reer as secretary of the Board. This study
> indicates that any characterization of Mann as
> a conscious, deliberate destroyer of religion
> in education is without foundation in fact.
> (Dunn's footnote: In his last years when
> President of Antioch College, a private
> institution at Yellow Springs, Ohio, Mann
> constantly encouraged religious instruction
> and practice in the lives of the students.
> [Cf. Mary P. Mann, Life, pp. 435, 464, 467,
> 468.])[2]

---

[1]Dunn, What Happened to Religious Education, p. 179.

[2]Dunn, What Happened to Religious Education, p. 180.

It was only in attempting a solution to the other difficulty that Mann aroused the opposition of Catholic leaders. In striving to eliminate indoctrination, Mann was adamant in eliminating any sectarian doctrine. Dunn maintains that what Mann wanted left in the schools were "the basic principles of Christianity to be garnered by the children from listening to the reading of the Bible."[1] It is perhaps in this peculiar dilemma that much misunderstanding has arisen regarding the Catholic solution forged during these years. The large number of Bible cases which revealed that Catholic children were forced to read Protestant Bibles aroused the simple faith of the immigrant groups. Their clergy likewise held a basic distrust of the sincerity of the non-sectarianism of the public schoolmen and well they might, for the non-sectarianism in operation often meant simply a non-sectarian Protestant education. Viewed in this light, one can see why the Church Fathers even at this date still were willing to cast their lot with the public school system, provided that adequate provisions were made to insure that their children would be given truly public training, and not a secret form of Protestant indoctrination. To see in the program evolved by the fourth council, as Diffley does,[2] the turning point of parochial education seems

[1]Dunn, What Happened to Religious Education, p. 181.
[2]Diffley, American Catholic Reaction, pp. 263-269.

again to be anticipating the problems which did eventually
force Catholics to abandon all hope of practical participation
in the public schools. The reasons, however, which were given
in the later struggle are not the same as those presented in
this council. It is evident from the Pastoral issued at its
conclusion that the participating Fathers were still searching
for a pattern of cooperation with the public schools. There
was much optimism as regards the public support of the already existing schools and only later were the members of the
hierarchy completely convinced that this pattern of public
and private education was impossible. It would be equally
wrong, however, to imagine that the hierarchy were beginning
to give way in their lengthy battle against the prejudices
which they had experienced during the course of the previous
fifteen years. Quite the opposite, in fact, seems to have
been the case. Some were not quite alive to the seriousness
of the situation and were much too sanguine in their optimism,
but others were acutely aware of the explosive situation, but
they hoped that the worst had passed and that the Church could
now embark on a period of growth. Eccleston wrote to the
mission societies in France, praising the missionary opportunities in this country. Understandably, he was showing the
bright side of the missionary field, since he had reason to
expect more funds from these supporters if there was good
hope of success.

> In my opinion the public mind will never
> be more favorably disposed toward the Catholic
> Religion than at present. The observations I
> had occasion to make in my late visitation of

this extensive diocese, confirm me in this
opinion. I everywhere remarked a laudable
desire to know the truths of the Catholic
doctrine; and I am convinced that many, if
they had instruction, would renounce their
prejudices and their error.[1]

A contrary opinion was given by John England in the following
year. From the context of his report, it appears that the
public school movement had not yet reached the Charleston
diocese. Knight supports this contention.[2] In describing
the terrible losses to the Church, England reports:

The causes of this loss, in my opinion,
are: 1. the dispersion of countless Catholic
emigrants in a country where no preparation
had been made to enable them to practice their
religion; where, on the contrary, numerous
and almost insurmountable obstacles were
thrown in their way;
2. the want of religious establishments to
educate Catholic children in the religion
of their parents;
3. the deplorable position of many of
these children, who, by the death, misfortune,
or misconduct of their parents, were thrown
in the Protestant schools, where the adopted
plan of education soon weaned them from the
true faith. . . .[3]

Among the suggestions sent in by the prelates in preparation
for their meeting, there is an interesting chapter of midwestern educational history. This is the story of the relationships of Benjamin Bosworth Smith (1794-1884). This

[1]Annals of the Propagation of the Faith, Sept., 1838;
quoting a letter from Eccleston at Baltimore, Jan. 31, 1838,
p. 302.

[2]Edgar W. Knight, A Documentary History of Education
in the South before 1860, 5 vols. (Chapel Hill, N.C.: The
University of North Carolina Press, 1953), vol. 5, 1-210 passim.

[3]Annals of the Propagation of the Faith, Feb. 1838,
no. 11, p. 101. Letter of Dr. England, Bishop of Charleston,
to the Central Committee of the Institution.

man was a Protestant Episcopal Bishop and in 1840 was chosen
Superintendent of Public Instruction for the state of Kentucky.
In this capacity he worked diligently for the spread of the
public system in Kentucky. Consequently, his activities in
this regard brought him into contact with the Catholic hierarchy who were at the same time making great efforts to establish a solid system of parochial education in that state.
This incident gives us an understanding of the difficulties
that arose for all concerned in the movement on the frontier.
Understandably, the fears of the Catholic Bishops were heightened when they received invitations to join a system of public
education which was directed by a Protestant Episcopal Bishop.
Bishop Smith himself seems to have envisioned for the state
of Kentucky a system of schools, dominated by sectarian groups,
yet supported by public funds. With this end in view, he
passed a resolution at the Conference of the Methodist Episcopal Church approving the system and at the same time recommended that all preachers and people extend encouragement
to the system.[1] Quite naturally, Smith was eager to include
the Catholics in the program, because by this time they had
begun to represent a sizeable portion of the Kentucky population. He was quick to establish contact with Martin John

[1]The most inclusive article on the Educational and
Episcopal work of Benjamin Bosworth Smith is that by W. Robert Insko, Historical Magazine of the Protestant Episcopal
Church, vol. xxii (June, 1953). This entire issue is devoted
to the work of Smith. Particularly useful for the work of
Smith as Superintendent of Public Instruction also was Barks-
dale Hamlett, History of Education in Kentucky (Kentucky Department of Education, Louisville, 1914). Much of the information given here is also contained in Dunn, pp. 266-267.

Spalding of Bardstown and at the latter's suggestion, Smith
prepared a letter to be sent to Bishop Flaget, who was then
in charge of the diocese. Included in the same letter is
an explanatory note which Smith wrote to Spalding in asking
him to forward the letter to Flaget. The letter to Spalding
follows:

Agreeably to your suggestions I have addressed a letter to Bishop Flaget on the subject of common School Education, & herewith
inclose it to your care, to be handed to the
Bishop. The more I reflect upon the subject,
the deeper becomes my solicitude that the Roman
Catholic community in the state should cooperate with their Fellow Citizens in this
great cause. Out of my natural official solicitude in this behalf, & in the spirit of
genuine kindliness & candor allow me to express
to you the grounds of this solicitude. I deprecate the neglect of the education of thousands of the children of our plain farming
interest; which must, I fear, result from the
declinature of the Roman Catholic interest, to
fall in, with the common school system. I as
deeply (perhaps more deeply) deprecate, that
more fierce exacerbation of sectarian bitterness, which I foresee must be the result. I
should also exceedingly deplore the loss to
your population of the benefits of their share
of the public bounty; & their exposure to a
kind of taxation, in the advantages of which
they could not participate. For though I
should certainly, under the condition mentioned in my letter to the Bishop, move the
Legislature to relieve you from this unfair
burden, it is by no means certain that they
would be disposed to do so. It would be exceedingly unfortunate for the Protestant Population,
in mixed neighborhoods, & in some sense hard and
unfair, to be deprived of the benefits of the
Public Fund & of the Common system, by their being too few to form a school; and that, (as
they would of course think) on account of the
unreasonable prejudices of their Roman Catholk

Fellow citizens, against a noble work. I
am, further, exceedingly anxious to anti-
cipate, & by anticipating to prevent, the
imputation to which our Roman Catholic Fellow Citizens will, in such case, certainly
expose themselves; that after all their
zeal for Education, they are not the friends
of universal popular education; that they
are content that thousands of children of
the plain farming interest should remain un-
educated; and that they, in fact, sustain
their Colleges and large Female Schools for
the sake of the funds which they derive from
Protestant patronage; and of the insensible
influence which they exert over the plastic
minds of Protestant children, in favor of
their own peculiarities. The time is near
at hand when the practical decision of the
country portion of our Roman Catholic Fellow
citizens, must be had; & I am therefore the
more anxious that the whole question in all
its bearings, should be before your leading
minds.

    with sentiments of sincere respect,
yours, etc. B. B. Smith[1]

Spalding dutifully presented Smith's letter to Bishop Flaget.

In this letter Smith does not emphasize so much the dangers

that might accrue to the Catholic body if they did not co-

operate in the movement. Presumably, Smith was on much more

intimate terms with Spalding than with Flaget or any of the

other leading churchmen of Kentucky and it was only to Spald-

ing that he was willing to convey his real intentions. The

letter to Flaget is a sincere and earnest attempt to find a

common basis of unity.

    I greatly regretted your absence from
Bardstown during my recent visit there, in
as much as I was anxious to hold communica-

---

[1] BCA 32A C 6 Smith to Martin John Spalding, no date.

tion with the heads of the Roman Catholic
Church, in my capacity as Superintendent
of Public Instruction, touching the question
of Common Schools in Roman Catholic country-
neighborhoods. As I failed the pleasure of
an interview, at the suggestion of the Rev.
Pres. Spalding, I address you by letter.
My first object is to give assurances on
the part of the Board of Education of the
State, of their disposition to respect the
private religious opinions of all classes of
Citizens, and to extend to them the benefits
of the public funds, & of the benign operation of the proposed system. Whenever, in
any school District the majority of voters
are Roman Catholic, the Law leaves all the
details in their hands. In mixed Schools,
the Board, if desired, will take pleasure in
giving instructions that, in the selection of
Teachers, regard shall be had as far as practicable, to the known wishes of the Roman
Catholics, & that every species of sectarian
aggression be strictly prohibited. Arrangements, no doubt, could be made, for separating
the children into different classes, if desired; for excusing Roman Catholic children
from Protestant prayers; for providing their
own translation of the Holy Scriptures for
their use, or for excusing them from employ-
ing them as a School Book. In case no such
understanding should satisfy the Roman Catholic community, & they should altogether decline any participation in the benefits of the
proposed System, as one of the Board of Education, I shall be prompt to move the Legislature
to relieve our Roman Catholic Fellow Citizens,
from the burden of the neighborhood tax, from
the advantages of which they may feel themselves excluded; on condition that some security be given for the education of every child
of Roman Catholic parents, between the ages
7 & 17 years: -- it seeming to me reasonable
that the State should insist, that no portion
of its population should grow up in ignorance.
After this communication on my part it would
be desirable if you have no objection,
that some communication should be

made on your part, informing the Board what
course it would be agreeable to their Roman
Catholic Fellow Citizens for them to take
in the premises.[1]

Instead of replying to Bishop Smith Flaget insisted
upon sending the communications to his own superiors. Accordingly, he bound the letters together and sent them to Francis
P. Kenrick of Philadelphia, who had the reputation among the
Bishops of being the most scholarly and therefore most able
to judge situations of this type. Flaget was not enthusiastic
about the proposal and in his letter to Kenrick indicated
that he was not eager to have his children in the public
schools, unless he was free to choose the teachers.[2] Bishop
England also wrote in preparation for this council, but in
spite of the fact that he mentions many other things, he
makes no reference to his educational problems or desires.
Benedict Fenwick from Boston gave vent to his irritation at
being called so frequently to these discussions:

Are we to have another council shortly?
I hope not. It is too often in our widely
extended Province for Bps. to meet. The last
business is not yet settled--nor has there
been time to settle it....Why not wait one,
two or even three years more?[3]

A few months later, when the council had been actually announced, he penned another note, in which he promised

---

[1]BCA 32 A C 6 Smith to Flaget.

[2]BCA 32 A C 6 Flaget to Kenrick, August 8, 1840.

[3]BCA 24 U 8 Benedict Fenwick to Eccleston, Boston,
November 26, 1839.

his attendance. At the same time, he indicated that he had
nothing at all to suggest, a hint at least that he did not consider his school problems as something that should merit
national discussion and airing.[1] Among the positive suggestions
located was one from Kenrick of Philadelphia, written long
before the letter from Flaget. Actually, Flaget's letter
did not reach Kenrick until after the meeting, but Smith's
proposal presumably had been made some time before that, and
therefore rightly belongs among the preparatory papers. Kenrick wrote among other suggestions for questions to be discussed at the council:

> Quid faciendum ut puerorum prospiciatur
> Christianae educationi, et quomodo cavendum
> est ne publico systemate scholarum pueris
> catholicis noceatur, vel fidei interatur
> praejudicium? Utrum publico systemati
> fovendum sit vel repugnandum?[2]

Kenrick here was succinctly and clearly placing the issue
before the mind of the Archbishop. Quite obviously numbers
of Catholic youth were still attending the public schools
and Kenrick wondered whether in his official capacity as
head of the Philadelphia Church he could encourage participation in the public system. Later remarks of his indicate

---

[1]BCA 24 U 9. Benedict Fenwick to Eccleston,
Boston, March 11, 1840.

[2]BCA 25 F 10. Francis Kenrick to Eccleston,
Philadelphia, February 8, 1840. Translation: What is to be
done in order to see to the Christian education of youth
and how can we be alert lest by the public system of schools
catholic youth be harmed or prejudiced against their faith?
Whether the public system is to be favored or rejected?

that he expected a negative reply to his query! Another
important letter came from the Bishop of the huge diocese
of Dubuque. Matthias Loras was to be a great spokesman for
the cause of Catholic education in the middle west and his
opinion was greatly respected. Consecrated in 1837, he remained a powerful force until his death in 1858. His early
interest in the field is displayed by this letter:

> Quoad quaestiones tractandas, mea humilis
> opinio est nihil majoris momenti proponi posse
> opium media ad suppeditandos ac etiam informan-
> dos Catholicos et competentes scholae magistros,
> v.g. ad instar Reverusm ep. Sti. Ludovici.
> Zelum Protestantium in ista materia omni nostra
> aemulatione dignum est et illi quidam ut
> corruptibilem coronam accipiant, nos autem
> incorruptam.[1]

The council opened in solemn session on May 17 and
closed again on May 24. The new Sees created in 1837, Dubuque,
Nashville, and Natchez, raised the total to fifteen suffragan
Sees, all but three of which were east of the Mississippi.
A conspicuous absentee from the deliberations was Bishop
Hughes of New York. Had he been present perhaps the legis-
lation enacted by the Fathers would have been more forceful.
A major pronouncement of the council was a reassertion by

---

[1]BCA 25 J 3; Loras to Eccleston, Dubuque,
February 10, 1840. Translation: In regard to the questions
to be discussed, my humble opinion is that nothing of greater
moment can be proposed than the best means of supplying and
training Catholic and competent school masters, after the
example of the Bishop of St. Louis. The zeal of Protestants
in this matter is worthy of emulation: and they indeed that
they may receive a perishable crown, we, an imperishable one.

the Bishops that they did not intend to tell their people
how to vote in the coming national elections. The pregnant
phrase:

> We disclaim all right to interfere with your
> judgment in the political affairs of our com-
> mon country, and are far from entertaining
> the wish to control you in the constitutional
> exercise of your freedom[1]

was a reassurance to Protestants that the hierarchy did not
intend to engage in the politics of the country.

The sixth decree of this council counselled pastors
to be aware of the nature of public education. Bearing in
mind the previous discussion it seems that here again the
Bishops were aware of the Protestant nature of public education and were inveighing against this influence. In this
particular decree, the Bishops seem to be asking for a truly
non-sectarian public school. Diffley concludes his analysis
of this decree and the accompanying Pastoral with the summary
remark that "an irrevocable decision had been made by all
the Bishops at the Fourth Provincial Council of Baltimore."[2]
The meagre archival materials available preclude a judgment
as to the universality of the decision, but the debates
which raged in the Third Plenary Council many years later
would seem to urge caution in expressing this uniformity
at such an early stage. The only available minutes for this

---

[1]Guilday, Pastorals, p. 142. Cf. also Ellis, American
Catholicism, pp. 71-75.

[2]Diffley, American Catholic Reaction, p. 269.

ouncil are those contained in the official printed copy,[1]
nd in reference to the present decree there in only the
imple statement that the decree was passed. It seems more
ikely to state that the dilemma which Horace Mann had
ecided in favor of the total exclusion of sectarianism from
he school was only now beginning to take full effect.
atholic Bishops, indeed the whole country, could not know
hat the relatively simple statement of a policy of non-
ectarianism as was announced by the New England school
oards would involve such far-reaching implications that the
upreme Court in 1963 would be called upon to find the
imple fact of prayer in the schools unconstitutional.
he fact that the clergy could not predict the course
f public education during these trying years was not
urprising. As indicated, many public officials them-
elves were not dedicated to the principle of non-sectarianism.
ishop Smith's vision of public education was a far cry from
hat sounded by Henry Barnard. It seems from statements
f the Bishops here in council that these men would have
ettled for a truly non-sectarian public school. Flaget
id not challenge the type of public school that Smith was
ffering; he doubted the sincerity of the Episcopal Bishop!
he defensiveness of the immigrant Catholic had not yet
iven way to the complete self-consciousness of a democratic

---

[1]Murphy, Concilia, p. 166.

citizenry. It was only when the clergy of the middle-western area had a full-blown educational system already in operation that the rest of the Catholic hierarchy were willing to legislate forcefully. In fact, one of the pressures used to secure the passage of the later stringent decrees was precisely the argument that schools already in existence would disappear unless strong measures were adopted. The Fourth Provincial Council is too early a period in which to locate this protective phase of Catholic education. At this time clergymen were still battling among themselves about doctrinal differences; the secularistic emphasis which so bothered the Bishops of the Third Plenary Council was to come only later.

The decrees as passed by this council were straightforward declarations that Catholics would not tolerate their children to attend schools in which Protestant influence was dominant. The pertinent decree reads:

> Cum constet publicae educationis rationem plerisque in his Provinciis ita iniri, ut haeresibus inserviat, puerorum catholicorum mentibus sensim sine sensu falsis sectarum principiis imbutis, monemus pastores ut omni quo valent studio catholicorum puerorum christianae et catholicae educationi prospiciant, et diligenter invigilent ne versione protestantica bibliorum utantur, vel sectarum cantica aut preces recitent. Ideo invigilandum erit,[1]

---

[1] Translation: Since it is clear that the purpose of public education in very many of these Provinces is so constructed as to favor heresies, the minds of catholic children being gradually filled without their knowing it with the false principles of the sects, we warn the pastors that with all possible zeal they look after the christian and catholic education of the catholic young and that they be alertly warchful so that they do not use protestant versions of the bible or recite songs or prayers of the sects.

ne in publicas scholas libri vel exercitia
hujusmodi introducantur,. cum fidei pietatisque discrimine. Constanter autem et moderate hisce sectarum conatibus ubique resis-
tendum est, eorum qui auctoritate valent
opportunum adhibere remedium implorato
auxilio.[1]

Bishop England once again compiled the Pastoral for
this council and by this time his remarks and thoughts concerning education had become standardized. Whether the more
prominent place given educational matters is indicative of
the higher importance that he placed upon these comments is
a moot question. At any rate, his paragraphs contained no
new advance upon his previous utterances. The statements,
as usual, are hard-hitting, and to the point:

> There are few subjects dearer to us than
> the proper education of your children, on this
> mainly depends their true respectability in
> this world, also the consolation of your own
> declining years, the prosperity of religion,
> the honor of God on earth, and your eternal
> salvation and that of your descendants. It
> is therefore that we have always deemed it to
> be one of our most pressing obligations to use
> our best and earliest efforts in providing es-
> tablishments where they may be carefully edu-
> cated by competent persons in all that is
> necessary for their prosperity in this life,
> whilst they were taught by admonition and
> example to walk in that path which leads to
> heaven. In general we have found our flocks
> disposed to profit by the opportunities thus
> afforded, but not always so ready to aid in
> defraying the expenses which should necessarily

---

[1]Murphy, Concilia, pp. 171-172. Translation: Therefore, they will have to be vigilant that books or exercises
of this kind not be introduced into the public schools, with
danger to faith and piety. Moreover constantly and with moderation they must everywhere resist these attempts of the sects,
imploring the help of those who have authority to use a fitting
remedy.

be incurred in having them secured and made
permanent. In many instances also, they who
belong not to the household of faith have
discovered the advantages which accompanied the
system of education in our schools and colleges; they have often been more industrious
to profit by them than have you, for whom
they were principally intended. We would
then admonish you, in a spirit of affectionate
interest for your own and your children's welfare, that we have in many instances observed
two serious mistakes upon this head. The first
that of parents, who altogether deprived their
offspring of that education to which they were
entitled, upon the plea that thereby they would
be better served by placing in their hands at
their entrance upon a life of industry, the
money which had been saved by the restriction
of their education. The second that of a mistaken and thriftless economy, which led them
to keep their children, especially females, at
an inferior school of less cost, until they had
nearly gone through those years allotted to
education, and then sent them for a comparatively short time to an establishment in which
they should have been placed years before.
The great evil in both cases is the danger to which they are exposed, of having their
faith undermined, the imperfect instruction
which they receive, if they get any, upon the
most important subject of religion, the nearly total abandonment of their religious practices and their exposure in their tender youth
to the fatal influence of that false shame
which generally arises from the mockery or
the superciliousness of those who undervalue
their creed. Beloved brethren we address you
not in the language of speculation or of abstract reasoning; our words are the faint effort to convey to you the deep impression which
long and melancholy experience has made upon
our minds; for we have witnessed the blastings
of our hopes in the ravages which have thus
been made.[1]

[1]Guilday, Pastorals, pp. 124-125.

This section of the Pastoral is then followed by a vindica-
tion of the teaching role of the Church and its authority.
Quite obviously, England felt constrained to demonstrate for
all that the Catholic Church did indeed revere and love the
Scriptures.

> In our country it is assumed by the larger
> portion of our fellow-citizens that versions
> of the Bible, not sustained by that evidence
> which we require, are the word of God; and more-
> over, that all individuals and all churches are
> liable to error in declaring its meaning, and
> they admit, as the mode by which we shall
> learn what God has taught, the opinions, con-
> jectures and judgment of each individual, for
> himself--all of which upon the ground that
> we have set forth is subversive of the purity
> of doctrine and the unity of faith; and the
> admission of which would be a dereliction of
> our duty. It is moreover generally prevalent
> that in public schools, some one of those ver-
> sions should be read by the children as the
> word of God, and frequently that the teacher
> who is an unauthorized individual, should
> give his own opinions as its proper interpre-
> tation, and that the child should be habituated
> practically to the principle, that it is the
> right of each individual to use his own pri-
> vate judgment, and not the public testimony
> of the Church as the standard of interpre-
> tation; whence you will at once perceive,
> the total opposition of the principle on
> which such schools are conducted, to the
> unchangeable doctrines and discipline of
> our Church.
> We are desirous that all under our charge
> should be as well acquainted with the doc-
> trine found in the Holy Scriptures as with
> any other portion of the word of God, we al-
> so highly approve of their being familiar
> with the edifying histories and admirable
> moral instruction which abound therein, we

therefore recommend that the authorised version be found in the houses of the faithful,
and that portions of it be frequently read
with the veneration which it so well deserves,
and meditated upon for the purpose of becoming better acquainted with the providential
ways of the Lord, for the amendment of life,
for the edification of the well disposed and
for the encouragement of virtue. We desire
that at an early period, children should be
instructed in the Sacred History, that they
may be made acquainted with the nature and
value of the divine volume, that they be gradually brought to its perusal with docile
hearts, and that in place of allowing them
an indiscriminate use of that which is difficult and liable to gross misconstruction,
together with what is simple and edifying,
they be judiciously led by proper selections,
under discreet and pious guides, to the right
use of this rich treasure. Moreover, we are
disposed to doubt seriously whether the introduction of this sacred volume as an ordinary class book into schools, is beneficial
to religion. It is thereby exposed to that
irreverend familiarity, which is calculated
to produce more contempt than veneration;
it is placed side by side with mere human
productions, with the fables of mythology
and the speculations of a vain philosophy;
it is thus too often made the subject of
a vulgar jest, it sinks to the level of
task-books, and shares the aversion and the
remarks which are generally bestowed upon
them by children. If the authorised version
be used in a school, it should be under circumstances very different from those which
are usually found in the public institutions
of our States, and this shows the necessity
of your better exertions to establish and
uphold seminaries and schools, fitted according to our own principles, and for the education of the children who are daily rising
up, and numbers of whom are lost for want
of such institutions.

There is another evil of which we have
still to complain. We can scarcely point

out a book in general use in the ordinary
schools, or even in higher seminaries, wherein covert and insidious efforts are not made
to misrepresent our principles, to distort
our tenets, to vilify our practices and to
bring contempt upon our Church and its members.
The system of which this is a part has been
of long standing, and is not peculiar to the
United States. It is no easy matter thus to
preserve the faith of your children in the
midst of so many difficulties. It is not
then because of any unkind feeling to our
fellow-citizens, it is not through any reluctance on our part, to contribute whatever
little we can to the prosperity of what are
called the common institutions of the country,
that we are always better pleased to have a
separate system of education for the children
of our communion, but because we have found
by a painful experience, that in any common
effort it was always expected that our dis-
tinctive principles of religious belief and
practice should be yielded to the demands
of those who thought proper to charge us with
error; and because we saw with great pain
the differences which an attempt to combine
and conciliate principles, which we have never
been able to reconcile, has produced in a distant
Church which has always been found faithful.
We are happy to perceive the existence of a
spirit to sustain the efforts recently made
to supply our schools, and our families with
some books, which whilst they remove the dis-
colourings of fiction, and vindicate the
truth of history, will rescue from unmerited
censure a portion of our illustrious dead,
without doing violence to the feelings of
even our opponents. We are anxious that
truth and charity should have dominion in
every place, but especially in our schools.
We should be gratified to behold the books
of earlier instruction also prepared upon
the same principle, and we strenuously recommend to you to encourage and to sustain
those who, being properly qualified, may
undertake the task.

It is but a few years since the schools
which the female religious orders and congregations so usefully superintend, were ex-

tensively spread abroad through our Union;
already you have gathered rich fruits from
the exertion of those virtuous and laborious sisters. The peculiar blessing of heaven appears to rest upon their work, calumny
has failed in her vile efforts to taint their
fair fame: popular frenzy has been excited
by every bad art to effect their ruin, but
with one notorious exception, it has been
restrained and rebuked, and now we may feel
confident, under the blessing of heaven,
that in a short period, under your auspices
our female children will have secured to
them, whether they be blessed with the goods
of this world or tried by poverty, the mighty
boon of as perfect a system of education as
need be admired; nor shall we be subject
to the partisan spirit of political leaders,
nor dependent upon the unsteady and contested
votes of legislative halls for its continu-
ance.[1]

In this lengthy section it becomes apparent that the

sectarian Bibles were beginning to raise tempers. Catholic

insistence that their subjects read only a version author-

ized by Catholic authorities was generally ignored by public

officials. Consequently, Catholic authorities tended to

insist with a great deal of truculence upon their rights in

this matter. Once again, the available documents from the

transactions of the College of Propaganda do not reveal any

discussions in regard to the sixth decree. In replying to

the American Bishops in regard to the council acts, Gregory

XVI on December 19, 1840, wrote, among other things, in

---

[1]Guilday, *Pastorals*, pp. 132-135.

praise of the desire of American Bishops to take the means
necessary for forming in Catholic children solid virtue and
true faith.[1]

Without doubt the period between 1840-1850 was truly
crucial for the development of the Catholic system as such.
The issue had been clearly put by Kenrick in his suggestions
to the previous councils: should the hierarchy encourage
the efforts of the nation at public education in general or
should they begin to extend their efforts at their own system. It would be logical therefore to expect that the three
councils which were held during the period would also come
to grips with educational issues and set forth guidelines
for priests and people. Unfortunately such was not the case
at all. Although the work had been begun in 1840, the legislation at each of these succeeding councils was disappointingly brief and almost nothing was mentioned in regard to
education itself. Certainly there were plenty of alterca-
tions throughout the nation to keep attention focused on
these matters. In their national meetings, however, little
was said and done to alleviate the strained relationships.
Gone, too, were the rousing Pastorals of Bishop England who
had died in 1842.

---

[1] Shearer, Pontificia, pp. 212-213. The major document is entitled: Sagra Congregazione de Propaganda Fide
onente L. Emo. e Rmo. Sig. Cardinale Giacomo Filippo Fran-
oni Praefetto Ristretto. Per la revisione degli Atti e
ecreti del Concilio Quarto Provinciale di Baltimore cele-
ratosi nel Maggio 1840; Novembre, 1840. Both the Acta and
the Scritturi have a considerable number of papers dealing
with this council.

In studying this period it seems that one overlooked
aspect has been the sheer force of numbers which thrust itself upon the nation in general and the Catholic population
in particular, especially through immigrations. The natural
increase in work that grew apace with the numbers of Catholics
may perhaps have so occupied the time and energies of the
clergy that what little strength remained from the simple
ministrations of the sacraments was not sufficient to stem
the popular movement towards public education in public
schools. The Catholic increase in population of this period
may be explained in threefold fashion: first, there was a
large influx of European immigrants. With them came their
traditions of large families, so Catholic population increased
rapidly through this channel; secondly, the annexation of a
large area of traditionally Catholic country as a result of
the Mexican War added large groups of Catholics to the American Church; and, finally, the Church itself, in spite of
nativistic assertions of foreign domination, was becoming
increasingly Americanized and more attractive to other Americans. Several prominent converts, such as the indomitable
Orestes Brownson, began to spread the Catholic message in
truly American fashion.

If there be any truth to the frontier thesis then
we can look to the middle west for the picture of the Church,
for it was during this period that the frontier amalgamation

was taking place there. Certainly also it was during this
period and in this area that the immigrant was most able
to lose himself and devote himself to the clearing of the
land, untortured by the conflicts that met his less fortunate
brother, jammed in the seaboard cities. Large German set-
tlements, however, grew up in the midwest and refused to be
absorbed by the sparse native elements and in these large
masses we find a source and a force for real parochial Catholic education. These settlers, eager to see their language
and their traditions preserved, quickly followed the leadership of their Bishops in setting up and supporting parochial
schools, taught by "their own." An example of this support
and its results can be found in the diocese of Cincinnati
which under Purcell had become the foremost diocese in ad-
vocating educational progress and reform. From the pages
of the Catholic Telegraph in the forties and fifties poured
a series of articles extolling the schools of the Catholic
Church and urging the people to support them. As an example
of this influence, the following article is adequate:

> And now that such facilities are en-
> joyed by the female youth of the diocese,
> how greatly do we not regret that similar
> advantages are not afforded to the boys.
> In this respect our German brethren, at
> least in this city, are far ahead of us.
> They have built a large and commodious school
> house at St. Mary's; they are preparing to

build two more, one at Holy Trinity, where
a large basement has hitherto served for
this purpose, and another adjoining the
new church of St. John the Baptist. Teachers are provided at considerable expense,
which is, however, generously and nobly
disregarded; and the enlightened attention
of the pastors of those congregations is
directed to the placing of those different
schools on such a footing as will leave
nothing further to be desired by Catholic
parents but the faithful correspondence of
the youth with the graces and blessings thus
liberally provided for them by our Holy
Religion.
   For the English-speaking youth of our
churches equal if not superior advantages
will, at last, we trust, be secured by the
opening of a Free School for boys on part
of the premises ceded for religious and
educational purposes to the fathers of the
Society of Jesus by the bishop. When this
arrangement is once made, we shall have
done much towards furnishing ample resources
for the right kind of education to all the
youth, both male and female, of the Catholic
congregations of the city, and as many
others as are willing to comply with the
rules in order to avail themselves of their
benefits.[1]

As Catholics in all sections of the country made

serious efforts to gain a portion of the public school funds,

or at least lodged vigorous protests against the Protestant

nature of public education, it was natural that controver-

sies should arise. The most celebrated of these occurred

in New York City. There under the leadership of John Hughes

and with the cooperation of Governor Seward, Catholics made

their most determined bid for a share of the public funds.

---

[1] The Catholic Telegraph, August 21, 1845.

The debate ended with a refusal of state funds after a pro-
tracted and bitter dispute. The Maclay Bill caused much ill
will and its close passage in the Senate was a true indication of the power and influence which the Protestant religion
had over the public schools in that area. Basically, the
Maclay Bill merely assured that non-sectarian treatment in
the schools would be guaranteed. Hughes had no reason to be
satisfied with his minimum victory. Down in Charleston,
John England followed the debates with great interest and
on their conclusion, he inserted the following notice in the
Miscellany:

> We this day insert the addresses made
> by Bishop Hughes and the Very Reverend Doc-
> tor Power to an adjourned meeting of the
> Catholics of New York, on the subject of
> the recent decision of the city council
> respecting the right of the Catholics to
> a share of this fund. Both addresses are
> worthy of the orators; each is excellent
> in its kind. For our own parts, we were not
> disappointed by the result of the applica-
> tion to the council. Indeed we expected
> nothing else. We write deliberately when
> we state that, probably, there is not a
> town or city council in the United States
> that would not have decided in the same way.
> Do we then think the decision just? No.
> Do we think the council dishonest? That
> is not the ground of our opinion. What then
> is it? We do not think it likely that a
> public body can be found in the United States
> which does not, without its own consciousness
> or suspicion, think and act under the influ-
> ence of great prejudice against Catholics,

their claims, their rights, their principles,
their religion, and their politics. Nor is
it strange that such would be the case.[1]

Emphasizing the prejudice that everywhere existed against

the Catholic minority, England continues on the next page:

> . . . It is, therefore, that we said that the
> Catholic cannot expect justice from any
> public body in this country, because every
> such body is more or less under the influ-
> ence of that prejudice which we have so
> imperfectly described. What else can ac-
> count for the injustice of Massachusetts,
> the bigotry of Boston, the criminality of
> its public courts of justice, the gross
> indecency of the very best and most fit-
> ting representative of Charlestown, and
> the absence of all sense of shame as well
> as of equity.[2]

The importance of the reaction of the clergy to these debates

cannot be over-emphasized. While more complete sutdies have

indicated that both bodies were limiting their horizons by

self-imposed rules, we are concerned with the influence of

these debates on the subsequent course of educational legis-

lation. Without doubt, the influence of Hughes in New York

was a potent factor and his experience in New York convinced

him that Catholics could not expect a share of the public

funds. Having made this decision, he cast all his energies

into the development of a private system. "The time has

almost come," he told his people in an oft-repeated pastoral

---

[1] U. S. Catholic Miscellany, Vol. XX, No. 34, 1841.

[2] U. S. Catholic Miscellany, Vol. XX, No. 34, 1841

of 1850, "when we shall have to build the school-house first
and the church afterward."[1]

In terms of the actual violence caused, no outbreak
was more severe than that precipitated by Kenrick of Phila-
phia in 1844 when he protested the enforced use by Catholic
children of the Protestant version of the Bible. The subsequent riots have been described in detail in another place[2]
and it is of importance here only to note that the crux of
Bible reading continued to plague public educators for many
years. Perhaps the most unfortunate outcome of the Philadelphia experiences was the widespread belief among Protestants that the Bishop had forbidden Catholics to read any
version of the Bible; consequently, they were able to picture themselves as ardent defenders of the Bible, thereby
adding fuel to the already flaming debates. Kenrick himself

---

[1]The story of the work of Bishop Hughes and his disputes with the New York Public School Society have been sufficiently told. The most complete monograph is that of Henry
J. Browne, "Public Support of Catholic Education in New York,
1825-1842: Some New Aspects," Historical Records and Studies
of the United States Catholic Historical Society, Vol. 41,
1953, pp. 14-41. Next in line would certainly be the detailed
analysis presented by Lawrence Cremin in his study of the development of the public school movement, The American Common
School, passim. . Likewise of importance is the study by Edward Connors, Church-State Relationships in Education in the
State of New York (Washington, D. C.: Catholic University
Press, 1951).

[2]Hugh P. Nolan, The Most Reverend Francis Patrick
Kenrick: Third Bishop of Philadelphia, 1830-1851 (Washington,
D. C.: Catholic University Press, 1948), pp. 288-342; Billing-
ton, Protestant Crusade, pp. 220-237.

discussed the issues involved in the altercation and disclosed

his deep concern about the schools in a report he penned for

Propaganda officials a year later:

> . . . Caeterum illud dolendum pueros Catholicos
> plerosque in scholis publicis, quae legis
> auctoritate erectae sunt, institui cum cae-
> teris quamvis enim lege cautum sit ne paren-
> tum religionis praejudicium fiat, facile
> tamen contingit animos magistrorum artibus
> devios agi, et falsis imbui praeceptis.
> Scholae hae reguntur a quibusdam electis a
> populo, et libri adhibentur his probati.
> Voluerunt jusseruntque Bibliorum quandam
> portionem singulis diebus legi scholae ini-
> tio, ut pia coepisse viderentur: et versionem
> Protestanticum legendam tradiderunt. . . .

In the midst of all this confusion, however, there

was still a firm, solid movement which continued to emphasize

the need for popular education, whether it came from public

or private sources. The following description of the ignor-

ant person and his woes comes from a leading Catholic news-

paper of the period, but it might well have appeared in Mann's

portfolio.

---

[1]"Relatio Status ecclesiae Philadelphiae in Statibus
foederatis Americae Septentrionalis, S. Cong. de Propaganda
Fide facta ab episcopo Philadelphiensi," Scrit. Rif., May 20,
1845. Translation: In addition, it is to be regretted that
the majority of the Catholic youth are educated in public
schools, erected by the authority of law, along with children of other sects. Although it is forbidden by law to do
anything prejudicial to the religion of the parents, it easily
happens that their minds are warped by the artifices of the
teachers, and they are imbued with false principles. These
schools are ruled by certain representatives elected by the
people, and the books to be used are approved by them. They
wished and demanded that a certain portion of the Bible be
read each day at the opening of the school, so that it might
seem to have begun piously: and they furnished a Protestant
version to be read.

> We cannot conceive a more pitiable
> being than he who cannot read or write.
> The one is condemned to a species of
> eternal slavery and humiliation. It is
> in vain that he acquires wealth. His peace
> and pride are destroyed by the poverty of
> his mind.
>
> He feels his inferiority in the pres-
> ence of his children and work-people, and
> then there is surely no state of feeling so
> painful. The grown woman, who cannot read
> or write is surely an object of pity. -- She
> cannot whisper the rudiments of knowledge
> to her infant, though beloved progeny. Her
> children grow up to learn that their mother
> was ignorant! Ignorant of the very alpha-
> bet! O saddening conviction! Each addi-
> tional year gives new poison to this corroding
> thought. Those children grow to maturity,
> observing each day, more distinctly the
> inferiority of their parents. Is it
> wonderful that such parents should be
> contemned and despised. No! It is natural.
> It will ever be so. And yet this is but a
> portion of the bitter fruits that await the
> ignorant parents of an intelligent progeny.[1]

The Fifth Provincial Council convened on May 14,
1843, and it closed the following week on the 21st. Only
two items of educational pertinence were located -- one a
letter from Bishop Hughes of New York in which he urges unified
action among the Bishops in regard to the publishing of books,
especially elementary books for the children in the schools.[2]
In the other manuscript the Archbishop of Baltimore had
indicated the topics he thought apt for discussion at the
congress of prelates:

---

[1]Boston Pilot, April 18, 1846, p. 6.

[2]BCA   25   E   7, Hughes to Eccleston.

De iis quae Archiepiscopo Baltimorens.,
consultis prius Baltimorensis Provinciae
Praesulibus, tractanda esse videntur in
quinto Concilio Provinciali, Baltimori
habendo die 14 Maii, 1843. . . .
12. De Prelo typographico: -- de usu
librorum catholicorum in scholis et
collegiis; de publicatione et diffusione
Tractatuum approbatorum, circa res fidei
etc.
13. Quid provideri possit et debeat pro
adolescentibus Catholicis qui in Navalibus
Scholis instruuntur (Navy apprentices) et
ibi compelluntur adesse cultui religioso
Protestantium?[1]

Once again, there is no evidence that the prelates came to
grips with the problems of a Catholic system or national
program of parochial education. In the final account of
the sessions there appears only a slight reference to the
Catholic press in the tenth decree. The Pastoral Letter was
written by Kenrick of Philadelphia and in view of the agi-
tation in that city, one would expect considerable discussion of the relationship of Catholics to the public schools;
Kenrick, however, was satisfied with a very brief paragraph
dealing with the education of the young. Presumably the

[1]BCA 27A R 2. Hand-dated in a later hand as
5-14-45. This date is obviously inaccurate. Translation:
Concerning those things which the Archbishop of Baltimore,
having previously consulted his provincial consultors, feels
should be discussed in the fifth Provincial Council, to be
had at Baltimore on the 14th of May,1843. . . .
12. About the Catholic Press -- concerning the use of
Catholic books in schools and colleges; the publication and
dissemination of Tractatuum approbatorum, dealing with
matters of faith, etc.
13. What can and should be done for Catholic young men who
are being trained as Navy apprentices and are being compelled
to attend Protestant devotions?

peacemaker in him was already at work and he was careful to
say or do nothing that would unnecessarily agitate the Protestant forces in his see city. One finds it hard to understand why the fiery Hughes or the eager Purcell did not secure the passage of rigorous and pertinent legislation.
Minutes are absent, so we cannot be certain that the matter
did not come in for more discussion, but we can be fairly
certain that educational discussions played no major role
in the deliberations, or some expression of its importance
would have found a place in the decrees or at least in the
printed minutes. The pertinent section in the Pastoral
Letter is as follows:

> The transmission of faith to their
> children was a special object of the solici-
> tude of our fathers; for which they
> thought no sacrifice too great. It must
> be your care, brethren, to let the precious
> inheritance descend without diminution.
> You must, therefore, use all diligence that
> your children be instructed at an early age
> in the saving truths of religion, and be
> preserved from the contagion of error. We
> have seen with serious alarm, efforts made
> to poison the fountains of public education,
> by giving it a sectarian hue, and accustoming
> children to the use of a version of the
> Bible made under sectarian bias, and placing
> in their hands books of various kinds
> replete with offensive and dangerous matter.
> This is plainly opposed to the free genius
> of our civil institutions. We admonish parents
> of the awful account they must give at
> the divine tribunal, should their children,
> by their neglect or connivance, be imbued
> with false principles, and led away from

the path of salvation. Parents are strictly bound, like faithful Abraham, to teach
their children the truths which God has revealed; and if they suffer them to be led
astray, the souls of the children will be
required at their hands. Let them, therefore,
avail themselves of their natural rights,
guaranteed by the laws, and see that no inter-
ference with the faith of their children be
used in the public schools, and no attempt
made to induce conformity in any thing contrary to the laws of the Catholic Church.[1]

The decrees were speedily approved by the Roman Congregation and their records indicate that by this time the
word of the American Bishops in regard to the establishment
of new dioceses and internal affairs of the American Church
was accepted without question. The procedures for approval
were smooth and there is no indication that any of the decrees were seriously questioned.[2] The final approval was
given by Cardinal Fransoni on September 30, 1843.

The council of 1846 was wholly silent on educational
matters. By this time the hierarchy had increased to twenty-
six and twenty-three of them were in attendance. Bishop
Fenwick of Boston sent his usual demurrer in spite of the
fact that he was on his death-bed; Blanchet from Oregon dared
not risk Indian attacks and swollen rivers so he declined
to attend. Benedict Flaget was now 83 years of age and

---

[1] Guilday, Pastorals, pp. 152-153.

[2] The Principal document here is: Sagra Congregazione
De Propaganda Fide Ponente L'Emo. e Rmo. Sig. Cardinale Giocomo Filippo Fransoni Prefetto Ristretto, con voto E Sommario
per la revisione degli atti, e decreti del Concilio Quinto
Provinciale de Baltimore tenuto in Maggio 1843. Septembre, 1843.

once again pleaded the infirmities due to his years. Although nothing is mentioned in the decrees themselves and the official minutes[1] and the Pastoral, again probably written by Kenrick,[2] there is evidence from the preliminary materials of the council that the topic of education was much in the eyes of all. Earlier, in 1845, Eccleston had written several letters regarding the publishing of Catholic books;[3] and in January of 1846 he sent the introductory letter calling the council for the fourth Sunday after Easter and at the same time proposed the questions for discussion. Among them we find:

> Enclosed are the questions which, after an attentive perusal of the letters of my venerable colleagues and on mature consideration, I propose for our deliberations, in the next P. Council which is to be opened on the fourth Sunday after next Easter. Although I have not yet heard from all the Bishops of the province, I believe that I consult the common wish, in no longer deferring this communication.[4]

Along with this letter there was an enclosure which listed the questions to be discussed. The eighth proposal was as follows:

---

[1] Murphy, Concilia, pp. 207-229.

[2] For the text see: Guilday, Pastorals, pp. 162-169.

[3] Cf. for example BCA 27A M 9 Eccleston to Kenrick, April 9, 1845.

[4] BCA 27A R 3 Baltimore, January 1846.

8. Quomodo puerorum, parentibus praesertim
pauperibus ortorum, Christianae Educationi
efficacius prospiciendum?[1]

This portion of the <u>tractanda</u> was assigned to a committee of

priests for study and implementation; they, in turn, sub-

mitted a report to the council. Their report is significant

because it was a well-thought-out appeal for a more ex-

tended program of education under Catholic auspices. The

committee was weighted in favor of the midwest and it is

small wonder that their report was in favor of more uni-

versal parochial education; represented on the theologians'

committee were the dioceses of Cincinnati (Edmund T.

Collins), Detroit (Charles C. Pise), and Nashville

(Charles J. Carter). The fourth member was the Rev.

John Barry of Charleston. Their report:

> The congregation to whom was referred
> Question no. 8 on the Christian education of
> Youth particularly the children of the poor
> beg leave to report:
>   They regard the question of paramount
> necessity, and would therefore most earnestly
> recommend the establishment of schools
> in every congregation thru the province and
> that when means are not sufficient for the
> support of a school, a charitable education-
> society should be organized and subscriptions
> and collections for this purpose taken
> up by the Pastor. And if it would not be
> too officious, they would humbly suggest the
> idea, that the Bishops on the occasion of
> their triennial visitations would vouchsafe
> to visit these schools, hold examinations
> etc, and impress on the Public the vital
> importance of such institutions in which
> Christian education together with morality

---

[1]BCA 27A R 3 enclosure. Translation: 8. How
can the Christian Education of youth, especially those born
of poor parents, be more effectively insured?

and religion is happily imparted, and urge
the necessity of sustaining them.
 This energy, zeal and active cooperation on the part of the clergy would in-
fuse themselves into the Laity, and would,
in the opinion of your congregation, produce a vast amount of good.
 The congregation hail with delight the
arrival and establishment in this city of
the "Brothers of the Christian Schools,"
whose labours have been crowned with sig-
nal success in France and other countries.
 From the representations of the zealous clergy, who superintend their school
<u>opened</u> here only in last September, the con-
gregation are assured that a marked improvement is visible in the litterary (sic), moral
and and (sic) religious character of the
boys in their charge.[1]

In addition to the above letter, there is extant also an appeal to the council fathers by the Rev. Julien Dulaune on
behalf of the Rev. E. Sorin, Superior of the Brothers of
St. Joseph in the United States. This letter is evidence
that priests and Bishops were looking for the means of extending the rudimentary system of education which had taken
root. The congregations of Sisters had begun to spread and
the hierarchy were especially eager that boys should be offered the same opportunities as girls. This was the occasion
for Fr. Delaune's appeal on behalf of these brothers.[2]

 These few papers indicate to some extent the involvement of this council in educational matters. Only five short

[1]BCA 27A R 8.

[2]BCA 29 A 1.

decrees were passed, the fifth of which was the setting of
the date for the next council. Action by the Roman authorities was once again swift and uneventful, even though Gregory
XVI had died on the 9th of June; but final approval was not
actually received by the American episcopate until July 3,
1847.[1]

   A factor which has up to this point been overlooked
is the effect that counter propaganda had upon the Catholic
masses. It was not, for example, immediately known to most
Catholics that a deranged Sr. Mary John had indeed appealed
to loyal Protestants for protection and has thus given some
basis in fact for the terrible burning of the Charlestown
convent.[2] Lack of communication on both sides hampered a
fair treatment; Catholic papers continued to report the
tragedies in terms calculated to stir the feelings of their
readers. The following extract from a report submitted to
European contributors to the American Church will serve to
illustrate the type of material that was circulated rather
widely. Certainly there can be little doubt as to the effect
of material of this calibre:

---

[1]The major document is: Sagra Congregazione De Propaganda Fide Ponente L' Emo. e Rmo. Sig. Cardinale Giocomo
Filippo Fransoni Praefetto. Ristretto com Sommario, E Voto
Sulla Revisione, negli Stati Uniti di America tenuto nel Maggio 1846. Decembre, 1846. Much material is also contained
in a summary to this document, listed in the Acta as Appendice.

[2]Robert H. Lord, John E. Sexton and Edward T.
Harrington, History of the Archdiocese of Boston in the
Various Stages of Its Development, 1604 to 1945 (New York:
Sheed & Ward, 1944), pp. 205-207.

In the middle of the tumult one of the
fanatics had ascended on the altar: I mention it in horror -- with sacrilegious hand,
he seized the holy Ciborium, emptied the
precious particles into his pocket, and,
swelled with the Satanic pride of Calvin,
he went to an inn of Charlestown. Surrounded
by a throng who were eagerly listening to
his sacrilegious exploits, narrated in the
presence of an Irish Catholic who listened
with profound awe -- the fanatic recognized
the Irishman. Suddenly he drew from his
pocket several hosts, and in a nseering
tone, "Here," said he, exhibiting them, "behold your God; what need you go any more to
seek him in the church?" The Irishman was
smote with horror. The sacrilegious man
then felt himself seized with a call of nature:
he went out. But a quarter of an hour -- a half-hour
elapsed -- he returned not. A vague fear
seized on the bystanders: by a presentiment
which they could not account for, they go
out and open the privy. The sacrilegious
man lay there dead -- dead by the death
of Arius.[1]

It is impossible to judge the extent or influence
of such reports. Suffice it to say that they were but another
of the factors which tended to complicate and obscure the
real issues and values which separated the nineteenth century
religious bodies. With the annexation of the large Catholic
territories of the southwest after the Mexican War, eastern
Protestant bodies again experienced a shudder of fear that
the Pope might be about to establish his residence in this
country. In their seventh meeting, however, in 1849, the
prelates again chose to make light of the movements of pre-

---

[1] Annals of the Propagation of the Faith, Vol. VIII,
1847, p. 3478. This is a communication from the Vicar General of Boston, Abbe Brasseur of Bourbourg, to the members
of the Association for the Propagation of the Faith.

judice and concentrated their attention on the organization
and administration of the American Church. As in the previous
council, there is little evidence that educational matters
played any important part in the council deliberations.
The preliminary papers contain little information. The most
pertinent item is from the pen of M. O'Connor of Pittsburgh,
in which he questions:

> Nonne recentiores praesertim Sedis
> Apostolicae decisiones sicut et ipsa ex-
> perientia expediri indicant ut scholae
> erigantur in omnibus Congregationibus
> Catholicis in quibus religio Catholica libere
> doceri posset et nulla auctoritas ecclesiae
> Catholicae infensa vel indefensus dominaretur.
> An aliquid et quid facere possumus nos ut
> hac obtineatur.[1]

There is also extant in the scheduled planning for the
meeting a list of items to be discussed in council, and
among those items are listed the following:

---

[1]BCA 24 0 7. This document is not dated by the
same hand as the rest of the letter. The date December 2,
1842 has presumably been added by one of the archivists.
Almost without doubt, the item refers to the Seventh Provincial Council and should therefore bear the date of 1848.
Supporting this date are the letters which O'Connor wrote
prior to this one. On October 26, 1848, he wrote (24 Q 8)
that he would shortly forward items for the next council.
On March 13, 1846, a letter clearly marked and dated
(24 0 5), he writes to Eccleston: "I have not sent any
questions to be treated of at this council. There is hardly
any thing that occurs to me to which I would call the
attention of the Fathers. It shall be my duty to listen
and try & learn wisdom from so many venerable characters,
with whom I feel myself so very unworthy to be associated."
Translation: Whether the recent decisions of the Holy See
and our own experience do not indicate that it is best that
schools should be erected in all Catholic congregations in
which the Catholic religion can be freely taught and no
authority hostile or alien to the Catholic Church can be
asserted. What steps can we take to bring this about.

De iis quae Archiepiscopo Baltimorensi,
consultis prius Baltimorensis Provinciae
Praesulibus, tractanda esse videntur in
Septimo Concilio Baltimori habendo die sexta
Maii 1849 . . . .

17o Nonne expedit ut Scholae erigantur in
omnibus Congregationibus Catholicis, in
quibus religio Catholica libere doceri
posset? -- ubi de Scholis Publicis?

18o De meliore methodo libros Catholicos
et Tractatus breves necnon et libros scholarum Catholicarum usui accommodatos, in
lucem edendi, ut vili pretio vendi possint
et ita magis magisque disseminentur.[1]

In the official Acta[2] and the subsequent Pastoral no mention

is made of educational matters.   The Seventh Provincial

Council should by all rights have been identified as a

plenary council, because by this time the country actually con-

tained three archdioceses.   Oregon had been erected on July

24, 1846, by the Bull Universi Dominici of Pius IX.[3]   Likewise,

on July 20, 1847, Pius IX erected the archdiocese of St. Louis

by the Bull Apostolici Muneris.[4]   The Ordinary of Oregon City,

---

[1]BCA   27A S 1. Translation: About those things
which the Archbishop of Baltimore, having consulted his
Advisers in the Province, felt should be discussed in the
Seventh Council of Baltimore, to be held on the sixth of
May, 1849 . . . .
No. 17. Whether or not it is opportune to erect Schools in
all the Congregations of Catholics, in which the Catholic
religion could be freely taught? Where are the Public
Schools to be treated?
No. 18. Concerning a better method of editing Catholic
books and short Tracts and books fitted for the use of
Catholic schools, so printed that they can be sold cheaply
and thus be more widely disseminated.

[2]BCA   27A S 2.

[3]Shearer, Pontificia, pp. 235-237.

[4]Shearer, Pontificia, pp. 249-251.

however, was unable to attend and Archbishop Kenrick of St. Louis elected to participate as a presiding prelate only.[1] Shortly before, Pius IX had been forced to flee Rome and in a spirit of filial concern the American Bishops had written and urged his attendance at this council, indicating that he might well stay in America until his European problems settled. The Holy Father responded in terms of grateful thanks for the invitation but declined:

> . . . . But, as in the existing times and circum-
> stances, it would be impossible for us to
> comply with your invitation, as your wisdom
> will easily understand, venerable brother,
> we request you to make known to the prelates
> these sentiments of our mind, and to inform
> them of the apostolical benediction, which
> from our inmost heart we affectionately im-
> part to you, to them, to all the clergy
> of that country, and to all your faithful
> people.[2]

In view of the prolonged riots which the visit of Archbishop Bedini precipitated a few years later, it is interesting to speculate what might have happened, had Pius IX agreed to come to the United States for this council.[3]

This concludes our discussion of the Provincial Councils of Baltimore. Obviously great progress both in ecclesi-

---

[1]Shearer, Pontificia, pp. 268-269.

[2]Shearer, Pontificia, p. 269. Little information on the Roman sources for the seventh council was available at Notre Dame, but what little was consulted made no references to educational matters in any fashion. Final approval was given on the tenth of August, 1850.

[3]James F. Connelly, The Visit of Archbishop Gaetano Bedini to the United States of America (June, 1853 - February 1854), (Romae: Gregoriana, 1960).

astical and educational affairs had been made since the time
of Carroll. The status and role of the American Church was
clearly defined; hierarchial procedure had been standardized;
the Church's interest in education was clear and unmistakable. It was left to the three succeeding plenary councils
to spell out the details of organization and effective implementation of these roles.

Chapter V

First Plenary Council

The general pattern of the development of public and
private education was well formed by mid-century. As Charles
Curran noted, Protestant churches had relinquished their efforts at private education and had more or less adopted the
programs of the common schools with more or less enthusiasm.
It is undoubtedly true that they had by this time ceased
their attempts to maintain private schools.[1] What is not
so clear is the degree to which the common schools reflected
Protestant influences and dogmas. If we are to believe Cubberly and Monroe,[2] the sectarian issue was clearly solved
by this period and no longer remained an item of contention.
Other authors, however, insist that for several decades beyond this point, Protestantism continued to dominate the
public schools in many areas.[3] Lawrence A. Cremin maintains
that by 1850 the common school had become a genuine part of
American life. The essence of America's commitment to common schools centered in four fundamental meanings, which he
describes as follows:

---

[1]Curran, Churches and the Schools, pp. 118-129.

[2]Elwood P. Cubberly, Public Education in the United
States (Boston: Houghton Mifflin Co., 1924, 2nd ed.), pp.
120 ff. Paul Monroe, Founding of the American Public School
System (New York: The Macmillan Co., 1940), pp. 295-388.

[3]Luther L. Gobbell, Church-State Relationships in
Education in North Carolina Since 1776 (Yale University:
unpublished doctoral dissertation, 1934).

Emerging out of the early life of the
American nation the common school by 1850
had in its own right become a genuine part
of that life, standing as a principal positive commitment of the American people. The
essence of this commitment had come basically
to center in four fundamentla meanings:
1. A common school was a school ideally
common to all, available without cost to the
young of the whole community.
2. A common school was a school providing students of diverse backgrounds with a
minimum common educational experience, involv-
ing the intellectual and moral training necessary to the responsible and intelligent
exercise of citizenship. It was careful to
avoid in the process those areas which in
terms of conscience would prove so emotion-
ally and intellectually divisive as to destroy
the school's paramount commitment to universality.
3. A common school was a school totally
supported by the common effort of the whole
community as embodied in public funds.
4. A common school was a school completely controlled by the whole community
(usually through its representatives) rather
than by sectarian political, economic, or
religious groups.[1]

Earlier in this same work Cremin located the emergence of

the American common school as an educational ideal -- an ideal

suited to serve the people of a democracy.[2] In many areas,

certainly, especially the efforts of support and control con-

tinued to be an ideal rather than an actuality. There is

ample evidence that during this period Catholics, particu-

[1]Cremin, American Common School, p. 219.

[2]Cremin, American Common School, pp. 151-178.

larly their prelates, expended a large amount of energy upon education and the building of schools. Roohan[1] lists this problem as the major effort of the period. The constant efforts of the clergy to stir the faithful to build their own schools undoubtedly led them to over-emphasize the differences between themselves and public educators. Hughes of New York was especially adamant in his pronouncements, to the extent that Billington cites him as a prime example of what he calls the Catholic blunder of the period, indicating that the intransigent stand of the clergy unnecessarily antagonized well-meaning Protestants who would otherwise have been more fair-minded. Others, notably the great Catholic convert, Orestes A. Brownson, defended the common schools and their efforts at eliminating prejudices. In one place he says: ". . . common school education is the order of the day, one of the pets of the times, and Catholics have enough . . . to weigh them down in our non-Catholic society without the additional burden of being thought to oppose it."[2] Understandably, relationships between Hughes and Brownson were strained throughout the period of their association; neither could stand the egoism and self-confidence of the other. However, Brownson was careful to maintain an

---

[1] James Edmund Roohan, "American Catholics and the Social Question, 1865-1900" (unpublished Ph. D. dissertation, Yale University, 1952), pp. 29-30.

[2] Brownson's Quarterly Review, Third Series, II (July, 1854), p. 372.

obedient attitude to the Archbishop. After a particularly

disconcerting letter from Hughes, he responded:

> In regard to education I certainly did not
> regard myself as saying one word against
> the policy you had been pursuing, and, if
> I had supposed that I was doing so, my ar-
> ticle would never have seen the light.[1]

The issue of the incorporation of Holy Cross College

in Worcester may well serve as an example of the status in

which earnest Catholics found themselves. Holy Cross College

has been deeded by Bishop Fenwick upon his death to George-

town College, and all the business of Holy Cross was trans-

acted under the charter of Georgetown. In 1849 the Jesuits

who were in charge of Holy Cross decided to apply to the

state of Massachusetts for a charter. Everything was in or-

der except the college's requirement that every student had

to profess the Catholic religion. On this basis the charter

was refused. It was only after severe debate that a recon-

sideration was granted and this time, again, the charter was

refused. It was only in 1865 under the sponsorship of Gov-

ernor Andrew that the Jesuits were finally able to obtain a

charter.[2] Wedges in between were the terrible Bible Wars and

the consequent ill-feeling between Catholic and Protestants.

---

[1] AUND, Brownson to Hughes, July 3, 1854.

[2] Lord, Sexton and Harrington, History of Archdiocese
of Boston, pp. 574-607.

Suffice it to say that the <u>Donahue vs. Richards</u> decision of
the Maine Supreme Court in 1854 did much to convince Catholics
that public schools were in fact Protestant schools and they
had little to hope from them.[1] Forced by this decision to
accept the hated King James version of the Scriptures, Catholics could readily see sectarianism in the "common" schools.

The conflict between Catholics and Protestants of the
1850-1860 period was also heightened by immigration. During
the decade over 2,500,000 immigrants entered America, and of
these nearly a million were Catholic, with Ireland furnishing
more than half the total and Germany contributing 250,000.[2]
Shaughnessy further estimates that in 1860 there were nearly
1,000,000 foreign-born Irish Catholics in this country.[3] Although their presence in such large numbers, especially in
the cities, gave the Know-Nothings plenty of cause for concern,
there are indications that amalgamation was proceeding at a
rapid rate. Theresa and Francis Pulszky give us an insight
into the progress that had been made:

---

[1]Reilly, <u>School Controversy</u>, pp. 18-20. See also
Oscar Handlin, <u>Boston's Immigrants 1790-1865 A Study in Ac-
culturation</u> (Cambridge: Harvard University Press, 1941), pp.
156-183, for a study of the role which the schools of this
area played in holding and Americanizing these groups.

[2]Shaughnessy, <u>Has the Immigrant Kept the Faith?</u>,
pp. 140-141.

[3]Shaughnessy, <u>Has the Immigrant Kept the Faith?</u>,
p. 142.

> The feeling against the Roman Catholics
> has much subsided here in recent times. A
> convent would not now be burned down by the
> mob as it was twenty years ago. An intelligent
> gentleman with whom I spoke on this subject
> told me that this turn in public opinion
> was entirely due to toleration, and not to
> an approach to the Roman Catholic dogmas;
> conversions were rare, and could almost
> always be traced to disappointment in love
> or ambition. Old maids sometimes make them-
> selves nuns, and unsuccessful literary men
> turn disciples of the Jesuits.[1]

It was against this background that the Bishops of
the United States gathered together in the First Plenary
Council. In addition to the archdioceses already mentioned,
Cincinnati, New Orleans and New York had been raised to arch-
diocesean rank. Eccleston had died the previous year (1851)
and Francis P. Kenrick was promoted from the See of Philadelphia to Baltimore. Pius IX appointed him apostolic delegate on August 29, 1851, for the purpose of convening a council and on November 21 he informed his colleagues in the
hierarchy that the council would open May 9, 1852.[2] An early
form of the Schema for the council matters was in the hands
of the participants late in April of 1852 and suggestions
were sent in by the Bishops.[3] Although none of these have

[1]Theresa and Francis Pulszky, White, Red Black quoted
in: Oscar Handlin, This Was America (Cambridge: Harvard
University Press, 1949), p. 248.

[2]John Tracy Ellis, "The Centennial of the First Plenary
Council of Baltimore," American Ecclesiastical Review, vol.
126 (May, 1952), pp. 321-350. This is the most authoritative
treatise of this council.

[3]John Tracy Ellis, American Ecclesiastical Review, p.
327. Cf. also: Francis J. Tscham, "The Catholic Church in
the United States, 1852-1868: A Survey," Records of the American Catholic Historical Society of Philadelphia, vol. LVIII
(June, 1947), pp. 123-133.

been located, the following rather lengthy document gives in
detail the educational philosophy of Kenrick, the prelate who
guided the deliberations of the council. Because of its
pertinence and comprehensiveness it may be taken as a sample
of the hierarchical thinking of the times.

Religion the basis of all Sound Education

Education is deservedly prized in our
age, as serving to promote civilization, to
render the intercourse of society agreeable
and useful, and to fit men for every station
in life. The advantages of religious education are not denied, unless by those who
are avowed enemies of religion, or who identify it with sectarism, and regard it as the
source of the errors and divisions that distract the world in regard to revealed doctrine. A due sense is not, however, enter-
tained of the importance of combining religion with education, so as to imbue the mind
of youth with a deep reverence for supernatural truth in all its fulness, and a moral
sentiment -- and feeling supported by the prom-
ises, and enforced by the threats of futurity.
The general state of society which is divided
into so many sects, and contains so vast a
number of unbelievers, or of men who avow no
belief, disposes men to separate education
from religion, and to train youth on principles common to all, and instruct them in
science and learning independently of doctrine.
This appears to prepare them for intercourse
in life, and for all social relations, which
the conflict of opinions is calculated to dis-
turb but it endangers and supplants Christian
principles, and prepares a generation of unbelievers,
since youth thus trained are likely to regard
with indifference doctrines sedulously kept
out of view. It is indeed impracticable
wholly to abstract from religion, or from
special doctrines, in any system of general
education, since, in one form or other, questions of this kind must arise, which cannot
be passed over without some answer: but the
effort to educate youth without giving any
religious tinge to the mind, tends to indifferentism and infidelity. It has been charged

that the popular system of education which
prevails in this country, and in many parts
of Europe, is the result of a combination
against Christianity, in order to supplant
it in the tender minds of youth, without the
odium of assailing its teachings. If it is
unjust to ascribe such a design to the promo-
ters of the system generally, it can scarcely
be denied that such a result might arise from
it, were it rigorously followed out, without
any of the counteracting influences which
happily preserve respect for religion. It
may seem expedient in some cases to adopt the
system by way of accommodation and compromise,
in small communities, where no particular
body of citizens can afford to provide a
teacher for their children. It may be admis-
sable by sects agreeing on certain tenets,
and careful to guard otherwise against any irreligious influence. For Catholics it is
always objectionable and dangerous: so that
if at any time they be constrained by law to
send their children to the Public Schools or
yield to the pressure of public prejudice,
they must take the necessary precautions,
and provide for their religious instruction.

The foundation of all instruction is the
knowledge of God, His works, the laws by which
the Universe is governed, and the moral laws
by which human actions must be regulated.
Reason leads us to inquire into the Author of
our being, and into the origin of all things,
and their mutual relations. If he has revealed
Himself to man, it must be our duty to ascertain the truths which He has made known, and
receive them with entire submission. If He
has implanted in our breasts, or proclaimed
externally, rules of action, we are bound to
obey them. It is a natural obligation of
parents to instruct their children in these
maxims. Compliance with this duty forms the
eulogy which God himself pronounced on Abraham:
"I know that he will command his children, and
his household after him to keep the way of the
Lord." (reference: Gen. 10:19). Teachers
enter into the place of parents, and instruct
their scholars in the existence of God, and
in the works of creation. Although they have
no divine mission, they are bound by natural
law to direct the mind of their pupils to God

their Creator and Lord. The revelation which
He has made should direct them in their lessons, that nothing may escape them contrary
to it, and that all may submit to its guidance.
They are not to take on them the office of
preachers or controvertists, but they should
teach nothing which does not harmonize with
revelation. It is inconsistent with the
Christian character to dissemble or hold in
abeyance any doctrine of Christ, when called
on to declare or explain it: since we should
be always ready to give an account of the
hope which we cherish. The curiosity with
which children make inquiries, the unreserved
confidence with which they receive the declarations of their teachers, and the tenacity
wherewith they retain early impressions, render it most important that the instruction
given them be unequivocal, unhesitating and
secure, that their belief may be firm. For
this reason Catholics who are guided by the
Church of God, which is the pillar and ground
of the truth, must necessarily found education on
religion, and should, as far as practicable,
select Catholic teachers of unquestionable
principles, who in conveying natural truths
or scientific discoveries, may never for a
moment weaken the conviction of divine truth.
Perplexity and confusion are the natural consequence when the teachings of the schoolmaster
clash with the catechism, or when his inciden-
tal observations cast reproach on the Church,
or its members. Every influence is desirable
to give full conviction to the minds of the
young. The mysterious character of the doctrines renders faith difficult. If they are
assailed, discredited or slighted by those who
are given as guides, it is not to be hoped
that children will retain faith. Is it rash
to say that the friends of the popular system
rely on its influence as certain to undermine
it?

The influence of religion is especially
necessary for moral training. Morality not
based on religion commends itself by human and
natural motives, which are not powerful enough
to restrain the passions. The punishments in-
flicted by the teacher, and the rewards of good
conduct and proficiency are not adequate to
determine youth to a virtuous course. If he

point not to futurity, he will not be likely
to deter them from vices especially of a secret character, or to stimulate them to virtue,
which in this life seldom receives a recom-
pense. He cannot urge future punishments without resting on Christian authority for their
belief. Tha moral principles themselves need
religious sanction and support, for although
they accord with reason, their development and
application depend greatly on the light of
revelation. The grievous errors against morals
into which the sages of Pagan antiquity fell,
show how imperfect the moral code would be
without the direction of Christian faith. Besides, the impotency of man, unaided from
above, to rise to the practice of virtue,
shows the need of religion to remedy the in-
firmity of nature, and keep under restraint
those passions which in youth display so great
violence. To train youth is no easy task
with all the appliances and aids of religion,
but without them, is it possible to effect
it? There may be some observance of School
discipline to avoid punishment -- some regularity of conduct to shun censure -- some goodness
and excellence arising from constitutional
dispositions: but morality without religion
is superficial, if not utterly fallacious.
It is plainly the duty of Christians to teach
the morality of Christ and it is all important
that it should be impressed on the minds of
the young by their teachers in the school
room, as well as by their parents, and by
the ministers of religion. Every moral principle should be strengthened by the Christian
law, and enforced by the threats of Christ
against transgressors. The aids of grace,
prayer, and the sacraments should be pointed
to, in order to supply human weakness, and
remedy the disorders of fallen nature. The
examples of the Saints should be opportunely
introduced, to stimulate the torpid. The
glory of heaven should be pointed to as the
reward exceedingly great of the virtuous and
devoted.[1]

---

[1] BCA note folder, no markings. The item bears a note
by Archbishop Spalding that it was presented for printing.
The item has bot been located in print; it bears no date.

Most significant in this statement of the aims and
purposes of Catholic education is the decided emphasis on
the absence of religion in the public schools. This trans-
ference from the attack on the sectarian bias of the public
schools to the emphasis on godlessness is the most perplexing
change in the history of parochial education. Whereas the
Protestant character of the schools was still de facto
bothering many Bishops, already the legal future of the public
school was beyond question -- non-sectarianism had won the
day; implementation of that state would take many years but
the issue had been decided. The hierarchy, too, were beginning to take cognizance of that fact. Protestants, also,
began to notice that control of the common school had begun
to slip from their grasp. On occasion, Protestant leaders
also began to speak of the lack of religion and its consequences for the public schools.

Within the council itself two committees were direct-
ly concerned with education. The first committee, composed
of prelates, had the following members: John Purcell of
Cincinnati; John Chance of Natchez; Vincent Whelan of
Wheeling; John McCloskey of Albany; Joseph Alemany of Monterey;
John McGill of Richmond; and John Neopomucene Neumann of
Philadelphia. With no exceptions, this committee was com-
posed of champions of the parochial school movement and could,

therefore, be expected to offer rigorous legislation favorable to parochial schools. In addition to the Bishops' committee a second was formed among the theologians present. Their report was presented on Tuesday afternoon of the council meetings and was signed by John McElroy as chairman; and by James Dolan, Josue M. Young, L. Obermeyer, and C. I. White. Their report follows:

> What provision should be made for the education of youth?
>
> The committee appointed for the examination of this question, respectfully submit that to provide for the education of youth may imply, either what mode or system should be adopted for the instruction of youth, or by what means is a fund to be raised for supporting this system of education.
>
> With regard to the first branch of interpretation of the question, it is the opinion of the committee:
>
> 1. That considering the lamentable evils which follow from the frequentation of the schools in which no impressions of true relition are made upon the mind of youth, the establishment of parochial schools is indispensable for the security of faith and morals among Catholic Children. By parochial schools are understood institutions, in which none but Catholic children are admitted, and which are conducted by teachers having the approbation of the pastor, exercising their office under his direction and superintendence, and making the catechism the frequent subject of their instructions to those under their charge.
>
> 2. As the parochial school is to be considered only as an auxiliary to the pastor and others who are charged with the proper education of young persons, he will not allow himself to grow remiss in the performance of his duty in this respect, on account of the

assistance which he may derive from such an
institution; on the contrary, he will remember that the efficiency of the school and its
successful operation depend essentially upon
the constant vigilance and attention which he
will give to it, and particularly upon his
wisdom in selecting teachers whose piety and
other qualifications render them competent
to such an office, upon his assiduity in cate-
chectical instruction, and fidelity and
firmness in urging upon parents and others,
from the pulpit and in the confessional, the
obligation of cooperating with him hin the religious education of their children, particularly by sending them to the school and to
Church, encouraging their application, and
confirming by word and example the salutary
influence which he exercises over them.

3. As they who devote themselves to the
instruction of youth, from supernatural motives, for the glory of God and their own
personal sanctification, are manifestly the
best qualified for this important task, the
pastor should endeavor by all prudent means
to secure the services of teachers who, by
their special consecration to the service of
God, apply themsleves to the education of
young persons as a means of promoting their
own spiritual welfare.

In regard to the second branch of this
question, which relates to the pecuniary provision necessary for the support of schools,
the comittee (sic) are of opinion:

1. that when the income of a Church is
more than sufficient for the support of the
pastor, which the ordinary of the diocess will
decide, a portion of it should be appropriated
to the maintenance of the parochial school.

2. that a revenue may also be derived
for this object, from schools in which those
who are able,will be required to make some
compensation for the instruction received.

3. that although the system of public
taxation for schools, as it exists in this
country, is loudly to be condemned, it is ad-

visable that an effort should be made, so far
as prudence will suggest, to secure a portion
of the public fund for the support of our
parochial schools.[1]

In analysis, this is quite a comprehensive report,
indicating that the dissatisfaction with public education
had reached high pitch; at the same time, however, the focus
of the report is on the parochial school itself. This is
probably the most detailed plea for a system of schooling
tied to the parish unit that had been given up to this time.
At the same time the final plea indicates that hope was
dwindling for a share of the public funds in support of a
private system. In germ, therefore, one might say that this
report is a pretty fair vision of the parochial system as
it was actually to develop. In spite of their conviction
that these schools deserved public funds, the many setbacks
had convinced them that there was little actual hope of ac-
quiring that aid.

The next afternoon, according to the minutes, the
theologians discussed the specific question of the public
schools themselves.[2] The committee report was probably prepared by the same group as the previous one, but it is different in tone and in spirit. Basically it is a harsh at-

[1] 32 B E 16. The minutes of the meetings indicate
that this report was read either on the 11th or on the 12th.
As the report next to be discussed is clearly marked as having been given on the 12th, this report must have been read
on the 11th.

[2] Acta, p. 28. Manuscript copy.

tack on the public system then in operation. The attack

centers on the exclusion of religion from these schools,

its Protestant nature, and the tendency to indifferentism.

> The Committee to whom the question -- "Quod remedium publicarum Scholarum abusui offerendum Sit" was referred, respectfully submit the following report.

> The question implies the existence of an abuse and the necessity of applying the proper remedy, if any can be found. Taking things in their proper order, the Committee have considered first the Abuse, and afterwards the Remedy.

> The radical disease of the public School System throughout this Country is the exclusion of all religion therefrom, in other words, its Godlessness, -- and this arises necessarily from the fundamental principle of the whole system -- the principle that the State, setting aside the parent & the pastor, has the right & is bound to educate the Children of the community.

> The organic law of constitution of every State or nearly every state of the Union declares, that the civil government shall not establish or teach any religion. Public Schools or schools established & controlled entirely by the Civil authorities are therefore essentially infidel & even atheistical; for to teach the existence of God and the duty of worshipping him, is to teach religion, which the State is in theory debarred from doing. The inconsistent, infidel-protestant advocates of the Common Schools take the ground, that such religious truths & duties are to be taught in them as all are agreed upon. No Catholic need be told how false & vicious in principle & fatal in its results must be such a system of instruction.

> But bad as the System is in theory, it is worse in practice; for in point of fact the public schools are very generally regarded & employed by Protestant sectaries & infidels.

as the great means of perverting & corrupt-
ing the rising generation & particularly the
children of Catholic parents. All intelligent observers must be aware of the existence
of a vast conspiracy to stop the spread of
the Catholic faith, and, if possible, to
crush the Catholic Church.

Though not formally organized or distinctly avowed, this conspiracy is not the
less active or dangerous. It has at its command no engine of such gigantic force, no weapon so formidable as our public school education. We have much less to fear from the press,
the pulpit & all the power, patronage & influence wielded by the enemies of our cause. If
we do not clearly see all the havoc it had
actually produced & is capable of producing,
it is because the system is still but develop-
ing its resources & preparing its instruments;
because its managers have been unwilling to
exhibit its true character, while there was
doubt of its strength & stability, &, above
all, because the immense accession to our
numbers by continual immigration blinds us
to the immense loss to the fold of Christ by
the seduction day by day & every where of the
lambs from the flock.

The Committee holds that this system is
in practice, both heretical and infidel. It
is in most parts of the country directly or
indirectly under the control of Protestant
ministers. It very generally adopts as a regulation the reading of the Protestant Bible,
and the reciting of Protestant hymns & sometimes of Protestant prayers; and when Catholics
object to these things, they are immediately
held up to public execration as enemies of the
Bible & of free institutions. That the system
is infidel in its principles, in its tendency & results, needs no argument or illustration.
Melancholy experience has shown the consequences
of all this. Catholic children exposed to insidious, if not open attacks on their religious
principles & practices, become ashamed of their
faith. Withdrawn from the care and vigilance
of their pastors & parents, obliged not unfre-
quently to use books offensive to their reli-

gious convictions & sentiments, they are at
the same time placed so effectually under
heretical and infidel influences, that it
is morally impossible, their faith should
not be weakened & their feelings warped.

Even the strict discipline & systematic
regularity in some respects of the best
public schools, are made so to work, (in exact
accordance, it is true, with their fundamental
principle -- Godlesness, --) as to withdraw
Catholic children from the instructions & pastoral care needed at the most important period
of their lives -- viz when about to prepare for
their first Communion & Confirmation.

Finally the dangers of evil communication
incident to all schools & presenting a most awful responsibility to the conscience of the
best Catholic teacher, are necessarily a hundred
fold greater in the mixed assemblage & unrestrained
intercourse, (apart from all pastoral or parental
care,) of the children of Catholics, Protestants,
Jews, & infidels. What horrible vices are
thus propagated & how rapidly & fearfully
they are spreading, the present moral condition
of the youth of our cities & larger towns, but
too clearly indicates.

The last abuse or evil, which the Committee
have felt called upon to notice, is this, that
in our cities & wherever there is a numerous
Catholic population, parochial or other Catholic
Schools could & would be established, were it
not for the public school supported by the
State. It is not only a heavy burthen, but a
flagrant injustice, in clear violation of the
theory of our laws and institutions that parents,
who cannot in conscience send their children
to the State Schools, should be taxed for
institutions from which they derive no
benefit & which they are bound to condemn as
hostile to true religion & the real welfare of
the community.[1]

---

[1]BCA 32B E 17.

The second half of the report, of nearly equal length, turns to an attempt at a solution of the basic weaknesses emphasized in the above portion.

Having examined, as well as circumstances permitted, the abuses of the Common Schools, the Committee proceeded to the consideration of the remedies, whether immediate or prospective.

They do not propose to assail the public School System, now generally established in this country & having a certain hold on the prejudices and affections of the majority of the people, especially the most bigoted among them. But they would remark, that in their opinion, it is a mistake to regard the system as so firmly fixed on the basis of popular will, that it may defy all efforts to modify the laws establishing & regulating it, to the extent called for by the exigencies of Catholic faith & feeling. There are many besides Catholics, who know, that it is a bad system & feel it as a grievance. In some places the Episcopalians will array themselves against it; in others the Presbyterians have declared war upon it--: the Jews and many others, who profess no particular religion & care for none, will be with us against it. Eminent statesmen have maintained in debates in Legislative bodies & conventions, that to make education universal, the public money must be given alike to all denominational schools, as well as those instituted by the civil authority. The Committee are moreover convinced, that the strength of the party in favor of the public schools as they are, is chiefly & for obvious reasons found in cities & the larger towns.

In country districts, the system is not cherished with ardent affection & in many places is positively unpopular & condemned as a failure.

The Fourth Provincial Council of Balt. adverting to the efforts already made to render the system of public education subservient to heresy & the corruption of Catholic chil-

dren, enacted in their 6th decree, that "these
efforts of the Sects should be constantly and
moderately resisted & the aid of those who
are in authority solicited to apply a suitable
remedy." The Committee have felt therefore
that they are sanctioned by this high authority of a provincial council in recommending,
1o. "that the Catholics everywhere, as soon
as it shall seem expedient, claim of the Legislative power such modification of the laws
on this subject, as will give to free schools,
asylums & academies furnishing education
gratuitously or cheap, as the public schools,
their proportional share of the public money.

    2o -- That the Bishops & pastors, in com-
pliance with the 34th Decree of the 1st Provincial Council of Baltimore should immediately
make united & powerful efforts to establish
free schools for the education of Catholic
children in our cities, & other places when
it is practicable to do so, & at the same time
should encourage & aid the institution of pay
schools under the direction of Catholic teachers approved by the Bp. & pastors.

    3o -- Whenever good Catholic schools exist,
the parents, who continue to send their children to the public schools to the great danger
of their faith & morals, should be strenuously
urged to withdraw their children from said
schools, -- & send them to Catholic Schools and
(with the approbation of the Bp.) should even
be required to do so on pain of being denied
the Sacraments.

    4o -- The Committee are of opinion that in
the place of any public appeal at this present
time on the part of the Catholic body at large
or their first pastors, which might have the
effect of exciting the Protestant community &
defeating the objects contemplated, the Bishops
& pastors in their respective stations should
without delay employ such instructions & influences as may arouse the Catholic community to a
sense of their rights & duties in this matter,
& secure at the proper time the necessary legislative action.[1]

One would be safe in assuming that the influence of

Purcell was evident in the stringent recommendations of this

[1]BCA 32B E 18.

committee. In many of the midwestern dioceses the question
of denying absolution to those who refused to send their
children to existing parish schools was beginning to be discussed and this committee was quick to make rigorous demands in this matter. On the other hand, many of their
remarks betray the traditional prejudices of the Catholic
body against the common schools. After such recommendations
it is surprising that the final decree was calm in tone and
lenient in its demands. Not only was there no mention of
the denial of absolution to guilty parents, but even the
general remarks have been toned down considerably:

> XII. Moneant episcopi sacerdotes curam animarum
> exercentes, ut institutioni juventutis in doc-
> trina christiana per se operam dent, nec putent
> ipsis licere quae sui muneris sunt negligere,
> rejecto omnino in alios onere juvenes, aliosque
> rudes, fidei morumque principia edocendi.
> XIII. Hortamur episcopos, et attentis gravissi-
> mis malis quae ex juventute haud rite instituta
> sequi solent, per viscera misericordiae Dei ob-
> secramus, ut scholas unicuique ecclesiae in
> eorum dioecesibus annexas, instituendas curent;
> et si opus fuerit, et rerum adjuncta sinant,
> provideant ut ex redditibus ecclesiae cui schola
> annexa sit, idonei magistri in ea habeantur.[1]

---

[1]Murphy, _Concilia_, pp. 46-47. Translation:
XII. Let the bishops warn priests who exercise the care of
souls to give their attention to the instruction of
youth in christian doctrine; nor may they think that
they can neglect what constitutes their duties, by completely placing the burden of teaching the principles of
faith and morals to youths and other uninstructed people
into the hands of others.
XIII. We exhort the bishops, and in view of the very great
evils which usually result from the defective education of
youth, we beseech them through the bowels of the mercy of
God to see that schools are established in connection with
the churches of their dioceses; and if it be necessary and
circumstances permit, tp provide, from the revenues of the
church to which the school is attached, for the support of
competent teachers.

The above decrees were passed by the fathers on the
18th.[1] That all the fathers were not totally agreed on the
peculiar necessity of parochial schools was apparent the
next day when the question of support was raised. It was
suggested that societies be erected whose purpose would be
the financial maintenance of Catholic schools, but the proposal was defeated fifteen to sixteen.[2] The Pastoral Letter
for this council was written by Arch. Peter Richard Kenrick,
the brother of the presiding prelate. Once again the letter
contains an eloquent passage on the necessity of Christian
education.

> No portion of our charge fills us with
> greater solicitude than that which our Divine
> Master, by word and example, has taught us
> to regard with more than ordinary sentiments
> of affection--the younger members of our flock.
> If our youth grow up in ignorance of their re-
> ligious duties or unpractised in their consol-
> ing fulfillment; if, instead of the words of
> eternal life, which find so full and sweet an
> echo in the heart of innocence, the principles
> of error, unbelief or indifferentism, are im-
> parted to them; if the natural repugnance,
> even in the happiest period of life, to bend
> under the yoke of discipline, be increased by
> the example of those whose relation to them
> gives them influence or authority,--what are
> we to expect but the disappointment of all
> hopes which cause the Church to rejoice in
> the multiplication of her children! We there-
> fore address you brethren, in the language of
> affectionate warning and solemn exhortation.
> Guard carefully those little ones of Christ;

[1] Acta, pp. 38 and 47.
[2] Acta, p. 37.

"suffer them to approach Him, and prevent
them not, for of such is the kingdom of heaven." (Mark x. 14). To you, Christian parents, God has committed these His children,
whom He permits you to regard as yours; and
your natural affection towards whom must ever
be subordinate to the will of him "from whom
all paternity in heaven and on earth is named."
(Eph. iii. 16). Remember that if for them
you are the representatives of God, the source
of their existence, you are to be for them
depositaries of His authority, teachers of
His law, and models by imitating which they
may be perfect, even as their Father in heaven is perfect. You are to watch over the
purity of their faith and morals with jealous
vigilance, and to instil into their young hearts
principles of virtue and perfection. What
shall be the anguish of the parent's heart,--
what terrible expectation of judgment that
will fill his soul, should his children per-
ish through his criminal neglect, or his obstinate refusal to be guided in the discharge
of his paternal duties, by the authority of
God's Church. (John xvii. 12). To avert
this evil give your children a Christian education, that is an education based on religious principles, accompanied by religious
practices and always subordinate to religious
influence. Be not led astray by the false and
delusive theories which are so prevalent, and
which leave youth without religion, and, consequently, without anything to control the
passions, promote the real happiness of the
individual, and make society find in the
increase of its members, a source of security
and prosperity. Listen not to those who would
persuade you that religion can be separated
from secular instruction. If your children,
while they advance in human sciences, are not
taught the science of the saints, their minds
will be filled with every error, their hearts
will be receptacles of every vice, and that
very learning which they have acquired, in
itself so good and so necessary, deprived of
all that could shed on it the light of heaven,
will be an additional means of destroying the
happiness of the child, embittering still more
the chalice of parental disappointment, and

weakening the foundations of social order.
Listen to our voice, which tells you to walk
in the ancient paths; to bring up your children as you yourselves were brought up by
your pious parents; to make religion the foundation of the happiness you wish to secure
for those whom you love so tenderly, and the
promotion of whose interests is the motive
of all your efforts, the solace which sustains
you in all your fatigues and privations. Encourage the establishment and support of Catholic
schools; make every sacrifice which may be
necessary for this object: spare our hearts
the pain of beholding the youth whom, after
the example of our Master, we so much love, involved in all the evils of an uncatholic education, evils too multiplied and too obvious
to require that we should do more than raise
our voices in solemn protest against the system
from which they spring. In urging on you the discharge of this duty, we are acting on the suggestion of the Sovereign Pontiff, who in an encyclical letter, dated 21 November, 1851, calls
on all the Bishops of the Catholic world, to
provide for the religious education of youth.
We are following the example of the Irish Hierarchy, who are courageously opposing the introduction of a system based on the principle
which we condemn, and who are now endeavoring
to unite religious with secular instruction of
the highest order, by the institution of a
Catholic University, -- an undertaking in the
success of which we necessarily feel a deep
interest, and which, as having been suggested
by the Sovereign Pontiff, powerfully appeals
to the sympathies of the whole Catholic world.[1]

There can be little doubt that these council enactments represent a decided advance on the pattern of Catholic
parochial education. From this point onward, no one was able
to offer to the hierarchy a serious challenge against parochial schools. Even the opposition party at the Third Plenary

[1]Guilday, Pastorals, pp. 189-191.

Council did little more than object to the stringency of the
requirement of sending children to these schools. Diffley
maintains that at the time of this council, there was a decided policy of establishing parochial elementary schools.[1]
In view of the fact that the Council Fathers were not willing
to accept the more severe recommendations of the committee
report and settled for less detailed decrees, it seems
that at best the policy was still largely an unspoken and
unwritten one. There was still much evidence that many of
the participants in this council hoped to modify the common
school system to the point where these could be considered
Christian. Others, having despaired of any modification
in the common school, still strove mightily to obtain a share
of the school fund for denominational schools. Consequently,
it seems unlikely that the members of the council had in
mind the pattern of private education, supported entirely
by free-will offerings, which was eventually to evolve.

The decrees of the council were entrusted to Bishop
Van der Velde of Chicago for transmission to Rome, but approval
was slow in coming. Pius IX wrote in July to the American
hierarchy congratulating them on their efforts to promote
the American Catholic Church.[2] It was a whole year later,
however, before the Holy See began to act on the suggestions of
the council; at that time the new Sees called for by the
council were established.[3] The general approval of the

[1]Diffley, American Catholic Reaction, p. 286.

[2]Shearer, Pontificia Americana, pp. 272-274.

[3]Shearer, Pontificia Americana, pp. 274-291.

decrees had come previously on the 30th of August, 1852. The
Propaganda agents had been led in their discussions by Raphael
Cardinal Fornari and the document of approval was given on
September 26.[1] In the preliminary discussions, Bishop Van der
Velde had been asked his opinion of the decrees and he made
the following remarks on the sections under discussion:

> Ad Decr XII: Hoc decretum servari quidem
> potest in urbibus et in locis ubi Pastor seu
> Missionarius residet, non autem rure et in
> locis quae semel tantum in mense visitantur,
> ubi pueri vel a Ludimagistro vel ab aliis
> doceri debent. Posset tamen commendari ut
> in talibus locis Pastor pueros statutis tem-
> poribus in doctrina christiana examinet.
>
> Ad Decr. XIII: In multis dioecesibus datur
> maxima difficultas inveniendi magistros ido-
> neos, et media quibus sustententur, Optandum
> esset ut ubicumque fieri potest, fratres Doc-
> trinae Christianae adhibentur; sed in multis
> locis difficillimum, ne dicam impossibile est
> ipsorum sustentationi subvenire. Ubi dantur
> scholae publicae, pueri catholici illas adeunt,
> cum ex aenario publico sustentantur, et nihil[2]

---

[1]_Acta_, pp. 56-57.

[2]Translation: Decree XII: This decree can be kept
in cities and in places where a pastor or missionary lives,
but not in the country and in places which are visited only
once a month, where the boys ought to be taught by a schoolmaster or by others. It could, however, be recommended that
in such places the pastor ought to examine the children at
stated times in Christian doctrine.

Decree XIII: In many dioceses there is great difficulty in finding suitable teachers and the means to support
them. It would be desirable that wherever possible the Brothers of Christian Doctrine were employed; but in many places
it is difficult, if not to say impossible to obtain the means
to support them. Where there are public schools, the Catholic boys go to them since they are supported from the public
treasury and nothing (quotation and translation continued
next page).

a parentibus solvendum est, et cum ibi permixti sunt cum pueris omnibus sectarum, multi
religionem gradatim amittunt, et fiunt vel
protestantes vel indifferentes. Hoc videtur
maximum malum in America, cui, in pauperioribus
Dioecesibus, nullum remedium hujusque ad-
ferri potuit.[1]

The Jesuit, Giovanni Perrone, was also called in as

one of the consultors of the Propaganda officials and his

report is very similar to that of Bishop Van der Velde. Even

a casual reading of the two reports indicates that they

must have planned their reports in common:

Hoc decretum potest executioni mandari in
urbibus; non autem in pagis in quibus ut
plurimum nulli degunt sacerdotes aut missionarii,
ab aliis proinde instrui debent. Posset
autem injungi sacerdotibus, ut cum loca haec
visitant, ipsi examinent pueros an bene
didicerent res fidei.[2]

---

[1] is paid by the parents, and since they are mixed
with youth of every sect, many lose their religion gradually
and become either protestant or indifferent. This seems to
be the greatest danger in America to which the poorer dioceses
can offer no remedy. Source: Sommario Decreta Concilii
Plenarii totius Americae Septentrionalis Foederatae Baltimori habitum a die 9 ad 20 Maii. A. R. S. 1852. Acta della
S.C. de Propaganda Fide, anno 1852, vol. 214, bundle 36,
Num. XXIV, pp. 53-55.

[2] Translation: This decree can be ordered for
execution in the cities but not in the tutal areas where
most frequently no priests or missionaries have permanent
residences; then the instruction ought to be given by others.
It could be required of the priests, however, that when they
visit these places they themselves should examine the
youngsters to see whether they are learning the matters
of faith satisfactorily.

XIII. Certe valde optandum esset, ut ubicumque
scholae instituerentur; imo ut fratres doctrinae christianae propagarentur; sed hoc
pendet a statu temporali uniuscujusque dioe-
ceseos. Interdum vel non inveniuntur sacerdotes idonei, vel non habentur proventus ad
eorum sustentationem. Ideo dicerem: ubicumque
id fieri potest adnitantur Espiscopi ut scholae
instituantur etc.[1]

There was more discussion in regard to the decrees but the
documents examined do not reveal that anything further was
done to modify the decrees.[2] This, therefore, completes
the discussion of the decrees of this council. By these decrees Bishops were charged with the responsibility of directing their pastors to erect schools which were to be connected
with the parishes. It is this latter fact, the parochial at-
tachment of these schools, that represents the greatest advance
of the legislation of these decrees. In tone, of course,
there is nothing to indicate the rigid decrees that were to

[1] Translation: It is certainly to be hoped that schools
be constructed everywhere; also that the Brothers of the
Christian Doctrine be increased; but this depends upon the
temporal status of each diocese. In the meantime either
suitable priests are not available or the means are not available for their support. Therefore, I would say: wherever it
can be done the bishops should command that schools be built,
etc. Acta, Parte III Folios 27-37. Voto del Rmo. P. Giovanni
Perrone delle Campagni di Gezu, Consullore della S.C. de Propaganda Fide.

[2] Cf. Sagra Congregazione Di Propaganda Fide Ponente
L'Eminentissimo e Reverendissimo Sig. Cardinale Raffaele Fornari Ristretto com Sommario Per la parte che rimaneva a deci-
dersi reguardo all' ultimo Concilio Baltimorense Giugno, 1853.
Also: Sagra Congregazione Di Propaganda Fide ponente L'Emeren-
tissimo e Reverendissimo Sig. Cardinale Angelonai. Ristretto
con Sommario e Voto Sopra i Decreti e le Instanze del Sinodo
celebrato dai Vescovi degli Stati Uniti de America. Agosto,
1852.

follow; the fact that many dioceses had already legislated
more strongly than this council indicates that the difference
of opinion in regard to the necessity of privately-supported
schools had begun to have practical effects upon the school-
building policies of various dioceses. Bishops, especially
those in the midwest, who had decided in favor of a completely
separate system,matched their decision with action and continued
to expand their school efforts.[1] Others, especially those in
the east, who were not yet completely convinced of the impossibility of a compromise with the public system, continued
to rely on a share in the public fund. Consequently, the
expansion of these diocesean systems proceeded at a slower
pace.[2]

---

[1]In addition to the study by Connaughton, cf. also
Spalding, Life of M. J. Spalding. PP. 195-215 indicate that
Spalding was also interested in obtaining public funds for his
local schools but proceeded without such aid. The relationship
between Spalding and Bishop Smith has already been explored.

[2]In addition to the comments of Bps. Timon and Bayley,
which are quoted elsewhere in this work, cf. A. J. Heffernan,
A History of Catholic Secondary Education in Connecticut
(Washington, D.C.: The Catholic Education Press, 1937), pp.
4-16. Also useful for a study of development in the New York
area are the pertinent chapters from Edward M. Connors, Church-
State Relationships in Education in the State of New York.

Chapter VI

Second Plenary Council

During the years between 1852-1866 efforts at Catholic education continued apace. Nearly every diocese either instituted or enlarged their pattern of school-building.[1] Evidence from the studies which have been completed on regional levels clearly shows that henceforward the program of parochial education was being increasingly accepted. And even the existence of a truly non-sectarian public school would no longer satisfy Catholic leaders. It was during this period, it seems, that the emphasis passed almost entirely away from the Protestant nature of public education to the presently more familiar arguments of godlessness and secularism. This phase of the program of Catholic education has been designated as follows:

> The maintenance by the Church of a costly system of parochial schools is the most revealing testimony of her criticism of non-sectarian, i.e., non-Catholic public education, and is the only course of action in keeping with the pontifical claims of sole responsibility in the Christian education of youth. Members of the clergy who refuse openly to brand the public schools as nests of atheism are conspicuously few in number.[2]

---

[1]Connaughton, *History of Education in Cincinnati*, pp. 44-65. Klinkhamer, *Historical Reasons*, pp. 86-90.

[2]Frederic Eugene Ellis, "Attitude of the Roman Catholic Church towards the Problem of Democratic Freedom and American Public Education" (Harvard: unpublished Ph.D. dissertation, 1948), p. 337. This is a study of the parochial system from the viewpoint of a present-day militant Protestant. He goes on to praise the work of Dr. Edward McGlynn, a priest opponent of the parochial system.

In this passage we have demonstrated the impression that the
activities of the Church in the matter of education has made
on nearly all students of this activity. Another interesting
document of the period is the manuscript which Archbishop
Hughes of New York prepared for the College of Propaganda in
March of 1858.[1] This lengthy document was entrusted by Hughes
to Rev. Bernard Smith, O.S.B., an Irish professor in Rome,
and was intended for the Cardinal Prefect of Propaganda, Alles-
sandro Barnabo and the Secretary, Gaetano Bedini.[2] Early in
the document he gave an outline of the headings which he intended to cover and the second topic was:

> Second--The education of Catholic Children,
> under a system of protestant, or rather infi-
> del training established by law, and having
> for its main object to seduce those children
> from the Catholic faith--there being no
> means provided for their education under
> the sanction of their parents and of their
> religion.[3]

In the report itself he narrates how after going to Europe in
1839 to obtain funds for St. John's College, he returned to
find his diocese in turmoil:

---

[1]Archives of the Congregation of the Propaganda Fide
Scritture riferite nei congressi. Cf. also Henry J. Browne,
"The Archdiocese of New York A Century Ago A Memoir of Arch-
bishop Hughes 1838-1858," United States Catholic Historical
Records and Studies, vol. XXXIX-XL, (1952),pp. 129-190.

[2]Browne, United States Catholic Historical Society
Records and Studies, vol. XXXIX-XL, pp. 134-135.

[3]Hughes, Memoir, pp. 502-503.

...The bone of contention was public education, but unfortunately for me, it had already
lapsed into political considerations--and, as
the Catholics were almost universally devoted
to the party sustaining public common school
education, as it then was, I had to enter the
lists not only against that party, but to a
great extent, in opposition to the Catholics
themselves, who had not taken the pains to
comprehend how the legalized system of education was insidiously undermining their every
hope to preserve their own children in the
faith of the Church of God. They had been
brought over to the idea that in a Republican
State which repudiated every notion of an established Church, in which the government ignored every special creed--in which the adult
population lived, and was expected to live,
in all the political, commercial, and social
relations of life, harmoniously without any
strife, or Sectarian zeal, as regarded any
one creed--so, to prepare the future citizen
for the proper discharge of his duties, it was
deemed expedient that the children from earliest
years, should be brought up in a blissful com-
panionship, without allowing any one religion
to find place among them in the public schools,
as an apple of discord. Such was the theory
of what was then called the public school society in this City--and Catholic parents, to a
great extent, had fallen into the trap which
had been thus cunningly laid for them.[1]

He then goes on to describe his fight with the public school

society and his involvement in the political affairs of the

period. Apparently, he felt it necessary to explain that he

was not really trying to invade the political arena, but in

this one occasion was forced by circumstances. He particu-

larly dwells on his unsuccessful attempts to obtain public

funds. He summarizes as follows:

---

[1]Hughes, Memoir, pp. 504-505.

Now, however, having been refused by the
City Council, we had a right to appeal to the
justice of the Legislature. This we did, and
in despite of all the influence which the
Public School Society brought to bear upon the
Legislative body, we obtained a law of partial
redress; the best effect of which, was to break
up that wicked monopoly which claimed to take
charge of the minds and hearts of Catholic
children. The popular feeling at our tryumph (sic)
could not restrain itself; and accordingly,
on the night in which the news reached the
City, a mob passed along, somewhat rapidly,
before the Episcopal residence, and having
hurled stones, and brick-bats into nearly every
window of the House (except the windows
of my own room, the only ones they aimed at,)
they passed on their way rejoicing. From that
period the political papers, out of personal
ill-will in the first instance, began to denounce
me as a "politician," as "meddling with the civil
affairs of the State," as one on whose "will
and feat" depended the success or defeat of any
party, or any individual aspiring to public
office. This, I have just remarked, was begun
with a view to hold me up to popular odium; but
it was repeated in such variety of form, and so
perseveringly, that at length it came to be
somewhat of a settled belief, in the public mind:
and to this day, vast numbers are very sincere
in the conviction that the first step towards
success, which a candidate should take, is to
have the approval of the Archbishop of New
York. I have often disclaimed this imputed
political influence; but the more I disclaimed
it, the more the conviction to the contrary
became strong and settled.[1]

The Archbishop next repeated the report of James Gordon
Bennett of the New York Herald which indicated that at the time
6,100 girls and 4,800 boys were under Catholic instruction. His
faith in the future of Catholic education is clearly demonstrated
in the following section:

[1]Hughes, Memoir, pp. 504-505.

158

Immediately after the breaking up of the
Public School Society, a new system was introduced, very different indeed, from what I
would have recommended; but yet an immense
improvement on the one which it replaced.
I was obliged to tolerate the attendance of
our poor children at these schools until we should,
with time and the blessing of Almighty God,
be enabled to erect schools of our own for
their exclusively Catholic training. In
this we have not been unsuccessful; although
yet much remains to be done.[1]

And elsewhere:

You must not suppose, that on the subject of
education we have reached anything like a fair
supply of School houses & teachers, to meet
the wants of our Catholic Children. But the
work must be continued, and by the time it
will be completed, I have very little doubt
that there will be such a change in the law,
as will result in our obtaining a share of the
public funds, which are employed for State
education of youth. . . .[2]

In spite of Hughes' optimism and his continued efforts
and those of other churchmen in later years, the issue of
public support of private education had been pretty well
solved; few private schools were successful in bidding for
public support after this date. Lawrence A. Cremin has char-
acterized the period:

The fight for free schools was a bitter
one, and for twenty-five years the outcome
was uncertain. Local elections were fought,
won, and lost on the school issue. The tide
of educational reform flowed in one state,
only to ebb in another. Legislation passed
one year was sometimes repealed the next.

---

[1]Hughes, Memoir, p. 505.

[2]Hughes, Memoir, p. 506.

State laws requiring public schools were
ignored by the local communities that were
supposed to build them. Time and again the
partisans of popular education encountered
the bitter disappointments that accompany
any effort at fundamental social reform.

Yet by 1860 a design had begun to appear, and it bore upon it the marks of Mann's
ideal. A majority of the states had established public school systems, and a good half
of the nation's children were already
getting some formal education. Elementary
schools were becoming widely available; in
some states, like Massachusetts, New York
and Pennsylvania, the notion of free public
education was slowly expanding to include
secondary schools; . . . The southern states,
with the exception of North Carolina, tended
to lag behind, and did not generally establish popular schooling until after the Civil
War.[1]

In general, after 1860, or indeed somewhat before,
the threefold ideal of tax-supported, non-sectarian, public
education became an established fact. Continued immigration
of German and Irish groups and the positive efforts of prelates
continued, at the same time, to advance the standards of the
Catholic parochial school. In view of the role which he was
to play in the Second Plenary Council of Baltimore, the efforts
of Martin John Spalding at the councils of Cincinnati are
of import. In the Pastoral Letter of the first council of
that province, he wrote:

Earnestly do we desire to see a parochial
school in connection with every Catholic

[1]Lawrence A. Cremin, The Transformation of the School
Progressivism in American Education, 1876-1957 (New York:
Knopf, 1961), p. 13.

Church in this province; and we hope the day
is not far distant when this wish nearest
our hearts shall be fully realized. With all
the influences constantly at work to unset-
tle the faith of our children, and to pervert
their tender minds from the religion of their
fathers, and with all the lamentable results
of these influences constantly before our
eyes, we cannot too strongly exhort you to
contribute generously of your means to enable
your pastors to carry out this great work.
The erection of Catholic schools is, in many
respects, as important an object as the building
of new churches. . . .[1]

His attitude was also clearly expressed in a letter

which he wrote to Archbishop Kenrick shortly after the first

plenary council:

The street brawler Kirkland delivered
inflammatory addresses here on yesterday,
(Sunday). I have published a Circular in
all the morning papers, warning the Catholics
to remain away from his meetings. I think
he will do but little harm in Louisville. He
attempted to speak again on Monday evening
but was driven away by the people. The evil
one seems unchained in this country; he is
evidently uneasy, it is a good sign. We have
lately received several converts of distinguished position in society. The chief object
of our enemy seems to be to pervert our youth
through the wretched school system. It will
be some time before we will be able to obtain
justice, but the time will come. I intend
to open several additional parochial schools
soon, & "to run opposition" to those of the
city. After a while, perhaps, people will
come to their senses on this & other subjects.[2]

Likewise active at this time was the minister, Horace

Bushnell. In a sermon preached at Hartford and later published,

---

[1]Pastoral Letter of the First Provincial Council of
Cincinnati to the Clergy and Laity (Cincinnati: Walsh, 1855),
p. 8. Cf. also Spalding, Life of Archbishop Spalding, p. 201.

[2]BCA 32A N 7. M. J. Spalding to Kenrick, Louisville, July 18, 1853.

the Congregationalist voiced the indignation of a good many
of his fellow countrymen at the antics of Catholics who were
challenging the public schools:

> . . . The withdrawing of our Catholic children
> from the common schools, unless for some real
> breach upon their religion, and the distri-
> bution demanded of public moneys to them in
> schools apart by themselves, is a bitter
> cruelty to the children, and a very unjust
> affront to our institutions. We bid them wel-
> come as they come, and open to their free
> possession, all the rights of our American
> citizenship. They, in return, forbid their
> children to be Americans, pen them as foreign-
> ers to keep them so, and train them up in
> the speech of Ashdod among us. And then,
> to complete the affront, they come to our
> legislatures demanding it, as their right,
> to share in funds collected by a taxing of
> the whole people, and to have these funds
> applied to the purpose of keeping their chil-
> dren from being Americans.
>
> Our only answer to such demands is,
> "No! take your place with us in our common
> schools, and consent to be Americans, or
> else go back to Turkey, where Mohammedans,
> Greeks, Armenians, Jews are walled up by the
> laws themselves, forbidding them ever to pass
> over or to change their superstitions: there
> to take your chances of liberty, such as a
> people are capable of when they are trained
> up, as regards each other, to be foreigners
> for all coming time in blood and religion."[1]

In order to complete the picture, it is necessary to read
similar paragraphs from the writings of the Catholic churchmen who were encouraging their people to desert the public

---

[1]Horace Bushnell, A Discourse on the Modifications
Demanded by the Roman Catholics Delivered in the North Church,
Hartford, on the Day of the Late Fast March 25, 1853 (Hartford:
Case, Tiffany & Co., 1853), p. 10.

schools and throw their energies into the private system.

> That the fierce spirit of intolerance
> has been lately evoked in this once free coun-
> try, no candid observer of passing events
> will deny. Christians of a particular denom-
> ination have been selected, as its first vic-
> tims; but no one who has studied human nature,
> as it is developed in the facts of history,
> will for a moment suppose, that the ruin of
> Catholics in this country will satisfy the
> cravings of this fierce Moloch of religious
> bigotry. As with the tiger, the taste of
> blood will but sharpen its appetite for new
> victims. So it has been in the past; so it
> will be in the future.[1]

Later in the work, he defines the attitude of the Catholics in
America towards the common schools:

> . . . 2. But we are not friendly to the common
> schools. [This is the charge that Spalding
> is refuting.] Our answer is at hand. Let
> the Protestant majority, in this country,
> make those schools such as not to wound the
> religious feelings, nor endanger the reli-
> gious faith of our children, and then may
> they, with some show of reason, taunt us
> with not cheerfully uniting in patronizing
> them. Let them remove from them all sectarian
> books, all sectarian influences, all teachers
> who abuse their position for purposes of
> proselytism; let them not force upon any chil-
> dren the reading of a version of the Bible,
> which in common with four-fifths of Christen-
> dom, we consider neither a genuine nor a com-
> plete rendering of the divine word:@ and then

> @
> and in which a committee of Protestant minis-
> ters, lately assembled in New York for the
> purpose of preparing a revised edition of the
> Bible, discovered no less than twenty-four
> thousand errors of translation!

> they will make it not only our interest, but
> our pleasure to unite with them in supporting

[1] An Address to the Impartial Public, on the Intolerant
Spirit of the Times, Being the Introduction to the Miscellanea
of M. J. Spalding D.D., Bishop of Louisville (Louisville: Webb
& Levering, 1854). p. 3.

the common schools, It will be our interest;
for, in common with our fellow citizens, we
pay our taxes for the erection and maintenance of those schools; . . . If we could
conscientiously do so, we have every possible
motive to patronize the public schools; but
we hold that it is better far to suffer any
earthly loss, rather than to jeopardize our
faith or that of our children.[1]

Although the details of the Eliot school case are
outside the area of this thesis, a quotation from the court
brief of this case will show the attitude of many militant
Protestants. Need we add that this sort of argument was
indeed a powerful factor in the final resolution of churchmen to proceed at all costs with their plans for private
schools, in which Catholic children would not be exposed
to the philosophy of this brief:

For years we have enjoyed the highest
blessing which even a free government can
bestow upon its citizens -- the blessing of
education, unbought, unsold -- free to all,
common to all, without distinction of birth,
or sect or race. Under the wise and parental
system of the public schools, our children
were taught to-gether as one free, and happy,
and united family. The children of the emi-
grant and the alien sat side by side with
the son of the free-born American -- they learned
from the same book -- they shared the same instruction, profited by the same culture -- and
they left the school to-gether to enter upon
the broad highway of life with the same lights
of learning behind them, the same stars of
hope and promise before them, free and equal
under the laws.
    This was the story of yesterday; but
to-day we find a sad and mournful and ominous

---

[1] Spalding, Address, p. 33.

change. Suddenly -- at the absolute will of
one man -- by the exercise of a dark and dangerous, a fearfully dangerous power, hundreds
of children of tender years, children who
were living in the full enjoyment of liberty
and of learning, are not only arrayed in
open rebellion against our established regulations, and in open violation of our
laws, but are deliberately taught that they
are to sacrifice all the benefits and blessings
of free education, and are led out by
their priest from the protecting roof of
their school-house to the temptations, the
dissipations and crimes of the streets. This
course is even now justified and persevered
in; the same influences are still at work in
our schools, and we are told to-day by the
advocate of those deluded children, that this
dangerous and unscrupulous priest was in the
right, that the laws under which my client
justifies himself, were rightly denounced
from the altar, were properly set at defiance
by the pupils, and are destructive of the
liberty of conscience, intolerant, illegal,
unconstitutional and void.

Who is this priest who comes here from
a foreign land to instruct us in our laws?
For whom, and on whose behalf, is this charge
of intolerance -- this charge that we are violating the sacred liberty of conscience --
brought against the people and the laws of
Massachusetts? Can it be that one of the
Society of Jesus is the accuser? I wish to
discuss this case as calmly as I may. I
wish to say nothing to arouse feelings which
cannot easily be allayed; but there are mem-
ories which we can never banish from heart
or brain; there are records on earth and in
heaven which can never be blotted out; there
are pages of history written in letters of
fire, and of blood; and the man who leads
forth his flock of children, and boldly ar-
rays them in open defiance of our established
laws, who audaciously and ungratefully assails
our established regulations as intolerant
and unchristian, and as violating the sacred
liberty of conscience, would do well to
look behind him, as well as before -- would

do well to pause and reflect if _he_ is in
a position which authorizes such grave
accusations, or justifies such violence.[1]

An educational champion of this period who shows
the contrast which existed in Catholic circles is Orestes
Brownson, the bluff defender of individualism who was converted to Catholicism in 1844. Through his celebrated _Quar-
terly_ his work was well known to his contemporaries and his
views carried much weight because of their wide distribution,
both inside and outside the Catholic Church. In one of his
articles, written in 1862, he stated:

> . . . All Catholics feel, or should feel, that
> education, either under the point of view of
> religion or of civilization, is useful
> and desirable no further than it is Catholic.
> Catholic truth is universal truth, is all
> truth, and no education not in accordance
> with it is or can be a true or a useful
> education, for error is never useful, but
> always more or less hurtful. Every Catholic,
> then, indeed every man who loves truth and
> wishes to conform to it, must be in favor
> of Catholic schools and Catholic education,
> if they are Catholic in reality as well as
> in name.[2]

Brownson himself was always a fearless defender of right and
truth as he saw it, and in the school question he was not
hesitant to judge and criticize the Catholic system as well as
the public one. He was not satisfied with a Catholic education

[1]_Defence of the Use of the Bible in the Public Schools:
Argument of Henry F. Durant, Esq. in the Eliot School Case_
(Boston: Ticknor & Fields, 1859), pp. 6-7.

[2]Orestes Brownson, "Catholic Schools and Education,"
_The Works of Orestes Brownson, collected and arranged by Henry
F. Brownson_ (Detroit: Nourse, 1884), vol. XLI, p. 496.

in name only; he demanded an education of quality. Perhaps his sharpest retort about the quality of Catholic
schools was his charge that Catholic schools failed to
educate youngsters for their role in the world:

> . . . They come out ignorant of contemporary
> ideas, contemporary habits of mind, con-
> temporary intelligence and tendencies, and
> large numbers of them sink into obscurity,
> and do nothing for their religion or their
> country; or, what is worse, abandon their
> religion, turn their backs on the church and
> waste all their energies in seeking pleasure,
> or in accumulating worldly wealth.[1]

However severe his criticisms may have been he was not willing
to encourage the abandonment of the private system. The
following quotation clearly delineates his position:

> That we are to have schools and colleges of
> our own, under the control of Catholics, we
> take it is a "fixed fact." Whether the movement
> for them is premature or not, it is idle, if
> nothing worse, to war against it. Let us
> say, then, to those who regard the education
> actually given by Catholics as we do, and
> who have not seen their way clear to the
> support of primary schools under the control of
> Catholics as a substitute, in the case of
> Catholic children, for the common schools
> of the country, that we regard it as our
> duty now to accept the movement, and labor
> not to arrest it, or to embarrass it, but
> to reform and render truly Catholic the whole
> system of Catholic education, from the highest
> grade to the lowest. Let it be our work
> not to destroy Catholic education, but to
> reform and advance it.[2]

---

[1]Brownson, _Works_, vol. XII, p. 501.

[2]Brownson, _Works_, vol. XII, p. 512.

Brownson's final thought on the relationship of secular Catholic education may be found in three proposals which he made in 1870. His first solution offered was the exclusion of the Bible and all religious teaching from the school. Almost as quickly, however, as he made the proposal, he rejected it as not being a solution at all, for Catholics could not accept it, and the majority of Protestants were not willing to abandon the Bible.[1] He recognized that Catholic thought had begun to reject the secular school with as much sureness as it had once rejected the Protestant-dominated public school. This led to his second proposal: the abandonment of public education and the adoption of a voluntary system of education. Since there would be no state fund, state support and control would thereby be ended. Brownson felt that Catholics could readily adapt to this program, since they were already maintaining their own voluntary schools.[2] This proposal, too, Brownson recognized as inadequate and incomplete.[3]

His third proposal was simply to divide the schools between the sects and have each group educate its proportionate share. By this arrangement Catholics were to be allowed

---

[1] Orestes Brownson, "The School Question," Works, vol. XIII, p. 247.

[2] Brownson, Works, Vol. XIII, pp. 250-252.

[3] Brownson, Works, vol. XIII, pp. 253-256.

their own religion in their schools and Protestants could
apply their religion in their schools. This suggestion,
although not strikingly different from the demands which
Archbishop Hughes was pressing unsuccessfully in New York,
was accepted by Brownson as an adequate solution to the
school situation.

Perhaps more than any other factor which would tend
to represent the Protestant nature of public education during
the period under consideration is a study of the textbooks
which were used. In his study of the McGuffey readers, Dr.
Richard Mosier analyses in detail the moral and social
virtues as they are presented in the tales. His conclusion
is that the ethic of the readers is a composite of Protestant culture and middle-class values:

> The great moral synthesis of the Ameri-
> can middle class, though enjoined by the
> Puritan and Protestants, was the work of
> generations of Americans who achieved so
> striking a synthesis of Christian and middle
> class virtues as to put the Puritan fathers
> in the shade. Those New England divines were
> sufficiently acquainted with the heavenly
> ordinances to labor diligently as stewards
> with both personal and public responsibili-
> ties; but the stewardship of later generations,
> of those who read the McGuffey readers, came
> to mean primarily the personal duty to acquire
> and possess, with only an occasional gesture
> of charitable or public activity. The great
> achievement of the McGuffey readers is the
> complete integration of Christian and middle
> class virtues; and in that respect, they are
> the great textbook product of American middle

---

[1]The question of Brownson's views on education has
been made the subject of a special study by Edward J. Power,
"Brownson's View on Responsibility in Education," Records of
the American Catholic Historical Society of Philadelphia,
vol. LXII(December, 1951), no. 4, pp. 221-252.

class culture. Though quick enough to heed
the Lord's calling to labor and acquire,
they could hardly embrace any political doctrine which threatened material possessions
or hindered the enjoyment of the fruits of
acquisition.[1]

The fact that forty million readers were sold during
the period from 1850-1870[2] makes it legitimate to appeal to
the readers as an indication of the spirit and temper of the
schools in which they were used. In large measure, of course,
the ideals of the McGuffey readers were identical with those
of Catholics, because both agreed on a large area of general
Christianity. The point is made here to illustrate the fact
that although the schools were becoming much more secular,
there was still a large residue of Protestant Christianity
left at this time. The Catholic clergy were caught in the
middle of a new dilemma; they recognized the increasing secularism of the schools as a real danger, but at the same time
they were not in a position to side with Protestant leaders
to halt this trend. The tragedy of their struggle often led
the hierarchy to impassioned outbursts against the injustice
of their position -- outbreaks which probably were more deeply
emotional than accurate. Thus Bishop John Timon of Buffalo
cried out in 1859:

---

[1]Richard D. Mosier, Making the American Mind: Social
and Moral Ideas in the McGuffey Readers (New York: King's
Crown Press, Columbia University, 1947), p. 164.

[2]Mosier, McGuffey Readers, pp. 168-169.

> Were Catholics the majority in this
> country, and did they frame such a school
> system for Protestants, how awful would be
> the outcry? Did a Catholic majority tax a
> Protestant minority for the purchase of
> school libraries full of books that insult,
> ridicule, and malign Protestantism, how
> would not Protestants protest? Did Catholics
> tax them for schools in which the Catholic
> Bible would be read and studied; tax them
> for Normal schools, in which all the students,
> educated at great cost to be the future
> teachers of youth, were Catholics; tax them
> in order to pay high wages, almost without
> exception, to Catholic teachers, who, in
> many ways, by word or by gesture, would
> show their contempt for Protestantism; tax
> them for splendid school houses, in which
> poor Protestants could not study without dan-
> ger of being, by a thousand appliances, made
> ashamed of the faith of their fathers; oh,
> were this the case, how the world would ring
> with Catholic injustice, and Protestant suf-
> fering.[1]

A powerful factor which contributed much to the breaking down of prejudice against the Church was the record of
American Catholics in the Civil War. Although the Know-Nothing
party was able to gain control of a number of state legislatures
and also secure a representation in the national Congress in
1854 and 1855, they did not succeed in any fashion in execut-
ing the well-publicized campaign against Rome. Neither Re-
publicans nor Democrats wished to have anything to do with
the rabid minority group and the best they could muster was a

---

[1]Charles G. Deuther, The Life and Times of the Rt.
Rev. John Timon (Buffalo: the author, 1870), pp. 274-275.

series of anti-Catholic debates in Congress. Within the states
Know-Nothingism proved somewhat stronger and Massachusetts
even appointed a "Nunnery Committee" whose purpose was to
investigate religious institutions in the state.[1] The national
crisis of the Civil War, however, stilled effectively any campaign against the Church.[2] It was not until after the Third
Plenary Council that another wave of anti-Catholic prejudice
was to sweep the country with the advent of the American Protective Association. The slavery issue had been diligently
avoided in the First Plenary Council, so that when the Civil
War was raging, the hierarchy of the Catholic Church did not
find itself split in allegiance. True, members of the hierarchy did play some role, notably Hughes and his commission
to Napoleon III, and Bishop Lynch of Charleston who was
sent by the Confederate States of America to secure diplo-
matic recognition from Rome.[3]

Archbishop Kenrick had died during the darkest hours
of the Civil War. While news was still coming back to Baltimore of the terrible casualties at Gettysburg, Catholics of

---

[1]Billington, Protestant Crusade, pp. 407-414.

[2]The only serious blot upon the Catholic record was
the New York draft riot.

[3]Ellis, American Catholicism, p. 95. For a more tho-
rough discussion of the Church during the Civil War period, cf.
Robert Joseph Murphy, "The Catholic Church in the United States
During the Civil War Period (1852-1866)," Records of the Amer-
ican Catholic Historical Society of Philadelphia, vol. XXXIX,
(December, 1928), no. 4.

the city turned out for the funeral of their beloved primate,
who died on the 8th of July. In an attempt to find a suitable
incumbent for the delicate Maryland See, the choice finally
fell upon the erudite Martin J. Spalding. As Bishop of Louisville, he had successfully learned the temper and mood of
both North and South. As a son of Baltimore emigres, moreover,
he could trace his ancestry to old Maryland stock.[1] His educational activity in Kentucky has already been touched upon.
The reasons for holding a national council at this particular
moment have been detailed by his nephew-biographer:

> . . . first, that at the close of the national
> crisis, which had acted as a dissolvant upon
> all sectarian ecclesiastical organizations,
> the Catholic Church might   present to the
> country and the world a striking proof of the
> strong bond of unity with which her members
> were knit together. Secondly, that the col-
> lective wisdom of the Church in this country
> might determine what measures should be adopted
> in order to meet the new phase of national
> life which the result of the war had just in-
> augurated; for, though the Church is essen-
> tially the same in all times and places, her ac-
> cidental realtions to the world and the state
> are necessarily variable.
> Thirdly, that an earnest effort might be made
> to render ecclesiastical discipline, as far as
> possible, uniform throughout the entire ex-
> tent of the United States. The fourth motive
> I shall give in the words of Archbishop
> Spalding:
> "I think," he wrote, "that it is
> our most urgent duty to discuss the future
> status of the negro. Four millions of these
> unfortunate beings are thrown on our charity
> and they silently, but eloquently appeal
> to us for help. We have golden opportunity
> to reap a harvest of souls, which,neglected,
> may not return."[2]

[1] Spalding,Life of M. Spalding, pp. 298-299.

[2] Spalding, Life of M. Spalding, pp.298-299.

Archbishop Spalding himself had initiated discussion
for a new council in the College of Propaganda and Cardinal
Barnabo was equally in favor of calling a second plenary
council. On March 4, 1866, Spalding was able to write to the
Archbishop of St. Louis, Peter Richard Kenrick:

> Letters from Cardinal Barnabo, dated
> January 4, 31   authorize me as Apostolic dele-
> gate to convene the Plenary Council.[1]

The Papal Brief, Apostolici Ministerii Munus, is dated
February 16, but the mails were slow in reaching Baltimore
and it was only after several months delay that the Brief
was actually in the hands of Spalding.[2] He then jotted
down in his spare moments items for discussion at the coming
meeting; it was his intention to make the legislation of
this council a model for the entire world. One of the
earliest drafts shows that, at least for him, the issue of
public versus parochial education had been reduced to a
general complaint against the lack of religion in the
public institutions:

> Synodus Plenaria -- Puncta discutienda
> Cap.   De Juventute Catholici erudienda
> 1. De Scholis Parochialibus ubique instituendis
> Principia traduntur sana educationis --
> Scholae Publicae examinantur -- eorum de-

---

[1] BCA, Spalding to Kenrick, March 4, 1866, Spalding
letterbook, p. 208.

[2] BCA, SpB W 1. Cf. also: Charles Fisher: "Archbishop Spalding and the Preparation for the Second Plenary
Council of Baltimore," (Baltimore, St. Mary's Seminary:
unpublished Master's thesis, January, 1950), p. 12.

fectus principalis quod careant Religionis
elemento -- jura Catholicorum vindicuntur ad
proportionem aequam summo ex taxis communibus,
sicuti in Anglia et ubique terrarum. Educatio
deberet ope denominationales.
2. Quidquid sit, Scholae omnibus ecclesiis
adnexae habeantur . . . .[1]

On March 19, Archbishop Spalding sent a portfolio to
each of the Metropolitans and Bishops in the country. In
addition to the letters of convocation, he included an item
called the Acta Concilio Praevia.[2] This schema was more detailed than those of previous councils had been, very likely
because of Spalding's desire to make this council outstanding
in every way. Titulus IX of this preliminary document dealt
with education and was entitled: De Iuventute Instituenda
Pieque Erudienda. The entire section was divided into three
chapters, the first of which concerned parochial schools.
It stated, among other items:

Titulus IX: De Juventute Instituenda Pieque
Erudienda.
Caput I. De Scholis Parochialibus ubique
constituendis.[3]

_____

[1]Acta Episcopalia, die 31 Julii, 1864, p. 23.
Translation: Chapter 1. Catholic education of youth:
1. Regarding the establishment of Catholic Schools everywhere:
Sound principles of education are laid down. The public schools
are examined -- their principal defect is that they lack the
element of religion -- the right of Catholics to a proportionate
share of the common taxes is vindicated, as in Britain and
other lands. Education ought to be through denominations.
2. What must be done so that schools may be attached to all
the churches . . . . .

[2]Acta Concilio Praevia (Baltimori: Excudebat Joannes
Murphy, 1866).

[3]Title IX: About the Christian formation and
education of youth.
Chapter 1. About establishing parochial schools everywhere.

1. Decretis Baltimorensibus jam latis additur
amplior magisque explicita declaratio, de
malis quae Scholarum Publicarum instructioni
et administrationi insunt, de periculis quibus
pueri Catholici eas frequentantes exponuntur,
et de gravi injuria quae nobis hac in parte
irrogatur.
2. Statuitur Scholas Dominicales, vulgo Sunday
Schools, bene sub Pastorum oculis ordinatas,
in omnibus ecclesiis constituendas.[1]

These early remarks are followed by a discussion of
the manner in which pastors are to prepare the youngsters for
their First Holy Communion and Confirmation. Chapter Two
of the Acta was a thorough analysis of the steps which
Spalding thought ought to be taken to provide for the establishment of industrial and reform schools, so that youths
might be protected from dangers to their faith, both within
and outside the public houses of refuge. The final chapter of
this title was entitled: De Universitate Literarum Fundanda.
In this section Spalding initiated the idea of founding a
university in the United States after the pattern of the Irish
and Belgian schools.[2] He then entrusted the materials of
Titulus IX to Archbishop McCloskey of New York for implementation and on May 7, McCloskey sent the materials he had

---

[1]Acta Concilio Praevia. Translation: 1. To the
Baltimore decrees already enacted is added a broader and more
explicit statement about the evils which are present in Public
School education and administration, especially the dangers to
which Catholic children frequenting them are exposed, and the
grave injury which is done to us in this manner.
2. Sunday Schools are demanded in all parishes, under the
direction of the Pastor.

[2]For a detailed study of the Catholic University,
cf. John T. Ellis, The Formative Years of the Catholic University of America (Washington: Catholic Historical Society,
1946); pp. 44-51 deal with the council under discussion.

prepared in regard to this title.[1] These remarks were not
located; the only correspondence from McCloskey deals with
the foundation of the Catholic University. An interesting
series of letters written earlier by another participant,
Henry Elder, are enlightening, because they reveal conditions as they were in the South. Writing from the diocese
of Natchez, he was feeling at first hand the miseries of war
and famine. Elder was later moved to the Archdiocese of
Cincinnati where he became a leader in the parochial school
movement. In view of this later prominence, it is interesting
to note his earlier views on the matter:

> I have another great perplexity here,
> with regard to the schools. The Public In-
> stitute has such advantage in means, & in
> popularity both with rich & poor, that we
> cannot get our school on an equality as to
> school-house nor as to efficiency. Children
> prefer the Public School because they have
> more companions, & they regard it as fashion-
> able. Parents prefer it because they pay
> taxes for it. Our teacher is good -- really
> very good -- considerably above the ordinary
> level of teachers in Parish schools, but a
> single teacher cannot do as well as a number
> of teachers dividing labor. Parents send
> their children rather through an unwilling-
> ness to oppose us, than through hearty ap-
> proval of the school. This deprives the
> school of the requisite spirit & weakens
> even the enforcement of discipline. I have
> sometimes thought that if I had foreseen
> the difficulties when I first came, I would
> have suffered the children to go to the Pub-
> lic School, & said nothing about it. -- I
> do not know whether it would have been wise. --
> The Pastor was desirous to keep our school --
> and I thought I ought to cooperate with him
> & help him to improve it: & we have done

---

[1]BCA 35 E 10, McCloskey to Spalding, March 7, 1866.

so. It was a very miserable one then; it
is now a good one -- & if it had not such odds
against it, it would be the best in town.
But still it is not in good estimation. -- To
give it up would be -- I think -- a great injury
-- a confession of incompetency -- a triumph to
our enemies, & to the luke-warm Catholics who
send their children to the Public School.[1]

Elder was unburdening his fears in this letter to Kenrick,
but the struggle was a difficult one, especially since he
was trying to establish his school during the Civil War period. Four years later he wrote to Spalding and once again
complained of his lack of progress.

Ever since my first coming to Natchez,
I have felt the condition of our Schools to
be my greatest solicitude as regards the interests of religion in the town. -- One considerable cause of the embarrassment of my
finances which I have mentioned to you -- has
been the expense of keeping up schools. --
They have never yet been so satisfactory that
I could appeal with any confidence to the
people to make a vigorous effort to provide
for them. Many have sent their children
rather through a reluctant docility to our
instances, than through choice: -- & many
have persevered in sending to the Public
Institute -- which had the reputation of being
well conducted. -- At present the Institute
is not in such good condition, -- though it
still gives satisfaction considering the
circumstances of the times. -- But at the
same time our own schools likewise have lost
ground. -- They are taught now by two ladies.
The number of scholars is small -- the spirit
is poor: no ambition -- to (sic) little piety.
The ladies are well disposed: but there
has always been a lethargy over both boys
& parents: -- which I see no way of shaking
off, without a thorough change. And at the
same time the expense must be some $400 or

---

[1]BCA   29 D 11, Elder to Kenrick, April 12, 1861,
Natchez.

$500 per an. beyond the receipts. It has
been still greater in former years. -- An
observing Young Priest three years ago told
me if we made no improvement in the care of
our boys -- we might by the time they grew up
-- rent out the church -- for there would be no
congreg. He himself had charge of them with
a gentleman and a lady for teachers -- & under him for a few months there was great
improvement in their spirit. But he was
carried off by death. -- Neither of us here
now can revive the spirit -- whether because
we have not the tact -- or for any other cause.
-- There must be new persons & a new start.[1]

All the South, however, was not tortured by the apathy
which puzzled and discouraged Elder. A few months before the
opening of the second council, we find this article in the
New Orleans secular newspaper:

Education and Religion
The Catholic Church and Public Schools
His Grace Archbishop Leray Gives Hiw Views
Through The Item.

The clergy of this diocese having lately in
their exhortations to the faithful at mass
and at instructions, strongly condemned the
sending of children to the public schools,
The Item this morning called upon His Grace,
Monseigneur F. X. Leray, Archbishop of New
Orleans, to ascertain if he had issued a decree to the clergy in respect to public schools.
Monseigneur was found in the garden of his
archiepiscopal residence, enjoying his morning
walk and inhaling the sce nt of flowers
with which the balmy atmosphere was laden.
He received The Item with his customary
amiability, and said: "I have issued no orders or edicts in that respect. The clergy
are at liberty to say whatever they please.
Of course I am opposed to the sending of
Catholic children to public schools, especially
when our parochial schools are excellent. A

---

[1]BCA 33 U 5, Elder to Spalding, February 20,
1865, Natchez.

little child is apt to receive its first and
lasting impressions of morality in the schools;
educated in a Catholic institution, he is instructed in his religion, whilst the public
schools only afford a common education, without any religious training. I have had occasion to visit several of our parochial schools,
and I have assisted at many of their commence-
ment exercises, and I find their standard of
education to be of a high order. I do not
wish to detract from the usefulness and merit
of the public schools, but I say Catholic
parents should send their children to Catholic
schools. The priests do not ask a great deal
of money for tuition; when parents are poor,
we charge nothing. By all means, let the
children be sent to their parochial schools,
but there is no strict prohibition from sending
them to other institutions."

Monseigneur further remarked that in a
public school it necessarily follows that
there can be no religious training; the institution is a public one, and accepts all races
and sects. Some twenty-five years ago, after
a hard struggle, the clergy succeeded in having
the reading of the Bible abolished in those
schools, so that now children receive there
a good, common education, and learn their
religion at home, whatever their creed may be.[1]

The general picture before the council was much

changed from that of the previous council in 1854. The Church

had continued to grow rapidly and by the time of this council,

there were seven provinces, San Francisco having been erected

since 1854, and forty suffragan Sees. Many of the Bishops

present at that council had since died but most of the

leading figures of this council had been present at the previous

council in some capacity or other.[2] Because of the vast area

---

[1]Daily City Item, New Orleans, October 6, 1865.

[2]Murphy, Records of the American Catholic Historical
Society, vol. XXXIX, pp. 323-324.

which the Church now covered, it becomes increasingly difficult to speak of any Church policies as a whole. More and
more, divergent policies became evident in various dioceses,
and this is especially true of educational matters. James
Roosevelt Bayley, for example, was greatly troubled and concerned about the lack of educational institutions in his diocese of Newark, although it would be expected that this would
be an area strong in Catholic schools and institutions. In
appealing to the Society for the Propagation of the Faith for
funds to expand his school system, he pleaded:

> . . . In this country, more than in any other,
> the prosperity of the Church depends above
> all on the education given to the children.
> The evil influences to be met on every side
> are so destructive that the Catholic religion
> will disappear as quickly as it has spread
> unless we transplant it in a good soil, in
> training up with all possible care the chil-
> dren in the faith of their fathers. There-
> fore I have opened schools wherever there is
> a church and a resident priest. It is a great
> burden for our poor people, who are obliged
> not only to support Catholic schools, but
> also to pay taxes for the maintenance of
> free schools, which are carried on at an im-
> mense outlay and which present every attrac-
> tion to catch our children.[1]

Likewise of importance are the many other problems
which faced the members of the council. General Church legislation needed to be renewed and strengthened in order to
preserve the unity of north and south, east and west. Catholic

---

[1]Joseph Flynn, The Catholic Church in New Jersey
(Morristown, New Jersey, 1904), pp. 276ff. Cf. also Sr. Hildegarde Yeager, The Life of James Roosevelt Bayley: First
Bishop of Newark and Eighth Archbishop of Baltimore 1814-
1877 (Washington, D.C.: Catholic University of America Press,
1947), pp. 217-255.

journalism received a great deal of attention at this council likewise, indicating that the clergy were becoming more and more aware of the need for a more favorable image.[1] Even more important to bear in mind is the fact that this legislation was meant for the entire Church in the United States, not merely for individual sections or provinces. Authors frequently indicate that the legislation of this council was not as stringent as the legislation of earlier provincial councils of a local nature. This is especially true of the educational decrees. The Cincinnati province, under the leadership of Purcell, had passed several decrees in their councils which were of a more encompassing nature than those of this council. However, these decrees were meant for the entire country and the Bishops were slow to legislate matters that were difficult or impossible of fulfillment. Many authors, following Burns,[2] indicate that the province of Cincinnati had reached a much more advanced stage of legislation than did the Plenary Council itself. What most of these authors do not remark is that Spalding himself was a prime mover of both these councils; yet at the second he was satisfied to pass a milder decree.

---

[1]For a brief survey of the conciliar legislation as it affected Catholic journalism see Clifford J. Fenton, "The Councils of Baltimore and the Catholic Press," American Ecclesiastical Review, 136 (February, 1957), pp. 120-131.

[2]Burns and Kohlbrenner, History of Catholic Education, pp. 138-140.

In spite of the greater prestige of his position as Archbishop, Spalding was aware that not all sections of the
country were as eager and ready for privately-supported
parochial education as were the midwestern prelates.
The Schema of the council in regard to education was
little changed, another indication that Spalding had
rightly interpreted the minds of the assisting Bishops.
The theologians met early in May to deliberate and discuss the proposed legislation, but their notes indicate
that their discussion in regard to education was sparse.[1]
The action of the council proper began on October 4th, when
the Archbishops gathered for a secret conference; the
regular activities began on the seventh and lasted for a
full two week period, closing on the twenty-first. The
congregation which had been given the duty of discussing
the ninth title: De Juventute Instituenda, Pieque Erudienda,
was under the direction of the Bishop of Milwaukee, John
Henni; he was aided by Isaac Hecker, the controversial
founder of the Paulists, and by Michael Heiss, together
with fourteen others.[2] Though the minutes of the entire
council are quite detailed, there is no indication that the
decrees concerning education received any lengthy discussion

---

[1] BCA 39A A 3.

[2] Concilii Plenarii Baltimorensis II., In Ecclesia
Metropolitana Baltimorensi, a Die VII, ad Diem XXI, Octobris,
A. D. MDCCCLXVI., Habiti, Et a Sede Apostolica Recogniti,
Acta et Decreta. Praeside Illustrissimo ac Reverendissimo
Martino Joanne Spalding, Archiepiscopo Baltimoreensi, et
Delegato Apostolico (Baltimorae: excudebat Joannes Murphy,
1868.

or debate.[1] Because of the length of the entire section
on education, only the immediately pertinent sections will
be discussed here.[2] As already indicated, the question was
discussed under the general heading of the education of
youth. Three separate chapters were introduced; one of
which dealt with the founding of a university in this
country, a second considered the foundation and support
of industrial or protective schools, and by far the
lengthiest and most important section was devoted to the
need for parochial schools and the moral obligation of
parents to send their children to these schools. The
legislation in regard to the university and the industrial
schools is simple in nature; consequently, our attention
will be focused on the decrees dealing with the foundation
of parochial schools. Beginning with a defense of the
teaching role of the Church, the legislators go on to re-
emphasize the traditional interest and protective care which
the Church has always and everywhere lavished on the
education of youth.[3] In the next decree the Fathers point
out that the enemies of religion are constantly striving
to corrupt the minds of the young. Hence, they list their

[1] Concilii Plenarii, pp. lx-lxxxix.
[2] Cf. Appendix I.
[3] Decree nos. 423-424.

reasons for opposition to the public school system in the
following words:

> For daily experience enough and more
> than enough proves how serious are the
> evils, how intrinsic are the dangers which
> more and more come into the way of Catholic
> Youth from attendance at public schools
> in those areas. It can surely happen by
> the force of the system existing among them
> that often Catholic Youth will be exposed
> to great danger to faith and morals. And
> not merely for the sake of repetition, we
> see the strides which that taint of deadly
> Indifferentism, as they call it, has up to
> this time made and daily continues to make
> in this area. We see also the corruption
> of morals by which we tearfully notice that
> even the youngest among us are infected
> and destroyed. For the habit of those who
> foster either a false religion or none at
> all, of daily reading and meditating on
> authors who attack, slander and sprinkle
> with foul wit our most sacred religion and
> teachings, yea even the Saints themselves,
> gradually weakens in the minds of Catholic
> children the force and virtue of true Re-
> ligion. Their fellow-students, with whom
> they are in close association, are by their
> habits and examples, by that lawless free-
> dom of speaking and acting, such that by
> this close contact and intercourse with
> our youngsters, (even though excellently
> trained at home), all shame and sense of
> piety is quickly consumed and destroyed,
> just like wax in the presence of fire. The
> evils of this kind were not unknown to our
> predecessors as is clear from their decrees: . . .[1]

Having stated their grounds for their opposition to the
common school system, the Bishops repeat with approval
the decrees of the previous councils. Their own summary is

---

[1]Decree no. 426.

as follows:

> 430. It seems that the best, or rather the
> only, remedy that remains by which these
> very serious and troublesome evils can
> be met is that in every diocese, next to
> each and every church, Schools be erected
> in which the Catholic youth may be imbued
> with literature and the fine arts as well
> as with Religion and good morals. This was
> already provided for in the wise admonition
> by the Fathers of the previous Plenary
> Council:
>
> We exhort the bishops, and in view of
> the very great evils which usually result
> from the defective education of youth, we
> beseech them through the bowels of the mercy
> of God to see that schools are established
> in connection with the churches of their
> dioceses; and if it be necessary and cir-
> cumstances permit, to provide, from the
> revenues of the church to which the School
> is attached, for the support of competent
> teachers. (I. Balt., 90).
>
> 431. Therefore following the examples of
> our predecessors, we strongly urge the
> Pastors to apply their efforts in accord
> with their resources to construct Parochial
> Schools, wherever it can be done. In these
> Schools, under the careful scrutiny of the
> Pastors, shall be avoided the dangers which
> we have already said inhere in the public
> schools; the children shall be protected
> from that indifferentism now so rampant;
> they shall learn to walk in the Catholic
> way and to bear the yoke of the Lord from
> their youth.[1]

Many of the Bishops had already expended great effort

in the procurement of teachers for their parish schools,

so their thoughts next turned to teaching personnel, badly

needed to staff these schools.[2] Subsequent paragraphs

---

[1]Decrees no. 430-431.

[2]Decrees no. 432-433.

give detailed instructions to be followed in case the
parochial schools cannot be built and the pupils must
of necessity attend the public schools. The importance
they attached to religious instruction is apparent
from these commands:

> 437. Let him induce the parents with every
> means of which he is capable to do their
> parts. Let him stir them up with exhor-
> tations, let him instill fear with threats,
> and let him entreat them with prayers to
> send their children to Church for cate-
> chetical instructions at the proper time.
> Moreover, let him entice the children with
> little presents and rewards to come more
> quickly and to learn. Every day the
> teachers of heresy do this to draw the
> Catholic children to their schools, in
> order to steep them in the poison of error
> and to inflict them with eternal punish-
> ment; will not the minister of God and our
> most holy Religion carefully and diligently
> do the same in order to preserve his own
> and not lose any one of those whom the
> Father has given to his Anointed One?
> (John, xvii., 12; xviii., 9).[1]

The major advance in the decrees of this council was
the transfer of attention from the Protestant nature
of the public schools to the charge of fostering and
inducing indifferentism. The relative importance of
this move is sometimes overlooked. Following Burns,[2]
most authors are satisfied to state that little progress
was made at this council. However, the length of the
decrees of this council conceal much of the real import
of the transition which was completed in this council
from the attack on the Protestant nature to the godless-

---

[1]Decree no. 437.

[2]Burns, Growth, p. 187.

ness argument. This is highly important because it does mark
a real stage of development in the thinking of Catholics.
Had the fathers been satisfied to send the children to public
schools which were completely non-sectarian, they might have
won the few sectarian battles that were still to crop up and
the truly non-sectarian school would have emerged within that
decade. However, having moved on to indifferentism as the
major obstacle against reunion with the public schools, the
Bishops here in this council prepared the way for the thinking
of the later council. A portent of the trend which future
legislation would take had already been given in the arguments
of the theologians prior to the meeting. In reference to num.
434, some of the theologians wished to inject the words: "Nisi
forte alicubi contingat publicas quasdam scholas non vertere
in detrimentum Catholicae religionis," immediately after the
phrase ordering pastors and parishioners to erect and maintain
parochial schools. The suggested amendment, however, was defeated, with only six of the group favoring such a change.[1]
If the usual division of the American hierarchy into liberal
and conservative elements has any force or validity,[2] mani-
festations of it can best be demonstrated by the attitude which

[1] BCA 39A D 3 Relationes Congregationum
Theologorum Ad Titulum IX (May 18th, 1866, Sessio V), p. 10.

[2] For a general treatise of the validity of this type
of division, cf. Robert Cross, The Emergence of Liberal
Catholicism in America (Cambridge: Harvard University Press,
1958).

the groups took toward the problem of public education.
More than any other issue, this difficulty tended to split
the clergy into opposing groups.

The Pastoral Letter for this council was written
by Archbishop Kenrick of St. Louis, although Spalding himself
gave very detailed instructions as to its content and arrangement. Kenrick himself was strongly disturbed by the conduct
of the meeting, but he seems to have prepared the letter before
he arrived at the deliberations and left it unchanged, in
spite of his objections to the proceedings of the council.
The section of the Letter dealing with education follows:

> VII   Education of Youth
> We recur to the subject of the education
> of youth, to which in the former Plenary Coun-
> cil, we already directed your attention, for
> the purpose of reiterating the admonition we
> then gave, in regard to the establishment and
> support of Parochial Schools; and of renewing
> the expression of our conviction, that reli-
> gious teaching and religious training should
> form part of every system of school education.
> Every day's experience renders it evident,
> that to develop the intellect and store it with
> knowledge, while the heart and its affections
> are left without the control of religious prin-
> ciple, sustained by religious practices, is
> to mistake the nature and object of education;
> as well as to prepare for parent and child the
> most bitter disappointment in the future, and
> for society the most disastrous results. We
> wish also to call attention to a prevalent
> error on the subject of the education of youth,
> from which parents of the best principles are
> not always exempt. Naturally desiring the ad-
> vancement of their children, in determining the
> education they will give them, they not unfre-

[1]Fisher, Spalding, pp. 74-76.

quently consult their wishes, rather than
their means, and the probable position of
their children in mature age. Education, to
be good, need not necessarily be either high
or ornamental, in the studies or accomplish-
ments it embraces. These things are in themselves unobjectionable; and they may be suitable and advantageous or otherwise, according
to circumstances. Prepare your children for
the duties of the state or condition of life
they are likely to be engaged in; do not ex-
haust your means in bestowing on them an education that may unfit them for these duties.
This would be a sure source of disappointment
and dissatisfaction, both for yourselves and
for them. Accustom them from their earliest
years to habits of obedience, industry, and
thrift: and deeply impress on their minds
the great principle, that happiness and success in life, as well as acceptance with God,
do not so much depend on the station we fill,
as to the fidelity with which we discharge its
duties. Teach them, that the groundwork of
true happiness must be placed in habitual and
cheerful submission of our wills to the dis-
pensations of Providence, who has wisely consulted for the happiness of all, without, however, bestowing on all an equal share of the
goods of fortune.[1]

As usual, the decrees were immediately submitted to
Rome for approval. The published Acta show clearly that the
Propaganda agents again spent much time and effort in discussing and amending the decrees, but there is no evidence that
they offered any changes in the decrees regarding education.[2]
The final approval was granted by Cardinal Barnabo on the 24th
day of February, 1868.[3]

---

[1]Guilday, Pastorals, pp. 215-216.

[2]Concilii Plenarii, passim. The materials at Notre
Dame do not include the Second Plenary Council as of this date,
and hence the coverage of the Roman side is limited.

[3]Shearer, Pontificia Americana, pp. 330-333.

Chapter VII

Third Plenary Council

Between the adjournment of the second council and
the calling of the third, nearly twenty years were to elapse.
These were years of rapid development within the country as a
whole. The nation endured the trials of reconstruction and
the thrill of western settlement. Industrialization went
hand in hand with settlement; large fortunes were built in
steel, land speculation, textiles and railroads. It was also
a period of maximum growth for the public elementary and
secondary school. William T. Harris took charge of the St.
Louis system the year after the close of the second council,
and his career stretched on into the twentieth century. Harris'
view of religious training in the schools may be taken as representative of the difficulties one has in studying this
period. Although deeply convinced of the need for public and
private morality, especially as defined by Hegel,[1] he was much
more eager than many to push the separation of Church and
State to the logical conclusion of totally separating secular
and religious instruction. In his Fifteenth Annual Report
he pleads that the public school system was, indeed, regulated
by a sincere desire to respect the feelings and wishes of
all. Therefore, he insisted, let the community see to it
that the public schools be free from all sectarian bias, and

[1]McCluskey, Public Schools and Moral Education,
pp. 118-144.

let the Church be free to fulfill its own mission.[1] Harris
therefore was insistent that Bible reading and prayer be excluded from the St. Louis public system. In many ways, he
represented the truly sincere public school man of his age.
He saw clearly the impossibility of integrating sectarian
doctrine and public universal education. He had prefaced his
general treatment of the subject with the remark that the
question of religious education in the schools was not a question of the importance of religion itself; it was rather one
of the guarding of the rights of private conscience and the
separation of Church and State.[2] In opposition to this line
of thought, Catholic educators during this period continued
their justification of the parochial schools along both traditional and new lines. One of the most interesting developments in later years was represented by John Lancaster Spalding, but the view itself traces its origins to this time
period. The clearest exposition of the concept is given by
Bishop John Wright of Pittsburgh in a present-day symposium,
but the ideas expressed were found among many of the educators
of this early period:

> Q. What has been the effect, do you think,
> of the nineteenth century decision by Ameri-
> can Catholics to resolve the problem of
> education by establishing their own school

---

[1]William Torrey Harris, Fifteenth Annual Report, p. 22.

[2]McCluskey, Public Schools and Moral Education, p. 160.

system rather than, as some Catholics then advo-
cated, entering fully into the public school
system? How has that affected the character
of American Catholics and the extent to which
they are engaged in the work of the general
community? Has it taken them automatically
and inexorably out of a large part of the main-
stream of community life, and, if so, is this
a significant factor?
Wright: Perhaps it is, but not in the way
that is sometimes feared. Indeed, I sometimes
think it will prove a significant factor in
enriching the authentic American tradition in
a way that may never have been expected, certainly not in the way that I once expected. I
am in a peculiar position on this matter. Not
only did I go to public school, but I am
very happy that I went to my specific public high
school at the time when I did, because I fear
it would no longer be equally worthwhile to
go there now. It has changed, as have all
things else. Now I find myself believing, and
passionately believing, that a principal contribution of the Catholic school system to
the American educational tradition may be as
a means and instrument for the preservation
of the very freedom of education. I am not
paranoid on this matter, but I have talked
with people involved in it often enough to be
aware of the forces in the land that are bent
on establishment of a single public school
system, a monolithic educational system under
state, even federal, control.

     As of a couple of generations ago I
might have wished we Catholics had gone, in
the nineteenth century, fully into the public
school system. Now I consider this would
have been an unmitigated political and educational disaster. Let's face it, totalitarianism is present, seed fashion, in every purely
secular government as it would be in any
theocracy; the moment you say that ours is a
purely secular state, at that same moment you
provide a basic formula for one or another
form of totalitarianism and you come perilously
close to Mussolini's concept: "everything
within the state, nothing outside the state."
The separate school system is a major and
healthy obstacle to such a situation.[1]

---

[1]Religion (Santa Barbara, California: Center for the
Study of Democratic Institutions, 1962), pp. 36-37.

It would be misleading, however, to pretend that this point of view was either widespread or even representative of a large group of the hierarchy. By and large, the majority of the arguments that were brought against the public schools repeated the earlier charges of Protestantism with a generous amount of godlessness thrown into the balance. Even as late as the Third Plenary Council Bp. Dwenger launched a biting attack upon the immorality of the public schools, and even after that council, there were many denunciations of the public schools as a hotbed of vice. The division in the ranks of the clergy and hierarchy is shown by the following report of the New York Freeman Journal, indicating that not all citizens had yet agreed upon even the fundamental question of the right of taxation, much less upon the right to be taxed for schools which Catholics could not attend. After a discussion of the struggles in 1850 and the extension of the free-school system over the entire state, the author charges:

> . . . The aim of our vehement appeals was not yet understood by the Radicals -- for, in 1850, there was not in the whole of New York one Catholic parochial school for boys! Our appeal to Catholics was to get up their own schools, with their own money -- and to ignore the Public Schools, for whose support, they, with others, were taxed. The Radicals thought we were preparing to renew the old agitation for a division of the public school money. We, on the contrary, denied the right of the State to tax the people for school money -- divided or undivided.[1]

---

[1] New York Freeman's Journal and Catholic Register, November 24, 1866.

Perhaps no problem has plagued the courts and school
officials alike more than the Bible issue. The delicate issues involved have challenged the courts down to the present
time; at the period in question, however, there was no resort
to arguments about admitting the Bible as literature. All
generally admitted that the Bible was the foundation of morality and was needed in the schools. Rather, the problem balanced
precariously on the delicate issue of sectarian versions. Because of the violence which the issue often caused, the editor
of the _Journal_ ventured this suggestion:

> The Catholic solution of this muddle
> about Bible or no Bible in schools is, "Hands
> off!" No State taxation or donation for any
> schools. You look to your children, and we
> will look to ours. We don't want you to be
> taxed for Catholic schools. We do not want
> to be taxed for Protestant, or for godless,
> schools. Let the public school system go to
> where it came from--the devil. We want
> Christian schools, and the State cannot tell
> us what Christianity is.[1]

Symbolic of the many debates and riots which accompanied these
public airings was the test case in Cincinnati during 1869-
1870. Because this court case is clearly a situation where
popular feelings overcame the integrity of the court, it may
be worthwhile to enter into its discussion here. The practice of daily readings from the King James version of the
Bible dated back all the way to 1829, when the public school

---

[1]_New York Freeman's Journal_, December 14, 1869.

system in Cincinnati had its beginnings.[1] In 1842 Bishop
Purcell had the regulation modified to the point where Catholic
students were permitted to read any version desired.[2] This
remained the situation until after the Civil War. At that
time in an attempt to merge the parochial and public system
into one, the public school board opened negotiations for the
possible purchase of the Catholic school properties and their
actual incorporation into the public system.[3] In order to
achieve Catholic cooperation the Board agreed to stop the
Bible reading in the public schools. The resolution effecting
this was introduced by Samuel C. Miller and the resolves came
to be known as the Miller Resolves. When news of the proposed
merger and the sacrifice of the Bible reached the ears of
the city's Protestants, the area was rocked with riots equal
in intensity to those of the Bedini visit. Protestants rallied
in an effort to keep the Bible in the schools. Although the
concessions had been made in order to allow the Catholics to
attend without violating their rights of conscience, Purcell
reiterated the conservative Catholic stand that Catholic youth
were bound to attend schools where their own religion was

---

[1] Harold M. Helfman, "The Cincinnati 'Bible War', 1869-
1870," The Ohio State Archeological and Historical Quarterly,
vol. 60 (October, 1951), no. 4, p. 369.

[2] John B. Shotwell, A History of the Schools of Cincinnati
(Cincinnati: School Life Co., 1902), p. 446. Connaughton,
Education in Cincinnati, pp. 30-42.

[3] Helfman, Ohio State Quarterly, pp. 370-371.

taught and hence Catholics had no desire either to join the public
system or to see the matter of the Miller Resolves passed favorably.[1]
As a result Miller and his backers were caught without either
popular or Catholic support, but they managed to win enough
support from the board to pass the resolves on November 1,
1869, by a vote of 22 to 15,thereby excluding the Bible from
the public schools. Enraged citizens carried a protest to
Judge Bellamy Storer of the Superior Court of Cincinnati and
requested an injunction. This granted, the scene of the argument moved from the halls of the School Board to the court-
room. The sessions began on November 9, 1869 and because of
the extreme importance of the case, all three judges sat in
the sessions. The defense lawyers based their plea on the
grounds that on trial was not the question of Bible reading
but the right of freedom of conscience. Their opponents, on
the other hand, used the traditional argument of the Bible
as the foundation of freedom and morality.[2] The trial lasted
almost a month and on February 15, 1879 the decision was announced. By a vote of two to one the tribunal reversed the
ruling of the board of education, indicating that by banning
the Bible the board had trespassed upon the sacred character of

[1]Helfman, Ohio State Quarterly, pp. 377-380, Quite
obviously, Miller and his group had expected the support and
cooperation of the Catholics in the city; seemingly Purcell
had also given some intimation of his support.

[2]Helfman, Ohio State Quarterly, pp. 381-383.

religion and, consequently, that the exclusion of religious
instruction from the public schools was unconstitutional.[1]

In addition to the storm of resentment that the parochial system created among Protestants, the system was not
completely and totally accepted without reserve by Catholics
themselves. We have already seen the comments of Brownson.
During the entire period of its development, others also continued to demand improvement in personnel and facilities.
Writing in 1884 Fr. H. A. Brann accepted wholeheartedly the
idea of Catholic private education but he deplored the meagre-
ness of the private school and its offerings. His major purpose in raising the issue was to demonstrate the ways in
which the system could be improved. He questioned, for example, the needless multiplication of subjects and brought
his heaviest criticism against the lack of organization. Each
parish, he maintained, went its completely separate way and
as a result the schools did not learn from each other as
readily as they should have. He urged also the establishment
of stronger training programs for the teachers themselves.[2]

As the Church became more and more involved in matters
of education, explicit statements concerning the right of the
Church to be involved in education came into vogue. Typical

[1]Helfman, Ohio State Quarterly, pp. 384-385.

[2]H. A. Brann, "The Improvement of Parochial Schools,"
The American Catholic Quarterly Review, vol. IX (April, 1884),
No. 34, pp. 238-253.

of these writings is one by Rev. James Conway. After giving
the traditional view of the Church's role in early primitive
education, he goes on to defend the Church's right to found
elementary, normal and training schools. Further, he vin-
dicates the Church's role in examining, approving and in-
specting the credentials of the teachers in these schools.
He then quotes from various papal briefs and bulls to justify
the involvement of the American Bishops.[1]

There is also much evidence that political maneuvers
became increasingly operative in the school issues. President
Grant attempted to distract attention from his own corrupt
regime and tried to gain momentum for his third term by in-
jecting the issue of public and/or private schools into the
campaign. His address at Des Moines on September 29 has
been widely reported.[2] Subsequently, James Blaine, one of
the Maine representatives, introduced an amendment which embodied Grant's suggestion. Having passed the House, it was
amended in the Senate to exclude Bible reading also and
lost. The bitterness of the campaign in which the school

---

[1] Rev. James Conway, "The Rights and Duties of the
Church in Regard to Education," The American Catholic Quarterly Review, vol. IX (April, 1884), pp. 650-669.

[2] John T. Ellis (ed.), Documents of American Catholic
History (Milwaukee: Bruce, 1956), pp. 407-409.

ssue became a major factor is described in detail elsewhere,[1]
nd the effect upon the parochial school movement is also
roperly assessed. The issue was not immediately settled
y the failure of the bill and the subsequent campaign; in
880 another hard-fought election saw Garfield win a solid
ajority in the electoral college but the popular vote had
een evenly split. Once again, the malcontents raised the
chool issue, and an anonymous writer accused the Republican
arty of being heavily weighted in favor of the Protestants
nd against parochial schools. The platform of the Republican
arty in 1876 had read: "The American school system of the
everal states is the bulwark of the American republic, and
ith a view to its purity and permanence, we recommend an
mendment to the Constitution of the U.S. forbidding the ap-
lication of any funds or property for the benefit of any schools
r institutions under sectarian control."[2] The author uses this
latform plank as a springboard to this suggestion to his fel-
ow Catholics as a temporary modus vivendi:

> Every denomination in which any real reli-
> gious spirit remains will form its own
> schools, as the only means of keeping Chris-
> tianity alive in the hearts of the young.

---

[1]Sr. M. Carolyn Klinkhamer, "The Blaine Amendment of
875: Private Motives for Political Action," Catholic His-
rical Review, vol. XLII (April, 1956), pp. 15-49.

[2]"The Anti-Catholic Issue in the Late Election. The
elation of Catholics to the Political Parties," The Ameri-
an Catholic Quarterly Review, vol. VI (January 1881), no.
1, pp. 36-50.

The Episcopal body has already moved, feeling that some step was necessary. They have
been violently assailed, but they are too
conservative a body to be easily deterred from
their course. Their example will be followed.
Every religious body that believes in God and
in redemption through Christ must establish
its own schools to save the coming generations, for in a few years the public schools
will be as hostile to Christianity as they
are now to Catholicity.

In any coming discussion as to the schools,
we Catholics may prudently abstain from any
part. We are taxed for them, and must submit
to that wrong. We shall ere long have plenty
of companions smarting under the sense of
wrong as bitterly as we do.

To remedy the injustice seems now impossible; we should merely arouse an unreasoning
and unconvincible hate. Providence will direct all wisely, and quite all for its own
purposes, while we are making sacrifice on
sacrifice, to do for our children what we feel
to be our highest and most imperative duty.
We must train our children as Catholics, knowing, loving, and practicing their faith, and
not to be lured or driven from it.

In the politics of the country our course
is plain. Our association should be guided
by our conscientious advocacy of all measures
tending to its greatest good, the benefit of
the whole country, and the greatest amount
of personal and local liberty consistent with
good government. As new parties arise, each
one of us entitled to the elective franchise
will exercise it conscientiously, giving his
preference for the honest and upright men who
will, as far as human judgment can determine,
advocate the soundest principles.[1]

It seems that the role of the Church in modern educa-

tion called for more attention than any of the other issues.

---

[1]"The Anti-Catholic Issue," The American Catholic
Quarterly Review, vol. VI, pp. 49-50. Cf. also Sr. Mary Angela Carlin, O.S.U., "The Attitude of the Republican Party
toward Religious Schools, 1875-1880," (Catholic University of
America, Department of Education, unpublished Master's thesis,
1953).

.lliam J. Onaham returns to this theme; like other authors,
 restates the history of the Church's traditional interest
 education through the centuries; then he continues:

> Indeed it is scarcely extravagant to
> assert that no charge and reproach against
> the Catholic Church is more familiar to the
> public ear, and no other is pressed with great-
> er vigor and pertinacity than this ridiculous
> and unfounded charge, that she is, or at all
> events has been hostile to popular education,
> unfriendly to common schools, and opposed
> to the enlightenment of the masses of the
> people. "Wherever that Church has been able
> to wield power and to employ her resources
> unfettered," say these hostile critics, "she
> has shown herself hostile to education; has
> everywhere sought to cramp and fetter the
> mental powers and the intellectual activity
> of her subjects--in a word has been a bar
> and an obstacle to the mental as well as to
> the social and political advancement of peoples
> and nations."[1]

In another article of similar import T. W. Marshall
:udied secular education both in the United States and in
gland. His purpose again was to justify the Church's role
 the schooling of children. He views secularism as rampant
 the schools and observes with American readers in mind.

> Only this incident was wanting to com-
> plete our estimate of Secularism, the agents
> by whom it is promoted, the motives on which
> they act, and the ruinous results to which
> their selfish and evil policy tends. Yet
> Secularism, as all classes concur in stating,
> is nothing but a product of "the utter impos-
> sibility of harmonizing multiform creeds."
> In other words, it is a product of the so-called

[1]William J. Onaham, "The Catholic Church and Popular
lucation," The American Catholic Quarterly Review, vol. VIII,
.pril, 1883), no. 30, pp. 264-281.

Reformation, and, we suppose, one of its
peculiar titles to the admiration of the human
race. Like many other results of that anar-
chic movement, of which we perceive more clearly every year the fatal action upon modern
society, it perplexes statesmen, puzzles preachers, and suggests to both that as religion
is a factor of human life so unpliant and in-
tractable, the only remedy is to get rid of
it altogether. And they get rid of it accordingly. If after being expelled from the school
it can contrive to maintain a precarious existence in the family, there is at present no
law, even in Prussia, prohibiting that expiring
effort. Modern legislation is yet content,
with benevolent forbearance, to refuse it all
public recognition, and, in once Catholic
England, to sweep the children of God into
the schools of Satan, with a coercive discipline of fines and imprisonment for all who
refuse to come, or tarry on the way. The de-
vout pupils of our Board schools, or at least
a good many of them, may be safely trusted to
pursue the system to its logical term, when
they assume in their turn the civic toga, and
to hunt religion out of the family, as their
teachers have hunted it out of the school.
And then people will be able to say of England,
as Dr. Edson says of America, that secular education has proved to be "only the first downward step to complete irreligion and infidelity,
and thence to a corruption of morals such as
was exhibited in the heathen world." Perhaps
when that auspicious era arrives, some Eng-
lishmen will still be found to say with Lord
Bacon, only using the past instead of the future tense: "The misery is that the most ef-
fectual means have been applied to the ends
least to be desired."[1]

One of the more common techniques used in expressing

one's point of view at this time was to choose a pamphlet or

[1]T. W. Marshall, "Secular Education in England and
in United States," The American Catholic Quarterly Review,
vol. 1 (April, 1876), no. 2, pp. 278-311.

speech of the opposition and to review it in critical detail.
This was done by Rev. P. Bayma of the Society of Jesus, who
chose as his medium a pamphlet written by Francis Abbot on
the public school question. The pamphlet was a standard interpretation of the times, indicating that the public system
of schooling was the only democratic answer to the religious
and educational problems here in America. By claiming to be
completely non-sectarian and disinterested, the author echoed
the views of many public schoolmen of the era. He made no
secret of his interpretation of the Catholic view as being
both partisan and sectarian. Fr. Bayma proceeded to answer
the charges of Abbot:

> Here Mr. Abbot again assumes that the
> Catholic view of the school question is "par-
> tisan" and "sectarian," whilst he pretends
> that the secularist view is "universal" and
> "strictly unsectarian." This is mere twaddle.
> Everyone knows that the word "sect" comes from
> the Latin secta, which is derived from seco
> (to cut off), or, as others teach, from sector
> (to follow): hence the word "sectarian" ap-
> plies to the followers of any peculiar reli-
> gious or irreligious system invented by in-
> dividual thinkers in opposition to the common
> doctrines of the true and divinely instituted
> universal Church. Calvinists, therefore,
> Lutherans, Unitarians, Presbyterians, and all
> those who have wilfully separated from the
> Universal Church, are sectaries. Free reli-
> gionists, too, and the members of all Masonic
> societies, whatever their name, are sectaries,
> as they are cut off from the universal Church.
> But to say that we Catholics are sectaries,
> is to forget that catholicity means universal-
> ity, and that there is a difference between
> the living branches of a tree and the dry

sticks which are consigned to the fire. Catholicity and sectarianism are so incompatible,
that all sects hate catholicity, though they
are often friendly to one another.[1]

He continues with this challenge:

We may ask him, would it be "equal justice to all," if the public schools were all
to be placed under the exclusive control of
the Roman Catholic Church? Would you think
it just to have all the citizens taxed, that
the boys and girls of opposite denominations
may be educated by nuns, by Christian Brothers,
by priests, and by Jesuits? We suppose that
such a system of public schools would not
please you. And yet it is quite certain,
that nuns, Christian Brothers, priests, and
Jesuits are the best instructors and educators
in the country; and accordingly, you free
religionists, who boast so much of your great
love of the country, should have no objection
against this kind of instruction. The pupils
educated by us compare favorably with those
of other institutions; they are, to say the
least, as well instructed, while their moral
faculties are much better trained, and their
evil propensities more effectually checked
and smothered by the help of Christian instruction, the example of their teachers, and
the practice of religious duties. Why then,
should you, Mr. Abbot, and your friends, object to such a good education being extended
to all the children of the country?[2]

These brief excerpts from the periodicals of the time

cannot, however, give one the entire picture which was so

complex and controverted as to defy treatment. In an attempt

to clarify the issues, The Catholic World published an article

which attempted a fair summary of Protestant and Catholic

[1]P. Bayma, "The Liberalistic View of the Public School
Question," The American Catholic Quarterly Review, vol. 11,
(January, 1877), no. 5, p. 5.

[2]P. Bayma, "The liberalistic View," The American Catholic Quarterly Review, vol. 11, p. 7.

views. The author sees the issues in this way:

> Therefore what lies at the bottom be-
> tween Catholics and Protestants in their dif-
> ference concerning the public-school question
> is not, as some fancy, a thing of secondary
> importance, but one of the highest and most
> weighty; and to insist that either party can
> or should accommodate itself to the other,
> or both should compromise, is an evidence of
> indifference in religious matters or of un-
> reasonableness.
> The education question, properly under-
> stood, is a religious question. It is a ques-
> tion of enlightened religious convictions
> --convictions the most sacred of the rational
> soul; and neither party, Catholic or Protes-
> tant, if intelligent and conscientious, can
> accept the views or convictions of the other.
> To expect that these can be accommodated or
> adjusted, or compromised on a common basis,
> is to ignore what is at stake. And all at-
> tempts to impose upon a minority of a commun-
> ity the religious convictions of a majority
> by the force of the ballot-box, or by legisla-
> tion or any other force than that of persua-
> sion, is a gross violation of the fundamental
> ideas of our free institutions, contrary to
> all reason, and a tyrannical act of religious
> bigotry.[1]

In order to understand best the workings of the third

council in the area of education it is necessary to study some

of the ideas which motivated the men who participated therein.

Foremost among the educational leaders at this time was the

young John Lancaster Spalding. His enthusiasm for education

was well known and his location in the middle-western diocese

of Peoria gave him many opportunities to speak on educational

---

[1] "What Does the Public-School Question Mean?," The
Catholic World (October, 1881), pp. 88-89.

matters. Although definitely liberal in view and outlook
his basic concern was to keep the government out of education
and far away from control. It was his view that as soon as
the State took over, man lost some of his individual freedom:

> ...We believe that the man is more than the
> citizen; that when the state tramples upon
> the divine liberty of the wretched beggar,
> the consciences of all are violated; that it
> is its duty to govern as little as possible . . . .
> For this reason we believe that when the
> state assumed the right to control education,
> it took the first step away from the true
> American and Christian theory of government
> back towards the old pagan doctrine of state-
> absoluteism.[1]

The major portion of Spalding's episcopal work was done after
the council, but his views especially in regard to the need
of a Catholic university carried great weight in the deliberations.

As an example of the actual school activity of this
period, we may again take the archdiocese of Boston. Slow
at first in undertaking schools, the archdiocese began to
build more rapidly after the Instruction of 1875 put the obligation more strongly. The number of parishes having schools
of one kind or another reached sixteen in 1879, but other
areas in the country had many more.[2] Archbishop Williams

---

[1]"The Catholic Church in the United States, 1776-1876,"
Catholic World, XXIII (July, 1876), p. 452. Cf. also John
Tracy Ellis, John Lancaster Spalding: First Bishop of Peoria:
American Educator (Milwaukee: Bruce, 1961), p. 52.

[2]Lord, Sexton, & Harrington, History of Archdiocese
of Boston, vol. 11, p. 79.

appears to have been somewhat less than a dynamic and forceful leader and it took a great deal of pressure to get schools
built and supported. Late in the seventies, moreover, Pro-
testant-Catholic conflicts continued to flare up in the city.[1]

Bernard McQuaid was the outstanding champion of parochial education in the eastern area. Stationed in Rochester
he wielded large influence through his personal friendship
with Archbishop Corrigan. McQuaid's sometimes brash boldness
kept him in the public eye and it must be admitted that he was
not one to shrink from the role thus thrust upon him. Faced
with the challenge of Dr. Edward McGlynn and his liberal
tendencies, McQuaid quickly suspended the unfortunate cleric
and refused to reinstate him until ordered to do so by Roman
authorities.[2] But it was in the movement for parochial
schools that he became best known. He feared the public schools
and wrote of parochial schools:

> Without these schools, in a few gener-
> ations, our magnificent cathedrals and churches
> would remain as samples of monumental folly
> - of the unwisdom of a capitalist who consumes
> his fortune year by year without putting it
> out at interest or allowing it to increase.
> The Church has lost more in the past from the
> want of Catholic schools than from any other

---

[1] Lord, Sexton, & Harrington, History of the Archdiocese of Boston, vol. 11, pp. 115-119.

[2] The story of Dr. McGlynn has been told fully in
two places: Frederick Zwierlein, The Life and Letters of
Bishop McQuaid (3 vols.; Rochester: Art Print Shop, 1925-
1927), and Stephen Bell, Rebel, Priest and Prophet A Biography of Dr. Edward McGlynn (New York: Devin-Adair, 1937).

> cause named by me this evening. The 2,500
> schools, with a half million of scholars,
> which now bless our country, tell Catholics
> and non-Catholics that the question of reli-
> gious education is settled, so far as we are
> concerned. The good work so well advanced
> will not halt until all over the land the
> children of the Church are sheltered under
> her protecting care. The establishment of
> these and their improvement in management
> and instruction is our surest guarantee of
> future growth and fixedness.[1]

McQuaid's struggles in education were on two fronts, both of
which he carried on simultaneously. He was tireless in his
efforts to establish more and more parochial schools and at
the same time he agitated for the recognition of the Catholic
right to tax money. The position he took is clearly displayed
in this address:

> Whilst we claim these rights for our-
> selves, we are equally strong in our convic-
> tions that the same rights belong to others.
> While we bring religion into our schools and
> mean always to have religion there, we say
> to our non-Catholic citizens, bring into your
> schools whatever religion you have -- bring in
> prayer and religious singing and Bible read-
> ing. These means of good you hold as sacred
> and precious; we would much prefer good Pro-
> testants of any kind to infidels and deniers
> of all revelation; we thank God for any and
> all truth, whenever we find it. If but the
> beginning of truth today, we pray God that this
> small beginning of truth may grow into the fulness
> of all truth.[2]

By these remarks he was urging a return to the early pattern
of American education. Other Catholic educators, however,

[1]Zwierlein, McQuaid, vol. 11, p. 305; quoting Memorial
Vol. III Plen. Council Balt., pp. 161-178.

[2]Zwierlein, McQuaid, vol. 11, p. 120.

ere still fighting the Bible battle and the Protestant na-
ure of public schools,[1] and McQuaid was definitely in the
inority in his plea for religion in the public schools. His
ajor effort at effecting a solution had been to lease public
chool buildings to the public school officials for a nominal
um; an arrangement which persisted even during the alterca-
ions which McQuaid waged with Ireland over the Faribault-
tillwater arrangement.[2]

A document of major importance for American education
as sent by the Congregation of Propaganda de Fide in 1875.
eemingly, this brief was sent at the request of several of
he American Bishops who were disappointed at the somewhat
ild legislation of the 1866 council. Because this document
uided the thinking of the Bishops in their subsequent concil-
ar legislation, it seems necessary to report it here in
canslation.

> The Sacred Congregation of Propaganda
> had been many times assured that for the
> Catholic children of the United States of
> America evils of the gravest kind are likely
> to result from the so-called public schools.
> The sad intelligence moved the Propa-
> ganda to propose to the illustrious prelates
> of that country a series of questions, with
> the object of ascertaining, first, why the
> faithful permit their children to attend non-
> Catholic schools, and secondly, what may be

[1]Zweirlein, McQuaid, vol. 11, pp. 119-153.

[2]Daniel F. Reilly, The School Controversy, pp. 74-77.

the best means of keeping the young away from schools of this description. The answers, as drawn up by the several prelates, were submitted, owing to the nature of the subject, to the Supreme Congregation of the Holy Office. The decision reached by their Eminences, Wednesday, June 30, 1875, they saw fit to embody in the following Instruction, which the Holy Father graciously confirmed on Wednesday, November 24, of the same year.

1. The first point to come under consideration was the system of education itself, quite peculiar to those schools. Now, that system seemed to the S. Congregation most dangerous and very much opposed to Catholicity. For the children in those schools, the very principles of which exclude all religious instruction, can neither learn the rudiments of the faith nor be taught the precepts of the Church; hence, they will lack that knowledge, of all else, necessary to man without which there is no leading a Christian life. For children are sent to these schools from their earliest years, almost from their cradle; at which age, it is admitted, the seeds sown of virtue or of vice take fast root. To allow this tender age to pass without religion is surely a great evil.

2. Again, these schools being under no control of the Church, the teachers are selected from every sect indiscriminately; and this, while no proper precaution is taken to prevent their injuring the children, so that there is nothing to stop them from infusing into the young minds the seeds of error and vice. Then evil results are certainly to be dreaded from the fact that in these schools, or at least in very many of them, children of both sexes must be in the same class and class-room and must sit side by side at the same desk. Every circumstance mentioned goes to show that the children are fearfully exposed to the danger of losing their faith and that their morals are not properly safeguarded.

3. Unless this danger of perversion can be rendered remote, instead of proximate, such schools cannot in conscience be used. This is the dictate of natural as well as of divine law. It was enunciated in unmistakeable terms by the Sovereign Pontiff, in a letter

addressed to a former Archbishop of Freiberg,
July 14, 1864. He thus wrote: "There can be
no hesitation; wherever the purpose is afoot
or carried out of shutting out the church from
all authority over the schools, there the children will be sadly exposed to loss of their
faith. Consequently the Church should, in
such circumstances, not only put forth every
effort and spare no pains to get for the children the necessary Christian training and
education, but would be further compelled to
remind the faithful and publicly declare that
schools hostile to Catholicity cannot in conscience be attended." These words only express
a general principle of natural and divine law
and are consequently of universal application
wherever that most dangerous system of training youth has been unhappily introduced.

4. It only remains, then, for the prelates
to use every means in their power to keep the
flocks committed to their care from all contact with the public schools. All are agreed
that there is nothing so needful to this end
as the establishment of Catholic schools in
every place,--and schools no whit inferior to
the public ones. Every effort, then, must be
directed towards starting Catholic schools
where they are not, and, where they are, towards enlarging them and providing them with
better accommodations and equipment until they
have nothing to suffer, as regards teachers or
equipment, by comparison with the public schools.
And to carry out so holy and necessary a work,
the aid of religious brotherhoods and of sister-
hoods will be found advantageous where the
bishop sees fit to introduce them. In order
that the faithful may the more freely contribute the necessary expenses, the bishops themselves should not fail to impress on them, at
every suitable occasion, whether by pastoral
letter, sermon or private conversation, that
as bishops they would be recreant to their duty
if they failed to do their very utmost to provide Catholic schools. This point should be
especially brought to the attention of the
more wealthy and influential Catholics and
members of the legislature.

5. In that country there is no law to
prevent Catholics having their own schools and
instructing and educating their youth in every

branch of knowledge. It is therefore in the
powers of Catholics themselves to avert, with
God's help, the dangers with which Catholicity
is threatened from the public school system.
Not to have religion and piety banished from
the school-room is a matter of the very highest interest, not only to certain individuals
and families but to the entire country,--a
country now so prosperous and of which the
Church has had reason to conceive such high
hopes.

6. However, the Sacred Congregation is
not unaware that circumstances may be sometimes
such as to permit parents to conscientiously
send their children to the public schools.
Of course they cannot do so without having
sufficient cause. Whether there be sufficient
cause in any particular case is to be left to
the conscience and judgment of the bishop.
Generally speaking, such cause will exist when
there is no Catholic school in the place, or
the one there cannot be considered suitable to
the condition and circumstances in the life
of the pupils. But even in these cases, before
the children can conscientiously attend the
public school, the danger, greater or less,
of perversion which is inseparable from the
system, must be rendered remote by proper safeguards and precautions. The first thing to
see to, then, is whether the danger of perversion, as regards the school in question, is
such as cannot be possibly rendered remote, as,
for instance, whether the teaching there is
such, or the doings of a nature so repugnant
to Catholic belief and morals, that ear cannot
be given to the one, nor part taken in the
other without grevious sin. It is self-evident
that danger of this character must be shunned
at whatever cost, even life itself.

7. Further, before a child can be conscientiously placed at a public school provision
must be made for giving it the necessary Christian training and instruction, at least out of
school hours. Hence parish priests and missionaries in the United States should take seriously
to heart the earnest admonitions of the Councils
of Baltimore, and spare no labor to give children thorough catechetical instructions, dwelling particularly on those truths of faith and
morals which are called most in question by
Protestants and unbelievers. Children are beset

with so many dangers that they should be urged
with tireless vigilance, and induced to frequent the sacraments, and pastors should excite
in them devotion to the Blessed Virgin and on
all occasions animate them to hold firmly to
their religion. The parents or guardians must
look carefully after those children. They
must examine them in their lessons, or if not
able themselves, get others to do it. They
must keep them from freedom and familiarity
with those of the other school children whose
company might be dangerous to their faith and
morals, and absolutely away from the corrupt.

8. Parents who neglect to give this necessary Christian training and instruction to
their children, or who permit them to go to
schools in which the ruin of their souls is in-
evitable, or finally, who send them to the
public school without sufficient cause and without taking the necessary precautions to render
the danger of perversion remote, and do so while
there is a good and well-equipped Catholic
school in the place, or the parents have the
means to send them elsewhere to be educated
--that such parents, if obstinate, cannot be
absolved, is evident from the moral teaching
of the Church.[1]

The general background of the country for the period

immediately preceding this council has been thoroughly stu-

died by Fr. McAvoy.[2] Our quick survey of the educational pat-

tern has purported to show that two general patterns within

the Church had begun to make themselves felt in regard to

---

[1]Instructio De Scholis Publicis Ad Episcopos Americae
Septentrionalis Foederatae. Acta et Decreta, pp. 279-282.

[2]Thomas T. McAvoy, "The American Catholic Minority
in the Later Nineteenth Century," Review of Politics, vol.
15 (July, 1953), pp. 275-302. Cf. also Thomas T. McAvoy,
The Great Crisis in American Catholic History, 1895-1900
(Chicago: H. Regnery, 1957), pp. 1-43.

the public schools. The one, championed by men like Ireland
and Spalding and aided by Gibbons, preached the value of education and encouraged it at every turn. Their relations
with public schools officials were generally cordial, Spalding and Harris being good friends; Ireland, too, had many
friends among public school officials and was as a result
invited to give the address to the 1891 N. E. A. assembly,
in which he uttered his oft-quoted:

> . . . The Republic of the United States has sol-
> emnly affirmed its resolve that within its
> borders no clouds of ignorance shall settle
> upon the minds of the children of its people.
> In furnishing the means to accomplish this
> result its generosity knows no limit. The
> Free School of America! Withered be the hand
> raised in sign of its destruction.[1]

These prelates were concerned that each man should receive his
basic right of suffrage and elimination of ignorance was a
highly desirable prerequisite to this right. The conservatives,
conversely, were doubtful of the values to be found in public
education and tended to focus on the evils of the system.[2]
Catholic growth during the two decades since the Civil War
had been enormous. By 1880, there were over 6,000,000 Catholics
in the United States.[3] By and large the Church was still

---

[1]John Ireland, The Church and Modern Society (St. Paul:
Pioneer Press, 1905), p. 202.

[2]Cross, Emergence of Liberal Catholicism, p. 131.

[3]Shaughnessy, Has the Immigrant Kept the Faith, p.
161.

drawing a large portion of its membership from the hyphenated
Americans, but a strong core of native Americans dominated
both the congregations and the hierarchy. There was little
effort by foreign parties to dominate the American scene and
the hierarchy became more and more free in their selection
of their own numbers. In spite of efforts, however, to Amer-
icanize the Church over the decades by prelates of the stature
of England, Purcell and the two Kenricks, Catholic traditions
continued to appear un-American to their fellow Americans;
the Nast cartoons struck the public fancy and had wide
circulation. Especially among many fundamentalist groups
the feeling against the Church of Rome ran high and there
were many who still felt that America had, at all costs, to
be protected from invasion by a temporal pope. Coupled as
the Church was with the immigrant groups of all the periods
of history, it is not surprising that even at this late period the Church was looked at with fear and misgivings.[1]

At the time of the third council, Blatimore was still
considered the center of Catholicism, having been awarded a
"primacy of honor" among the American dioceses, although New
York was the first archdiocese to be honored by the cardinal-
ate.[2] The Roman authorities of Propaganda, however, had turned

---

[1]Higham, Strangers in the Land, pp. 6-7.

[2]John Farley, The Life of John Cardinal McCloskey,
First Prince of the Church in America, 1810-1885 (New York:
Longmans, Green and Co., 1918).

to Gibbons for initiation of this council and the American prelates looked to him for the leadership they needed. McAvoy intimates that the character of the Church in this period is roughly geographically divided into a conservative eastern group, and a more liberal western group. In between were the progressive midwesterners who, shepherding immigrant groups, at one and the same time were conservators of the European traditions.of their subjects and strong pushers of legislation for schools and welfare agencies, both of which were designed to aid the immigrant groups. The general pattern is borne out by a study of the personalities of the Bishops in these areas. John Williams has already been noted for his leadership in Boston, as a "timid leader, noted rather for his performance of parochial functions than for public leadership."[1] New England Catholics were poor, uncultured and subjected to the most violent antagonism. Thanks to its quality of leadership by men of the stature of Cheverus and Williams, the tide of antagonism had been stemmed, but the Church was behind in its progress. Especially important in this area was the non-involvement of the ecclesiastical leaders in the political affairs of the localities.[2]

Cardinal McCloskey in New York was also a conservative, satisfied to leave controversies untried, but his suf-

[1]McAvoy, Review of Politics, vol. 15 (July, 1953), p. 281.

[2]McAvoy, The Great Crisis in American Catholic History, pp. 17-19.

fragan Bishop McQuaid and his coadjutor Corrigan, abetted
by the former, were constantly in the fray and they frequently involved themselves in the forum of political matters.
McQuaid was the most forceful of the eastern segment of the
hierarchy and there were not many of his foes who escaped
his snapping tongue or vitriolic pen. His conservatism
seems, however, to have been exaggerated. His role in the
Ireland controversy of later years as a defender of the parochial system has served to effectively screen the fact that
in his own territory he was using arrangements of the Pough-
keepsie type. McQuaid was devoted to Catholic education and
his diocese of Rochester was a model in many respects to the
other prelates. Continuing the conservative tradition, Arch.
Patrick Ryan of Philadelphia was vacillating and cautious.[1]
Philadelphia, though, was the cultural center of the Church
at this time, being the publishing home of the Catholic Quarterly Review. Gibbons in Baltimore was himself new in his
see but subsequent activities label him not a conservative
but more of an opportunist, ready to carry on tasks but not
eager to initiate them.

It was in the middle west that the Church was making
its most rapid strides and here too were its most controversial hierarchy. The giant of the territory was the enormously

---

[1]McAvoy, Review of Politics, XV, p. 282.

successful Ireland of St. Paul.[1] Having come to America as
an Irish immigrant himself, he was for a lifetime interested
in the immigrant and his plight. Thoroughly American in
thought and action and with frontier disregard for diplomacy,
Ireland spoke out against injustice, urban servitude, and
whatever else struck his fancy. Gifted with a magnificent
voice and physique, his intellectual vision suffered on occasion and embroiled him in many debates. His people loved
their champion though and supported his every action. Another
leader whose reputation has suffered a slight tarnish is
John Purcell of Cincinnati. Like Ireland, he was sincerely
concerned with the financial difficulties of the rural folk
and he sought to aid them by handling their banking transactions. Caught up in the financial disasters of the age,
his bank failed and he was left with an enormous debt. This
has tended to obscure the many other fine works accomplished
by this leader. Further west in Illinois was the intellectual leader, John Lancaster Spalding.[2] In the south and the
southwest the Church has suffered heavily from the post-bellum
depression and occupation but California represented a solid
center of Catholicism of a strong Spanish tradition. The
enthusiasm for a council seems to have come mostly from the
western and midwestern bishops seemingly because it was in

[1]James H. Moynihan, The Life of Archbishop John Ireland (New York: Harper & Bros., 1953).

[2]Ellis, Spalding.

their dioceses that the most rapid changes had taken place.
No one has definitely placed the beginnings of a request for
the Third Plenary Council. The first letter on record in
the archives of Baltimore was written in 1881 by Michael
Heiss of Milwaukee. He had consulted with Grace of St. Paul,
both of whom desired a council.[1] Gibbons was reluctant to
endorse a new council especially since it was apparent that
he would have to furnish the leadership.[2] Ellis ventures the
opinion that the unsettled conditions of the western dioceses
could alone hardly account for the eagerness of the western
contingency for a council. Immigrants and the problems they
created were more pressing here than in the eastern dioceses.
Ellis, therefore, sees in the demand for a council an expression of the venturesome spirit of the west and eagerness
for new solutions to their problems in contrast to the conservative influences of the east.[3]

Definitive action in regard to the council was finally taken by Cardinal Simeoni in May of 1883. Convinced
of the necessity for a council, he called the American hier-

---

[1]BCA 76 C 7 Heiss to Gibbons, August 26, 1881.

[2]John T. Ellis, The Life of James Cardinal Gibbons,
Archbishop of Baltimore, 1834-1921, 2 vols. (Milwaukee:
Bruce, 1952), vol. II, pp. 204-205.

[3]Ellis, Gibbons, p. 206.

archy to a preliminary meeting in Rome. Perhaps the best
source of information concerning the purpose and reasoning
behind this Roman meeting is two letters which Bishop John
J. Keane wrote to his friend, Gibbons, from Rome during
the summer prior to the meeting.[1] Keane hastened to reassure Gibbons that the Roman officials were not suggesting a council in the spirit of criticism, but were doing
so in order to foster better order among the American Church
and to reinforce the channels of communication between the
Bishops and Rome. The hierarchy summoned to this preliminary
Roman meeting opened their sessions on November 13, 1883
under the leadership of the Propaganda officials, Giovanni
Cardinal Franzelin, Ludovico Cardinal Jacobini, Arch. Domen-
ico Jacobini, and the prefect Giovanni Cardinal Simeoni. At
the first meeting held on that day, the Propaganda agents
presented a list of topics for the discussion of the American Bishops.[2] Almost immediately the temper of the American
Bishops became apparent and they protested the already framed
agenda. Eager to please, the officers of the Propaganda al-

[1]77-H-8 Keane to Gibbons, Rome, June 25, 1883.
77-I-1 Keane to Gibbons, Florence, July 4, 1883. Cf. also
Ellis, Life of Gibbons, pp. 208-209.

[2]Capita Praecipua quae Emi Cardinales S.C. de Propaganda Fide censuerunt a Rmis Archiepiscopis et Episcopis
Foederatorum Statuum A. S. Romae congregatis praeparanda esse
pro futuro Concilio.

owed the Americans to prepare a substitute document.[1] This

atter document was quite similar to the one presented by

ropaganda but the Bishops had the satisfaction of knowing

hat they were to be heard and their opinions respected. The

ertinent sections dealing with education in these two docu-

ents are relatively short. In order to understand the blos-

oming of the legislation as it was actually formulated in the

nsuing council we shall repeat here the proposals of these

oman meetings. Chapter X of the <u>Capita Praecipua</u> was entit-

ed: <u>De Scholis Parochialibus</u> and gave only general directives:

> Commendanda vehementer institutio et incre-
> mentum scholarum parochialium. Ceterum ser-
> vanda etiam est ea pars Instructionum SS.
> Congregationum, in qua declaratur sub quibus
> conditionibus pueri aliquando sine peccato
> ad scholas gubernii mitti possint. Vetandum
> igitur ne sacramentis priventur fideles qui
> ad scholas gubernii mittunt filios suos nisi
> adsit proximum periculum perversionis iuxta
> Instructiones iam datas. Haec privatio sacra-[2]

---

[1]Capita Proposita et examinata in collationibus, quas
oram nonnullis Emis Cardinalibus Sacrae Congregationis de
ropaganda Fide ad praeparandum futurum Concilium plenarium
abuerunt Rmi. Archiepiscopi et Episcopi Foederatorum Statuum
mericae Septemtrionalis (sic) Romae congregati.

[2]Capita Praecipua, p. 7. Translation: The establish-
ent and increase of parochial schools is to be vigorously
ommended. Especially to be maintained is that portion of the
nstruction of the Sacred Congregation in which are specified the
onditions under which children can sometimes be sent without sin
o the public schools. It is forbidden to refuse the sacraments
o the faithful who send their children to the public schools,
nless there is present the proximate danger of perversion,
ccording to the Instructions already given.

mentorum maxime quoad pueros ipsos vitanda
est. Porro servetur Instructio S. Congregationis circa scholas et convictus mixtos anni
1868, nec non Instructio S. Congregationis S.
O. anni 1875 circa scholas publicas gubernii.[1]

The parallel section in the companion Schema contains

nearly the same ideas and in almost exactly the same phraseol-

ogy. It read:

Urgenda et commendanda institutio et incrementum scholarum parochialium, ita ut Episcopi
contra Rectores Missionum hac in re culpabil-
itur negligentes pro rei gravitate poenis
etiam procedant. Ceterum servanda etiam est
ea pars Instructionum SS. Congregationum, in
qua declaratur, sub quibus conditionibus pueri
aliquando sine peccato ad scholas gubernii
mitti possint. Cavendum igitur, ne sacramentis
priventur fideles, qui ad scholas gubernii
mittant filios suos, nisi adsit proximum periculum perversionis iuxta Instructiones iam
datas. Haec privatio sacramentorum magis adhuc quoad pueros ipsos vitanda est. Porro
servetur Instructio S. Congregationis circa
scholas et convictus mixtos anni 1868, nec non
Instructio S. Congregationis S.O. anni 1875
circa scholas publicas gubernii.[2]

---

[1]Translation continued: This deprivation of the sacraments is especially to be avoided as regards the children
themselves. Moreover, the Instruction of the Holy Congregation
of the year 1868 concerning schools and mixed classes is to
be kept, and also the Instruction of the Sacred Congregation
of the year 1875 concerning public schools.

[2]Capita Proposita, p. 11. Translation: The establishment and increase of parochial schools is to be urged and commanded, to the point that Bishops may move against pastors grave-
ly negligent in this matter with penalties equal to the seriousness of the matter. Moreover that part of the Instruction of
the Sacred Congregation is to be preserved, in which it is declared, under what conditions children may legitimately attend
public schools. The faithful who send their children to public
schools are not to be deprived of the sacraments unless there is
danger of perversion according to the instructions already given.
This deprivation of the sacraments is to be especially avoided
concerning the youngsters themselves, Moreover, the Instruction
of the Holy Congregation of the year 1868 concerning schools and
mixed classes is to be kept, and also the Instruction of the
Sacred Congregation of the year 1875 concerning public schools.

these two passages the objectives of the American Bishops
re clear; they were going to preserve their schools at any
ost, even if it meant stringent regulations upon their own
astors. Likewise, it is interesting to note the consistency
ith which the Propaganda officials continued to emphasize
he undesirableness of refusing the sacraments to the faithful
ho sent their children to the public schools. In the light
f this passage, it is difficult to understand the arguments
hich arose in the general sessions of the Third Plenary Coun-
il. Relative to this point, the first reference to parochial
schools in the briefly recorded discussions of the Bishops
ame on November 29, when the tenth chapter was introduced.
n general, the legislation as proposed in the *Capita Praecipua*
nd the *Capita Proposita* was accepted by them as written. The
rchbishop of Oregon, Charles J. Seghers, asked a revealing
uestion, however, when he queried as to the expediency of
aving the clergy seek positions on the public school boards.
he opinion of the Cardinals was that if good could be expected
o come from their presence, the Bishop should be left free to
ecide whether or not to allow their presence on the board.
he Archbishop of Oregon asked further whether or not the coun-
il should enact a decree which would require, under a given
enalty, that missioners should build parochial schools within
 brief interval of time to be specified by the Holy See, as
he *Capita Proposita* had insisted. The Cardinals did not

favor such a decree because of the many difficulties in which
missionaries find themselves but conceded that Bishops
should insist on the building of schools with appropriate cen-
sures upon priests who proved themselves culpably negligent.
A final point of interest because of subsequent discussions
was initiated by Archbishop Heiss of Milwaukee who inquired
whether a Bishop could prohibit attendance at the public schools
in order to prevent harm from coming to parochial schools.
The Cardinals responded that if it were for this reason alone
then the Bishops could not attach a penalty to their prohibition.[1] The meetings closed in Rome on December 10, and the
members of the hierarchy returned to their dioceses. After
some panicky moments during which it was feared that a foreign
representative would be appointed to handle the council,
Gibbons was appointed Apostolic Delegate by Pope Leo XIII,
on January 4, 1884. Almost immediately he assigned a chapter
of the Capita Proposita to each of the Archbishops for discussion and report. The results of their deliberations were
then compiled and distributed in printed form. The tenth
chapter which concerned the parochial schools was assigned
to Archbishop Patrick Feehan of Chicago and the report is
brief enough to reproduce here in its entirety:

---

[1]Relatio collationum quas Romae coram S. C. de P. F.
Praefecto habuerunt Archiepiscopi pluresque Episcopi Statuum
Foederatorum Americae, 1883 (Baltimorae: 1884). There is also
a handwritten copy of these minutues in the Baltimore archives:
77 1 20. An English translation of these decrees was
published in The Jurist. The passage on schools appeared in
July, 1951 (vol. XI, no. 3, pp. 417-424).

The Bishops of this Province most earnestly urge the erection of Parish Schools, wherever possible, and the necessity of elevating them to a standard, equal at least to that of the Public School.

They suggest to the Bishops the importance of some uniformity of text books, in each diocese and especially the need of a Catechism, to be used everywhere.

The Bishops fully accept all that is said in Cap. X de scholis parochialibus, and also the Instruction of the S. Congregation of 1868, and those of the S. Congregation S. O. of 1875.

The question was discussed of establishing a school of higher education for priests, who have gone through the elementary studies of the Seminaries. The project was favorably received.[1]

The province of Milwaukee, under the leadership of Heiss, also contributed a few comments to this section, all of which dealt with the method and manner of support of parochial schools.[2]

In addition to the provincial meetings, Archbishop Gibbons selected theologians from every diocese in the country, whose task it was to prepare an advance copy of the legislation desired. These men worked diligently and by the time the council convened, each of the participants received detailed papers which listed the suggested legislation. During the months preceding the council, there was a flurry

---

[1]Relationes eorum quae disceptata fuerunt ab Illmis ac Revmis Metropolitis cum suis suffraganeis in suis provinciis super schema futuri Concilii praesertim vero super capita cuique commissa (Baltimore: 1884), p. 37.

[2]Relationes eorum, p. 37.

of correspondence and many of these letters are still on file.
Heiss of Milwaukee, remembering perhaps the items discussed
in the preliminary meetings, wrote:

> . . . In regard to the parish schools, everybody
> knows we ought to have them, to increase their
> number & to improve them. But the question,
> in which way, by which means this can be ef-
> fected.[1]

Corrigan from New York also remarked about the difficulty of
obtaining the necessary funds:

> . . . P.S. As the Holy See insists so much on
> our paying off the debt on Church property,
> would it be possible to come to an understand-
> ing in the Council, that, excepting always
> collections recommended especially by the Holy
> See, or for Peter Pence etc., no collections
> be allowed for extraneous purposes, until our
> own children are provided with schools and
> our indebtedness reduced to small dimensions?[2]

There is every indication, moreover, that communication channels
with the Holy See were kept quite open during the preparatory
period. A directive from the Propaganda came early in October, directing the American prelates to be certain to turn
their attention to school problems during the coming council:

> Et primo quidem de scholis. Procul dubio
> ecclesias aedificare optimum est consilium
> et quandoque necessarium ut fideles verbum
> Dei audire, sacro adesse, atque aliis reli-

---

[1]BCA 78 K 13 Heiss to Gibbons, August 17, 1884.

[2]BCA 78 Q 1 Corrigan to Gibbons, October 2, 1884.
From Tuscon, Salpointe writes that because the Rio Grande
was rampaging they were not able to gather together for comments on the Schema. BCA 78 G 1, June 10, 1884.

giosis officiis satisfacere valeant; sed
aeque necessarium est scholas aedificare ut
pueri in morum puritate et religionis sancti-
tate instituantur. Nonnulli tamen sacerdotes, si verum est quod asseritur, videntur
unice solliciti de ecclesiis aedificandis,
parum autem vel nihil de scholis, ita ut
parochiae non desint quae templum quidem
splendidum habent, schola vero parochiali
omnino careant; cui gravi puerorum institu-
tionis damno evitando opportune provideri
deberet. Scholae parochialis carentia efficit,
ut pueri scholas publicas seu Gubernii
adeant, quod a parochis ne eveniat totis
viribus curandum foret.[1]

When, late in November, fourteen archbishops,
fifty-seven bishops, seven abbots, thirty-one provincials
and religious superiors, and eighty-eight theologians
gathered in Baltimore, the council was opened in earnest.
The deliberations began almost at once and the business
of the council was underway. Once again the length of
the decrees on education prohibits their entire inclusion
at this point, but they are reproduced in their entirety

[1] Instructio S. C. De P. F., Romae, 3 Octobris,
1884. Translation: In the first place, concerning the
schools. Without doubt the best advice is to build churches
and that whenever necessary so that the faithful may be
able to hear the word of God, to participate in the sacred
action, and to satisfy their other religious obligations;
but it is equally necessary to build schools so that the
youngsters may be trained in the purity of habits and the
holiness of religion. Many priests, if what is said is
true, seem concerned only about building churches, with
little or no concern given to schools, so that parishes
are not lacking where there is a splendid church but no
parochial school; this latter ought to be provided in order
to prevent grave damage to the youngsters. The lack of
a parochial school forces the children to attend a public
school or State school, a situation which the pastors
should try to avoid with all their strength.

in Appendix II. The general outline of the educational
proposals follows closely that of the Second Plenary
Council. The sixth major division of the council proceedings was entitled: De Catholica Juventutis Institutione; this major section was subdivided into two chapters, one dealing with the topic of Catholic schools,
especially the parochial schools; the other, a somewhat
detailed discussion of higher education. The chapter
on parochial schools was further divided into two sections;
one dealing with the necessity of these schools, the other
with the means necessary for the promotion and support
of these schools. A quick survey of the more pertinent
decrees will serve as an introduction to the discussions
which arose in council. The first decree is a reassertion
of the necessity of Christian education in the modern
world:

> If ever in any age, then surely in this our age,
> the Church of God and the spirit of the world are in
> a certain wondrous and bitter conflict over the
> education of youth. Men, completely imbued with the
> spirit of the world, have for many years left no
> stone unturned in order to snatch away that which
> the Church received from Christ (Matt. 28, 19;
> Mark 10, 14); that is, the duty of teaching Catholic
> youth, and to turn this duty over into the hands
> of civil society or to subject it to the power of
> secular rule. Nor is this any wonder. For those
> most ruinous movements of indifferentism, naturalism
> and materialism have so invaded the minds of many
> that they foolishly imagine that the goal and happi-
> ness of man cannot be sought or found except in this
> passing life and material world; . . . .[1]

---

[1]Decree no. 194.

The argument against secular and godless education is
continued in the next decree and the final paragraph of
this number is a strong indictment of a merely secular
education:

> . . . it can hardly fail to happen that the
> young, steeped in the secular spirit from
> childhood, generally become by degrees and
> without their being aware of it not only lovers
> of the blind world, but by that very fact also
> haters of Christ and opponents of the Church.
> We are taught by the clearest testimony of as it
> were household enemies that the number of those
> who have defected from the Church chiefly for this
> reason, among others, that they have been instruc-
> ted in a merely secular education, is so great
> that only too abundant an opportunity and basis
> for rejoicing is given to the enemy, but for us
> only occasion for sorrow.[1]

The next appeal is to parents who are admonished to
provide for their children that truly Christian education which will protect them during the entire time
of their youth from the dangers of a purely secular
education. The previous enactments of the earlier
councils are then reviewed and approved. In addition
to the Instruction of 1875, the Bishops also appeal to
the Encyclical Letter of Leo XIII to the Bishops of
France. The quotation which they select from this
letter indicates their own acceptance and approval of
this letter:

> "It is important that the offspring of a
> Christian marriage as much as possible be

---

[1]Decree no. 195.

exposed early to the precepts of religion
and that those arts by which little children
are accustomed to be fashioned to the humanities be connected with religious instruction.
To separate the one from the other is the
same as to wish that the young minds be
moved in their duties toward God in neither
direction;[1]

One of the topics which always raised tempers
in the discussions relative to schools was the question
of refusing absolution to those parents who refused to
send their children to established parochial schools.
The issue had been settled by the Cardinals in the
Roman discussions and their views found expression in the
next canon to be enacted:

Nevertheless although from what has been said
the necessity and obligation of instructing
Catholic youth in Catholic schools is clearer
than light, it can sometimes happen -- just
as the instruction just praised intimated --
"that Catholic parents can in conscience commit
their children to public schools. They will
not be able to do this, however, unless they
have sufficient reason for so acting, and
whether such a sufficient reason in any
particular instance is present or not, will
have to be left to the conscience and judgment of the Ordinary; and then that will for
the most part be present when that which is
at hand is too little suited for properly or
suitably instructing the youths in accord with
their development . . . ."
Since therefore for a sufficient reason
approved by the Bishop, parents may wish to
send their children to public schools, provided
that the immediate dangers are removed by the
necessary precautions, we strictly enjoin
that no one whether Bishop or priest, because
the Pope through the Sacred Congregation clearly

[1]Decree no. 197, quoting the Encyclical Letter of
Leo XIII to the Bishops of France, Feb. 8, 1884.

forbids it, dare keep from the Sacraments
by rigorous threats or action parents of
this kind as though unworthy. This is much
more so in the case of the children themselves.
Wherefore let pastors of souls be exceedingly
careful when they warn the faithful committed to
their care of the dangers of these schools,
lest influenced by excessive zeal, they seem
by words or deeds to violate the very wise
counsels and commands of the Holy See.[1]

In the very next decree the Bishops put forth their plan

for Catholic education in their dioceses:

     1. Near each church, where it does not
exist, a parochial school is to be erected within
two years from the promulgation of this Council,
and it is to be maintained in perpetuum, unless
the Bishop, on account of grave difficulties,
judges that a postponement may be allowed.
     II. A priest who, by his grave negligence,
prevents the erection of a school within this time,
or its maintenance, or who, after repeated admonitions of the Bishop, does not attend to the matter,
deserves removal from that church.
     III. A mission or a parish which so neglects
to assist a priest in erecting or maintaining a
school, that by reason of this supine negligence
the school is rendered impossible, should be reprehended by the Bishop and, by the most effi-
cacious and prudent means possible, be induced to
contribute the necessary support.
     IV. All Catholic parents are bound to send
their children to the parochial schools, unless
either at home or in other Catholic schools they
may be sufficiently and evidently certain of the
Christian education of their children, or unless it
be lawful to send them to other schools on account
of a sufficient cause, approved by the Bishop, and
with opportune cautions and remedies.As to what is
a Catholic school, it is left to the judgment of
the Ordinary to define.[2]

[1]Decree no. 198.

[2]Decree no. 199.

These decrees represent the core of the legislation as it emerged from the council chambers. The
remaining decrees spelled out the manner in which these
decrees were to be effected. A great deal of attention
was given to the question of adequate personnel and a
system of teacher licensing was proposed. The final
section, as already stated, centered on higher education
and its relationship to the parochial school. The importance which the prelates attached to education is
apparent from the fact that nearly a quarter of the
total legislation passed at this council concerned schools
and educational matters. The disputations on the specific
topics have been printed in the private edition of the
Acta which was circulated before Roman approval of the
decrees was received. Hence, there are slight variations
in the texts. Discussion on the subject of parochial
schools centered on two specifics: dare the Bishops command and enforce by penalties the building and frequenting
of Catholic schools, even to the point of forbidding the
reception of the sacraments to those who refused to cooperate; and, secondly, what precisely was a Catholic school?[1]

---

[1]Acta et Decreta Concilii Plenarii Baltimorensis
Tertii in Ecclesia Metropolitana Baltimorensi Habiti A Die
IX, Novembris usque ad diem VII, Decembris A.D. MDCCCLXXXIV.
(Baltimore: John Murphy, 1884), pp. lx-lxix.

The discussion of Title VI began quietly with number 194
(219)[1] being passed without comment or change. In number
195 (220) only the latter part of the quotation from Matt.
was deleted. No. 196 (221) was an exhortation to Catholic
parents to procure for their children a Catholic education
in order to protect them from the danger of a merely secular
one, and this education was to be procured in Catholic, especially parochial, schools. Arch. Charles Seghers of Oregon suggested that only those schools be considered Catholic
which were supported by free collections and voluntary dona-
tions. James Healy, Bishop of the tiny diocese of Portland
in Maine, demurred and pointed out that many schools are accustomed to charge a small amount for attendance. Arch. Patrick
Ryan of Philadelphia noted the threefold division customary
in Catholic schools: parish, academy and private. If the
Catholic religion is taught in any of them, then they deserve
the title of Catholic. Seghers finally amended his proposal
to describe schools as parochial as long as they "quae sumptibus Ecclesiae sustentantur." Even with this emendation
the private minutes suggest that his proposal was not accepted at this time.[2]

---

[1]Because a number of decrees which were contained in
the Schema Decretorum were dropped from the final version, we
are including both numbers. The first number refers to the decree number in final redaction; the second number to the original Schema Decretorum.

[2]Acta et Decreta Concilii Plenarii Baltimorensis Tertii
in Ecclesia Metropolitana Acta Baltimorensi habiti a die IX.
Novembris usque ad diem VII. Decembris A.D. MXCCCLXXXIV (Baltimore: Murphy, 1884), p. lxi. In an handwritten version of
these minutes, BCA 78 T 20, there is also the remark: Proposi-
tio Oregonesis non placuit.

The prelates then plunged into a lengthy debate upon
the necessity of urging parents to send their children to
Catholic schools. The Schema spoke of commanding parents
to procure for their children a Christian education (non solum
paterno amore hortamur sed . . . praecipimus). Bishop Edward
Fitzgerald of Little Rock and Archbishop Alemany of San Francisco both felt that the council should content itself with
an exhortation rather than a command, a point of view which
would have been strongly in line with the final remarks of the
Cardinals at the Roman conference. Bishop Dwenger of Fort
Wayne strongly objected to toning down the strength of the
decree; he damned at length the public schools in which were
taught indifference and flabby morals.[1] Evidently his remarks
on the lack of morality in the public schools struck many as
exaggerated for Ryan of Philadelphia challenged Dwenger on
these remarks and came to a defense of the public schools in
his area. Fitzgerald then made a most telling remark, indicating his felling about the parochial schools: "We were
ordained to teach catechism not to teach school. If we know
that children are learning the catechism it is enough. No
just law can compel priests or parents to drive children into
[Catholic] grammar schools." There is some discrepancy of

[1]BCA 78 T 20.

meaning in his general remarks here. In the printed minutes
these remarks are so worded that he appears to be denying
the general question of obligation for anyone, priest or
parent, to send their children to any school, Catholic or
public, to learn merely secular subjects. The private written minutes suggest this meaning but the interpretation given
above, inserting the word Catholic seems also possible.[1]

The view of Fitzgerald was far too liberal to find
support among the conservatives of the East. And the midwestern bishops were so dedicated to the cause of immigrant
education in general that they too feared to endorse any of
the sentiment involved here. Arch. Feehan of Chicago, however,
also spoke against the idea of a precept, but he offered a
psychological reason for his lack of support: "A precept
when harshly pronounced," he countered, "begets a spirit of
resistence. Exhort them and see at the same time that they
have good schools & good masters and they will send their
children without fail."[2] However, he was immediately opposed
by his own neighboring Bishops, Dwenger of Ft. Wayne, Gilmour
of Cleveland, and Borgess of Detroit, all of whom spoke in
favor of the command. Borgess related that his schools were
occupied only after he had made it a reserved case.[3] Hennessey

---

[1] Private Acta et Decreta, p. lxi. BCA 78 T 20.

[2] BCA 78 T 20.

[3] BCA 78 T 20.

of Dubuque, Janssens of Natchez (where Elder had had so many difficulties), Watterson of Columbus, and Heiss of Milwaukee all supported the command, insisting that if the command were dropped, schools already existing would suffer, whereas no harm would be done to the already existing order by commanding attendance. Gilmour in his defense had appealed to the decision of the Propaganda (already quoted) in which he maintained that children before receiving holy communion must attend parochial schools for a year. Janssens, of Natchez, corrected this notion and demonstrated that the directive did not command at all. The Roman officials had only recommended that procedure and did not command it.[1]

The debate continued with nearly every Bishop being heard from. Ryan pointed out that commands should be laid down only for serious reasons and, more important, schools ought to exist before parents were commanded to send their children to them. Fitzgerald agreed and moved that the words of the decree "statuimus et decrevimus" be changed to "hortamur et urgimus," thereby considerably lessening the force of the decree. He maintained that new and formidable legislation was being introduced by this decree, legislation unknown to any country in the world. He gave statistics and wanted

---

[1]*Private Acta et Decreta*, p. lxi. Cf. also p. 213 of this dissertation.

to know the meaning of the term Catholic school. Then he
mentioned an awful case in Lancaster, Ohio, where a Catholic
taught school and in it catechism and was (herself and the
children) forbidden to approach the sacraments.[1] McQuaid
countered by saying that obviously no obligation existed where
no school was to be found. He took the opportunity to underscore his objections to the public schools, especially because
the friendships formed between Catholics and non-Catholics led
to mixed marriages. At the conclusion of his address, the
group adjourned. When the sessions were renewed, Bishop
Flasch of LaCrosse reopened the discussion with a defense of
the command to send children to Catholic schools. In an attempt to end the debates which had apparently become tiresome
for all, Healy offered the emendation that after warning parents against the evils of a merely secular education and after
commanding them to give their children a Catholic education,
the phrase "unless the Ordinary judges that otherwise it may
be done" should be appended, thereby giving the Bishop power
to lessen the obligation if he saw fit. This compromise suited
even Fitzgerald but he again impeded the progress of the meeting by returning to the question of the meaning of a truly
Catholic school. He again referred to certain schools which
he himself would consider Catholic, yet the Bishop apparently

---

[1] *Acta et Decreta*, p. lxii. BCA 78 T 20.

did not consider them such. Bishop Joseph Machebeuf, Vicar
Apostolic of Colorado, then related to the council members
some of the difficulties involved in maintaining schools in
his area. He noted that in his territory he had a school in
which for lack of a Catholic teacher, he was forced to use
the services of a non-Catholic teacher. This latter taught
not only the humanities but also prayers and the catechism
and all in all performed his duty in a most satisfactory manner.[1]

After other discussion William McCloskey of Louisville referred to the question previously raised by Seghers
in the Roman meeting about the penalties that might be exacted
of a pastor who was slow to build his schools. The Cardinals
had cautioned against setting a time limit in this matter;
Healy, in turn, argued that this was a point in favor of his
proposed amendment; apparently most of the council fathers
agreed, because they voted to accept Healy's suggested addition, forty-one to thirty-three.[2] The negative votes seem
to have been equally divided among those who thought the
legislation too severe and those who thought that it was not
strict enough.[3]

[1] Private Acta et Decreta, p. lxiii.
[2] Private Acta et Decreta, p. lxiii.
[3] BCA 78 T 20.

Several changes were then adopted in regard to number 199 (224), the paragraph which contained the core of the
council's legislation. Fitzgerald again argued for a less
stringent wording, recommending that the decrees should begin
with the words "we wish and urge" instead of "we decide and
decree." The Council Fathers rejected his more lenient reading.
Moreover, they recommended that the words from the 1875 Instruction be added to the fourth section, whereby it was indicated that parents who proved themselves contumacious were
to be denied sacramental absolution. The second section dealt
with the removal of a pastor who failed to erect a school within
the stated time; since Propaganda officials had already
cautioned against such severe legislation, it was felt that this
decree would not be approved, but the prelates decided to leave
the decree stand, since the length of time which would consti-
tute grave negligence was specified. The third section brought
out in an enlightening manner the radical differences of opinion
that actually existed in the council chamber. Healy moved
that in the decree dealing with the reprimand by the Bishop and
spiritual punishment, the notion of spiritual punishment should
be removed. No Bishop, he felt, would venture to put a
parish under interdict for such a slight and minimal cause.
He was brought up short, however, by Dwenger, who forcefully
insisted that not only would he do so but he had already done

so![1] The subsequent vote indicated better than anything
else the margin by which the severe regulations were carried.
Healy's motion was defeated by only eleven ayes.[2] A change
of six votes on this question would have altered greatly
the subsequent development of parochial schools, because
the threat of removal of the pastor and parish interdict
were indeed a mighty force to compliance.

At this point Arch. Peter Kenrick of St. Louis reopened the discussion of the nature of a Catholic school,
apparently feeling that the question had not been sufficiently
settled. Once again, it is disconcerting to note in the
discussion the wide variety of meaning which the concept had.
A strong group offered their opinion that any school was
Catholic which was held to be such in the judgment of the
Bishop. Elder and Ireland extended this view to mean that
a Catholic school was one which was subject to the authority
of the Bishop and subject also to ecclesiastical inspection
through the Bishop. After other discussion, Riordan apparently grew weary of the extended debate and, to settle the
issue, he urged that the question be referred to a special
committee. The Bishops refused, 26-35, to use this avenue
of escape. The thinking of another group is demonstrated
by the remark of Kenrick that the Fathers must be careful

[1]BCA 78 T 20. Private Acta et Decreta, p. lxiv.
[2]BCA 78 T 20.

not to violate the rights of private parties in this matter.
Unless it was apparent that the school was corrupt, no one
had the right to enter it [for purposes of inspection] and
civil law would not easily allow it. Quite obviously, Kenrick
and his supporters in this discussion were thinking in terms
of a state supported school which would at the same time be
subject to the inspection of the local pastor of Bishop.
Finally, tiring of the issue, the Bishops evaded the question
by declaring by an overwhelming majority that a Catholic
school was one which the Bishop judged to be such.[1]

The fourth section of this decree was now presented
for discussion. This last was probably the most important
portion of the entire decree for it stated that all Catholic
parents were bound to send their children to parochial schools
unless they provided for their Christian education either at
home or at other Catholic schools. Provision was made only
for extraordinary circumstances. A special committee of
Bishops (Heiss of Milwaukee, Gilmour of Cleveland, McNeirny
of Albany, and O'Farrell of Trenton) had already inserted
the additional phrase regarding the denial of the sacraments
to the contumacious. An original wording of debere in the
decree had also been changed into the more binding teneri.
Feehan began the discussion by suggesting that after the words
of the decree the phrase should be added: "After the judg-

[1]Private Acta et Decreta, p. lxv.

ment of the Bishop, who shall have the obligation of judging
the contumacy." Led by Gilmour the Fathers rejected this
suggestion by a vote of 30 to 41. Fitzgerald, of course,
objected to the entire section and this time he won support
from McCloskey of Louisville. Needless to say, they were not
supported by the majority of the council fathers. There was
considerably more discussion, but nothing of more significance in regard to these decrees.[1] The council closed on
December 7, and the decrees were submitted to Rome for approval. Three Bishops, John Moore of St. Augustine, Joseph
Dwenger of Fort Wayne, and Richard Gilmour of Cleveland,
were entrusted with the task of having the legislation passed
by Roman officials. It was only after a great deal of effort and correspondence that they finally managed to have
the legislation approved with only minor changes. Formal
approval was given by Leo XIII on September 10, 1885, and
the decrees went into effect. The official approval was sent
by Cardinal Simeoni on September 21, 1885.[2] In order to understand the effect of the Roman deliberations, we shall
here compare the 199th decree in the three versions, since
this is the most important of all the decrees. The Private

---

[1] For a more detailed discussion of this material cf.
Francis Cassidy, "Catholic Education in the Third Plenary
Council of Baltimore," Catholic Historical Review, XXXIV (October, 1948-January, 1949), pp. 257-327. For a more general
discussion of the council, cf. Ellis, Gibbons, passim.

[2] BCA 79 S 8 Simeoni to Gibbons, August 8, 1885.

<u>Acta et Decreta</u> had listed the first decree:

> Quibus omnibus bene perpensis statuimus et
> decernimus:
> 1. Prope unamquamque Ecclesiam ubi nondum
> existit, Scholam Parochialem intra duos annos
> a promulgatione hujus Concilii erigendam et
> in perpetuum sustentandam esse, nisi de ju-
> dicio Episcopi erectio vel sustentatio Scholae
> impossibilis sit.

In the Roman deliberations the following changes were intro-

duced:

> 1. Prope unamquamque . . . sustentandam esse,
> nisi Episcopus ob graviores difficultates
> dilationem concedendam esse judicet.

In this minor change, the Roman authorities were demanding a

bit more leeway for those pastors who were faced with diffi-

cult building programs. The second section dealt with the

removal of negligent pastors:

> Schema: 11. Sacerdotem, qui intra hoc tempus
> Scholam erigere eamve erectam in futuro bene
> dirigere graviter negligat, ab Ecclesia amoveri
> posse et debere.

Minor changes were introduced in this sentence during the

council deliberations and the Roman authorities amended it

to read:

> Sacerdotem qui intra hoc tempus erectionem
> vel sustentationem scholae gravi sua negli-
> gentia impediat, vel post repetitas Episcopi
> admonitiones non curet, mereri remotionem ab
> illa ecclesia.

Here, once again, we note that the Roman authorities softened

the harsh effect of the council's proposal. The third section

had read in the Schema:

> Missionem vel Paroeciam quae sacerdotem in
> erigendam vel sustentanda Schola adjuvare
> ita negligat, ut ob hanc supinam negligen-
> tiam Schola existere non possit ab Episcopo
> esse reprehendendam ac, si contumax fuerit,
> poenis spiritualibus afficiendam.

This decree was considerably altered in the process of the

Roman discussion and in final redaction read:

> Missionem vel paroeciam quae sacerdotem in
> erigenda vel sustentanda schola adjuvare
> ita negligat, ut ob hanc supinam negligen-
> tiam schola existere non possit, ab Episcopo
> esse reprehendendam ac quibus efficacioribus
> et prudentioribus modis potest, inducendam
> ab necessaria subsidia conferenda.

Finally the fourth portion of the Schema:

> Omnes parentes Catholicos prolem suam ad
> Scholas Parochiales mittere debere, nisi vel
> domi vel in aliis Scholis Catholicis Chris-
> tianae filiorum suorum educationi sufficienter
> et evidenter consultant, aut ob causam suffi-
> cientem, ab Episcopo approbatam, et cum oppor-
> tunis cautionibus remediisque eos ad alias
> Scholas mittere ipsis liceat.

During the council deliberations, the word _debere_ of the second
line had been strengthened to _teneri_. A final phrase had also
been added: Quaenam autem sit schola Catholica Ordinarii
judicio definiendum relinquitur. This decree was approved
by the Roman officials without change.[1]

The Pastoral Letter for this council was written by
that grand old patriarch who had witnessed so many of these
councils that he was literally a link with the fathers of
the early provincial councils, Peter Richard Kenrick. The

---

[1] All quotations taken from the _Acta et Decreta_.

section devoted to education reveals little that had not already been said to the people in previous letters:

     Scarcely, if at all, secondary to the
Church's desire for the education of the clergy,
is her solicitude for the education of the
laity. It is not for themselves, but for the
people, that the Church wishes her clergy to
be learned, as it is not for themselves only,
but for the people that they are priests.
Popular education has always been a chief
object of the Church's care; in fact, it is
not too much to say that the history of civilization and education is the history of the
Church's work. In the rude ages, when semi-
barbarous chieftains boasted of their illit-
eracy, she succeeded in diffusing that love of
learning which covered Europe with schools
and universities; and thus from the barbarous
tribes of the early middle ages, she built up
the civilized nations of modern times. Even
subsequent to the religious dissensions of the
sixteenth century, whatever progress has been
made in education is mainly due to the impetus
which she had previously given. In our own country notwithstanding the many difficulties at-
tendant on first beginnings and unexampled
growth, we already find her schools, academies
and colleges everywhere, built and sustained
by voluntary contributions, even at the cost
of great sacrifices, and comparing favorably
with the best educational institutions in the
land.

     These facts abundantly attest the Church's
desire for popular instruction. The beauty
of truth, the refining and elevating influences
of knowledge, are meant for all, and she
wishes them to be brought within the reach
of all. Knowledge enlarges our capacity both
for self-improvement and for promoting the
welfare of our fellow-men; and in so noble a
work the Church wishes every hand to be busy.
Knowledge, too, is the best weapon against
pernicious errors. It is only "a little learning" that is "a dangerous thing." In days
like ours, when error is so pretentious and
aggressive, everyone needs to be as completely
armed as possible with sound knowledge, -- not
only the clergy, but the people also that they

may be able to withstand the noxious influences
of popularized irreligion. In the great coming
combat between truth and error, between Faith
and Agnosticism, an important part of the fray
must be borne by the laity, and woe to them if
they are not well prepared. And if, in the old-
en days of vassalage and serfdom, the Church
honored every individual, no matter how humble
his position, and labored to give him the
enlightenment that would qualify him for future
responsibilities, much more now, in the era
of popular rights and liberties, when every individual is an active and influential factor
in the body politic, does she desire that all
should be fitted by suitable training for an
intelligent and conscientious discharge of the
important duties that will devolve upon them.

Few, if any, will deny that a sound civilization must depend upon sound popular education. But education, in order to be sound and
to produce beneficial results, must develop
what is best in man, and make him not only
clever but good. A one-sided education will
develop a one-sided life; and such a life will
surely topple over, and so will every social
system that is built up of such lives. True
civilization requires that not only the physical and intellectual, but also the moral and
religious, well-being of the people should be
promoted, and at least with equal care. Take
away religion from a people, and morality would
soon follow; morality gone, even their physical
condition will ere long degenerate into corruption which breeds decrepitude, while their
intellectual attainments would only serve as
a light to guide them to deeper depths of vice
and ruin. This has been so often demonstrated
in the history of the past, and is, in fact,
so self-evident, that one is amazed to find
any difference of opinion about it. A civilization without religion, would be a civilization
of "the struggle for existence, and the survival
of the fittest," in which cunning and strength
would become the substitutes for principle,
virtue, conscience and duty. As a matter of
fact, there never has been a civilization worthy
of the name without religion; and from the facts
of history the laws of human nature can easily
be inferred.

Hence education, in order to foster civilization, must foster religion. Now the three great educational agencies are the home, the Church, and the school. These mould men and shape society. Therefore each of them, to do its part well, must foster religion. But many, unfortunately, while avowing that religion should be the light and atmosphere of the home and of the Church, are content to see it excluded from the school, and even advocate as the best school system that which necessarily excludes religion. Few surely will deny that childhood and youth are the periods of life when the character ought especially to be subjected to religious influences. Nor can we ignore the palpable fact that the school is an important factor in the forming of childhood and youth, --so important that its influence often outweighs that of home and Church. It cannot, therefore, be desirable or advantageous that religion should be excluded from the school. On the contrary, it ought there to be one of the chief agencies for moulding the young life to all that is true and virtuous, and holy. To shut religion out of the school, and keep it for home and the Church, is, logically, to train up a generation that will consider religion good for home and the Church, but not for the practical business of real life. But a more false and pernicious notion could not be imagined. Religion, in order to elevate a people, should inspire their whole life and rule their relations with one another. A life is not dwarfed, but ennobled by being lived in the presence of God. Therefore the school, which principally gives the knowledge fitting for practical life, ought to be pre-eminently under the holy influence of religion. From the shelter of home and school, the youth must soon go out into the busy ways of trade or traffic or professional practice. In all these, the principles of religion should animate and direct him. But he cannot expect to learn these principles in the workshop or the office or the counting-room. Therefore let him be well and thoroughly imbued with them by the joint influences of home and school, before he is launched out on the dangerous sea of life.

All denominations of Christians are now
awaking to this great truth, which the Catholic
Church has never ceased to maintain. Reason
and experience are forcing them to recognize
that the only practical way to secure a Christian people, is to give the youth a Christian
education. The avowed enemies of Christianity
in some European countries are banishing religion from the schools, in order gradually to
eliminate it from among the people. In this
they are logical, and we may well profit by
the lesson. Hence the cry for Christian education is going up from all religious bodies
throughout the land. And this is no narrowness
and "sectarianism" on their part; it is an
honest and logical endeavor to preserve Christian truth and morality among the people by
fostering religion in the young. Nor is it
any antagonism to the State; on the contrary,
it is an honest endeavor to give to the State
better citizens, by making them better Christians. The friends of Christian education do
not condemn the State for not imparting religious instruction in the public schools as
they are now organized; because they well know
it does not lie within the province of the
State to teach religion. They simply follow
their conscience by sending their children to
denominational schools, where religion can
have its rightful place and influence.

Two objects therefore, dear brethren, we
have in view, to multiply our schools, and to
perfect them. We must multiply them, till
every Catholic child in the land shall have
within its reach the means of education. There
is still much to do ere this be attained.
There are still thousands of Catholic children
in the United States deprived of the benefit
of a Catholic school. Pastors and parents
should not rest till this defect be remedied.
No parish is complete till it has schools
adequate to the needs of its children, and
the pastor and people of such a parish should
feel that they have not accomplished their
entire duty until the want is supplied.

But then, we must also perfect our schools.
We repudiate the idea that the Catholic school
need be in any respect inferior to any other
school whatsoever. And if hitherto, in some
places, our people have acted on the principle

that it is better to have an imperfect Catholic
school than to have none, let them now push
their praiseworthy ambition still further, and
not relax their efforts till their schools be
elevated to the highest educational excellence.
And we implore parents not to hasten to take
their children from school, but to give them
all the time and all the advantages that they
have the capacity to profit by, so that, in
after life, their children may "rise up and
call them blessed."[1]

[1]Guilday, Pastorals, pp. 243-247.

Chapter VIII

The Present Status of Church Legislation

In order to complete the study of Church legislation
regarding parochial schools, it is necessary to say a few
words about the Code of Canon Law enacted on May 19, 1918.
The Code of Canon Law specifically states that local laws
enacted prior to the Code which were contrary to particular
elements in the Code were abrogated by canon 6, p. 1. Further portions of this same canon indicate that laws which
are not contrary to the Code, commonly called laws praeter
legem, remain in full force; this, at least, is the general
interpretation of the canon.[1] In the United States there have
been no councils called since 1884. The annual meeting of
the hierarchy has taken over any duties that previously would
have been taken care of by a council. Although the scope of
the legislation of provincial and plenary councils is somewhat limited by the Code, educational legislation is clearly
within the scope of these councils.[2] Likewise the binding
force of conciliar decrees, properly approved, has never been

----

[1] Elias Poblete, The Plenary Council: A Historical
Synopsis and a Commentary (Washington: Catholic University
of America, 1958), pp. 50-93.

[2] Poblete, Plenary Council, pp. 94-106. Cf. also Fran-
cis J. Murphy, Legislative Powers of the Provincial Council: A
Historical Synopsis and a Commentary (Washington: Catholic
University of America, 1947). Cf. also John Barrett, A Com-
parative Study of the Councils of Baltimore and the Code of
Canon Law (Washington: Catholic University of America, 1932).

seriously challenged. Therefore, the enactments of III Baltimore remain in force where they do not conflict with the Code.

The canons which directly affect Catholic education in public or parochial schools are few in number, so it will be useful to repeat them here:

> 1372. 1. Fideles omnes ita sunt a pueritia instituendi ut non solum nihil eis tradatur quod catholicae religioni morumque honestati adversetur, sed praecipuum institutio religiosa ac moralis locum obtineat.
> 2. Non modo parentibus ad norman can. 1113, sed etiam omnibus qui eorum locum tenent, ius et gravissimum officium est curandi christianam liberorum educationem.
> 1373. 1. In qualibet elementaria schola, pueris pro eorum aetate tradenda est institutio religiosa.
> 2. Iuventus, quae medias vel superiores scholas frequentat, pleniore religionis doctrina excolatur, et locorum Ordinarii curent ut id fiat per sacerdotes zelo et doctrina praestantes.[1]

---

[1]Translation: 1372. 1. All the faithful are to be so trained from childhood that nothing might be given to them which is contrary to the catholic religion and good morals; religious and moral training shall have a special place.
2. Not only parents according to the norm of can. 1113, but all the faithful who take their place have the right and the very serious duty of providing for the christian education of the children.
1373. 1. In every elementary school, religious instruction is to be given to the children, according to their age.
2. The young children, who attend middle or higher schools, are to be given a more full course of religion, and the local Ordinaries shall see that this training is given by priests outstanding in zeal and piety.

1374. Pueri catholici scholas acatholicas,
neutras, mixtas, quae nempe etiam acatholicis
patent, ne frequentent. Solius autem Ordinarii
loci est decernere, ad normam instructionum
Sedis Apostolicae, in quibus rerum adiunctis et quibus
adhibitis cautelis, ut periculum perversionis vitetur,
tolerari possit ut eae scholae celebrentur.
1375. Ecclesiae est ius scholas cuiusvis
disciplinae non solum elementarias, sed etiam
medias et superiores condendi.
1379. 1. Si scholae catholicae ad normam can.
1373 sive elementariae sive mediae desint,
curandum, praesertim a locorum Ordinariis,
ut condantur.
2. Itemque si publicae studiorum Universitates
doctrina sensuque catholico imbutae non sint,
optandum ut in natione vel regione Universitas
catholica conditur.
3. Fideles ne omittant adiutricem operam pro
viribus confere in catholicas scholas condendas
et sustentandas.[1]

It can be seen that there is nothing in these regu-

lations that countermands any specific aspect of the earlier

---

[1]Codex Iuris Canonici Pii X Pontificis Maximi (Romae:
Typis Polygottis Vaticanis, 1947). Translation: 1374. Catholic children shall not attend non-catholic or non-denominational
schools, nor mixed schools, that is, schools which admit non-
catholics. It is the right of the Ordinary alone in accordance
with the instruction of the Holy See to determine under what
circumstances and with what safeguards against the danger of
perversion that the attendance of catholics at such schools
may be tolerated.
1375. It is the right of the church to establish schools
of every level; elementary, intermediate, and higher.
1379. 1. If there are no catholic elementary or secondary
schools, according to the norms of canon 1373, the local
Ordinaries especially are to see to it that they are established.
2. Likewise if the public Universities are not imbued with
catholic doctrine and spirit, it is to be hoped that a
catholic University will be established in that nation or
province.
3. The faithful should not omit to aid according to their
ability in the building and maintaining of catholic schools.

legislation of the third council. Therefore, both continue
to govern the Catholic children of the United States.[1]

With this analysis of the present Code of Canon Law
our study of parochial school legislation in the United States
is complete. After an introductory analysis of the status
of Catholic education before the conciliar period, the work
of each of the ten councils has been examined in detail. A
particular effort has been made to reproduce here the documents and correspondence which shed light upon the course of
the development of the decrees. Particularly evident is the
fact that the resolve of the Catholic Bishops to build and
maintain a separate system was a reaction to the Protestant
nature of public education. In the latter portion of the
work an effort has also been made to show how the danger of
secularism and irreligion came to take the place of the general complaint against Protestantism. From the very beginning of their struggle the hierarchy were convinced of their
right to public tax monies and down to the final council of
1884 continued to insist upon the injustice of the use of
tax monies for public schools exclusively. Just how important a role this desire and hope for eventual public support

---

[1]Conrad Boffa, <u>Canonical Provisions for Catholic
Schools</u> (Washington: Catholic University of America, 1939);
Alexander Sokolich, <u>Canonical Provisions for Universities
and Colleges</u> (Washington: Catholic University of America,
1956).

actually played is impossible to determine, but it is certain that the hope of support was present and was a factor in the decisions.

The story of the legislation of the councils of Baltimore is the story of the Catholic Church in America. Barely tolerated at first, the Catholic Church grew and developed; its educational institutions grew and developed apace. During the half-century studied a consistent policy of education was evolved, tried, and finally made obligatory. By its nature, it was basically reactionary; consequently, as the educational program of the Catholic Church faces modern challenges, it may well be that the legislation of 1884 which is still in effect today will give way to other legislation which will be born of twentieth century practices and needs.

BIBLIOGRAPHY

Concilium Baltimorense. Provinciale Primum: Habitum Baltimori. Anno Reparate Salutis. 1829. Mense Octobri.
Baltimori: ex typis J. D. Toy, 1831.

Concilia Provincilia. Baltimori Habita ab Anno 1829. usque
ad Annum 1840. Baltimori: apud Joannem Murphy, 1842.

Concilia Provincilia. Baltimori Habita ab Anno 1829 usque
ad Annum 1849. Editio altera. Baltimori: apud Joannem
Murphy et socium, 1851.

Concilium Plenarium Totius Americae Septentrionalis Foederatae,
Baltimori Habitum Anno 1852. Baltimori: apud Joannem
Murphy et socios, 1853.

Decreta Conciliorum Provincialium et Plenarii Baltimorensium,
pro Majori Cleri Americani Commoditate simul Collecta.
Baltimori: apud Joannem Murphy et socios, 1853.

Concilium Plenarium Baltimorense Secundum Dominica Prima
Octobris. A.D. 1866. Aperiendum: Acta Concilio Praevia.
Baltimore: J. Murphy, 1866.

Concilii Plenarii Baltimorensis II., in Ecclesia Metropoli-
tana Baltimorensi. a Die VII. ad Diem XXI. Octobris. A.D.
MDCCCLXVI., Habiti. et a Sede Apostolica Recogniti. De-
creta. Praeside. Illustrissimo ac Reverendissimo Martino
Joanne Spalding. Archiepiscopo Baltimorensi. et Delegato
Apostolico. Baltimorae: excudebat Joannes Murphy, 1868.

Concilii Plenarii Baltimorensis II., in Ecclesia Metropolitana Baltimorensi. a Die VII. ad Diem XXI Octobris. A.D.
MDCCCLXVI. Habiti. et a Sede Apostolica Recogniti. Acta
et Decreta. Praeside Illustrissimo ac Reverendissimo
Martino Joanne Spalding. Archiepiscopo Baltimorensi, et
Delegato Apostolico. Secundum cuius editum. Baltimorae:
excudebat Joannes Murphy, 1868.

Concilii Plenarii Baltimorensis II., in Ecclesia Metropolitana Baltimorensi. a Die VII. ad Diem XXI. Octobris. A.D.
MDCCCLXVI., Habiti. et a Sede Apostolico Recogniti. Decreta. Editio altera, Emendata, et Approbata. Baltimorae: excudebat Joannes Murphy, 1876.

Concilii Plenarii Baltimorensis II., in Ecclesia Metropolitana
Baltimorensi. a Die VII. ad Diem XXI. Octobris. A.D.
MDCCCLXVI., Habiti. et a Sede Apostolica Recogniti: Acta
et Decreta. Editio altera mendis expurgata. Baltimorae:
excudebat J. Murphy, 1877.

Concilii Plenarii Baltimorensis II., in Ecclesia Metropoli-
    tana Baltimorensi, a Die VII. ad Diem XXI. Octobris, A.D.
    MDCCCLXVI., Habiti, et a Sede Apostolica Recogniti: Acta
    et Decreta. Editio altera mendis expurgata. Excudebat
    Joannes Murphy, 1894.

Acta et Decreta Concilii Plenarii Baltimorensis Tertii, A.D.
    1884. Baltimore: J. Murphy, 1884.

Acta et Decreta Concilii Plenarii Baltimorensis Tertii in
    Ecclesia Metropolitana Baltimorensi Habiti a Die IX.
    Novembris usque ad diem VII, Decembris A.D. MDCCCLXXXIV.
    Baltimore: John Murphy, 1884.

Acta et Decreta Concilii Plenarii Baltimorensis Tertii., A.D.
    MDCCCLXXXIV, Praeside Illmo, ac Revmo. Jacobo Gibbons.
    Baltimorae: typis Murphy et sociorum, 1894.

Decreta Concilii Plenarii Baltimorensis Tertii, A.D.
    MDCCCLXXXIV, Praeside Illmo, ac Revmo. Jacobo Gibbons.
    Baltimorae: typis Joannis Murphy et sociorum, 1894.

Decreta Concilii Plenarii Baltimorensis Tertii: A.D.
    MDCCCLXXXIV. Praeside Illmo, ac Revmo. Jacobo Gibbons.
    Baltimorae: typis Joannis Murphy Sociorum, 1901.

SECONDARY SOURCES

Books

Ahern, Patrick Henry. The Life of John J. Keane, Educator and
    Archbishop, 1839-1918. Milwaukee; Bruce Publishing
    Company, 1955.

An Address to the Impartial Public, on the Intolerant Spirit
    of the Times, Being the Introduction to the Miscellanea
    of M. J. Spalding, D.D., Bishop of Louisville. Louisville:
    Webb & Levering, 1854.

Barry, Colman J. The Catholic Church and German Americans.
    Milwaukee: Bruce Publishing Co., 1953.

Bell, Stephan. Rebel, Priest and Prophet: A Biography of
    Dr. Edward McGlynn. New York: Devin-Adair, 1937.

Billington, Ray Allen. The Protestant Crusade, 1800-1860:
    A Study of the Origins of American Nativism. New York:
    Macmillan, 1938.

Blanshard, Paul. American Freedom and Catholic Power. Bos-
    ton: Beacon Press, 1949.

Boles, Donald E. The Bible, Religion, and the Public Schools. Ames: Iowa State University Press, 1961.

Bourne, William Oland. History of the Public School Society of the City of New York. New York: William Wood and Company, 1870.

Brady, Joseph. A Confusion Twice Confounded: The First Amendment and the Supreme Court. South Orange, New Jersey: Seton Hall University Press, 1954.

Brent, John Carroll. Biographical Sketch of the Most Reverend John Carroll. Baltimore: John Murphy and Associates, 1843.

Brickman, William and Lehrer, Stanley. Religion, Government and Education. New York: Society for the Advancement of Education, 1961.

Brownson, Henry F. The Works of Orestes A. Brownson. 20 vols. Detroit: T. Nourse, 1882-1907.

Brubacher, John S. and Rudy, Willis. Higher Education in Transition. New York: Harper & Bros., 1958.

Burns, James A. The Catholic School System in the United States. New York: Benziger, 1908.

Burns, James A. The Growth and Development of the Catholic School System in the United States. New York: Benziger, 1912.

Burns, James A. Catholic Education: A Study of Conditions. New York: Longmans, Green and Co., 1917.

Burns, James A. and Kohlbrenner, Bernard J. A History of Catholic Education in the United States. New York: Benziger, 1937.

Bushnell, Horace. A Discourse on the Modifications Demanded by the Roman Catholics: Delivered in the North Church, Hartford, on the Day of the Late Fast March 25, 1853. Hartford: Case, Tiffany & Co., 1853.

Butts, R. Freeman. The American Tradition in Religion and Education. Boston: Beacon Press, 1960.

Carlier, Auguste. La Republique Americaine Etats-Unis. 4 vols. Paris: Guillaumin et Cie., 1890.

Clough, Shepard B. Basic Values of Western Civilization. New York: Columbia University Press, 1960.

Collectanea S. Congregationis de Propaganda Fide, 1622-1906. 2 vols. Romae: 1907.

Corrigan, Owen B. The Catholic Schools of the Archdiocese of Baltimore. A Study in Diocesean History. Baltimore: 1924.

The Council in Baltimore, 7-21 October, 1866; A Picture of American Life. Baltimore: Commercial Ptg. and Sta. Co., 1941.

Cremin, Lawrence A. The American Common School: An Historic Conception. New York: Bureau of Publications, Columbia Teachers College, 1951.

Cremin, Lawrence A. The Republic and the School. Horace Mann on the Education of Free Men. New York: Bureau of Publications, Columbia Teachers College, 1957.

Cremin, Lawrence A. The Transformation of the School: Progressivism in American Education, 1876-1957. New York: Alfred A. Knopf, 1961.

Cremin, Lawrence A. and Borrowman, Merle L. Public Schools in Our Democracy. New York: Macmillan Company, 1956.

Cross, Robert D. The Emergence of Liberal Catholicism in America. Cambridge: Harvard University Press, 1958.

Crowley, Jeremiah J. The Parochial School. A Curse to the Church, A Menace to the Nation. 2nd ed. Chicago: the author, 1905.

Culver, Raymond B. Horace Mann and Religion in the Massachusetts Public Schools. New Haven: Yale University Press, 1929.

Curley, Michael J. Venerable John Neumann, C.SS.R., Fourth Bishop of Philadelphia. Washington: Catholic University Press, 1952.

Curran, Francis X. The Churches and the Schools. Chicago: University of Loyola Press, 1954.

Curti, Merle. The Growth of American Thought. New York: Harper & Bros., 1943.

Curti, Merle. The Social Ideas of American Educators. New York: Charles Scribner's Sons, 1935.

Daley, John M. Georgetown University: Origin and Early Years. Washington: Georgetown University Press, 1957.

DeCourcy, Henry and Shea, John Gilmary. The Catholic Church in the United States. New York: Edward Dunigan & Brothers, 1856.

Defence of the Use of the Bible in the Public Schools: Argument of Henry F. Durant, Esq. in the Eliot School Case. Boston: Ticknor & Fields, 1859.

Deferrari, Roy J. Essays on Catholic Education in the United States. Washington: Catholic University of America Press, 1942.

Deuther, Charles G. The Life and Times of the Rt. Rev. John Timon. Buffalo: the author, 1870.

Dorchester, Daniel. Romanism Versus the Public School System. New York: Phillips & Hunt, 1888.

Dunigan's American Catholic Almanac and List of the Clergy, 1858. New York: Edward Dunigan and Brother, 1858.

Dunn, William Kailer. What Happened to Religious Education? The Decline of Religious Teaching in the Public Elementary School, 1776-1861. Baltimore: Johns Hopkins Press, 1958.

Dunne, Edmund F. Our Public Schools: Are They Free for All, or Are They Not? New York: 2nd ed. Egan, 1875.

Ellis, John T. American Catholicism. Chicago: University of Chicago Press, 1956.

Ellis, John T. (ed.). Documents of American Catholic History. Milwaukee: Bruce Publishing Co., 1956.

Ellis, John T. John Lancaster Spalding: First Bishop of Peoria: American Educator. Milwaukee: Bruce, 1961.

Ellis, John T. The Formative Years of the Catholic University of America. Washington: American Catholic Historical Assn., 1946.

Ellis, John T. The Life of James Cardinal Gibbons, Archbishop of Baltimore, 1834-1921. 2 vols. Milwaukee: Bruce Publishing Company, 1952.

Farley, John. The Life of John Cardinal McCloskey, First Prince of the Church in America, 1810-1885. New York: Longmans, Green & Company, 1918.

Foik, Paul J. Pioneer Catholic Journalism. New York: United States Catholic Historical Society, 1930.

Garraghan, Gilbert J. The Jesuits in the Middle United States. 3 vols. New York: America Press, 1938.

Greene, Evarts B. Religion and the State: The Making and Testing of an American Tradition. New York: New York University Press, 1941.

Guilday, Peter K. A History of the Councils of Baltimore, 1791-1884. New York: Macmillan Co., 1932.

Guilday, Peter K. The Life and Times of John Carroll, Archbishop of Baltimore, 1735-1815. 2 vols. New York: Encyclopedia Press, 1922.

Guilday, Peter K. The Life and Times of John England, First Bishop of Charleston, 1786-1842. 2 vols. New York: America Press, 1927.

Guilday, Peter K. (ed.). National Pastorals of the American Hierarchy, 1792-1919. Washington: National Catholic Welfare Conference, 1923.

Handlin, Oscar. Boston's Immigrants 1790-1865: A Study in Acculturation. Cambridge: Harvard University Press, 1941.

Hassard, John R. Life of the Most Reverend John Hughes, First Archbishop of New York. New York: D. Appleton and Company, 1866.

Higham, John. Strangers in the Land, Patterns of American Nativism: 1860-1925. New Brunswick: Rutgers University Press, 1955.

A History of the Third Plenary Council of Baltimore, November 9-December 7, 1884. Baltimore: John Murphy, 1885.

Hofstadter, Richard and Metzger, Walter. The Development of Academic Freedom in the United States. New York: Columbia University Press, 1957.

Huber, Raphael. The Part Played by Religion in the History of Education in the United States. Private Printing. Trenton: MacCrellish and Quigley Co., 1951.

Ireland, John. The Church and Modern Society. Lectures and Addresses. 2 vols. St. Paul: Pioneer Press, 1905.

Jackson, Sydney. America's Struggle for Free Schools; Social Tension and Education in New England and New York, 1827-1842. Washington: American Council on Public Affairs, 1941.

Jenkins, Thomas J. Christian Schools. London: Burns, Oates, and Washbourne, Ltd., 1890.

Kane, John J. Catholic-Protestant Conflicts in America. Chicago: Henry Regnery Co., 1955.

Kehoe, Lawrence. Complete Works of the Most Reverend John Hughes, First Archbishop of New York. 2 vols. New York: Catholic Publication House, 1865.

Knight, Edgar W. A Documentary History of Education in the South Before 1860. 5 vols. Chapel Hill, N.C.: University of North Carolina Press, 1949.

Lally, Francis J. The Catholic Church in a Changing America. Boston: Little, Brown and Co., 1962.

Lamott, John H. History of the Archdiocese of Cincinnati, 1821-1921. New York: Pustet, 1921.

Lord, Robert H., Sexton, John E. and Harrington, Edward T. History of the Archdiocese of Boston in the Various Stages of Its Development, 1604 to 1943. 3 vols. New York: Sheed & Ward, 1944.

McAvoy, Thomas T. The Catholic Church in Indiana, 1780-1834. New York: Columbia University Press, 1940.

McAvoy, Thomas T. The Great Crisis in American Catholic History, 1895-1900. Chicago: Henry Regnery Co., 1957.

MacCaffrey, James. History of the Catholic Church in the 19th Century (1789-1908). St. Louis: Herder, 1910.

McCluskey, Neil Gerard. Public Schools and Moral Education. New York: Columbia University Press, 1958.

McElrone, Hugh P. The Works of the Right Reverend John England. 2 vols. Baltimore: The Baltimore Publishing Co., 1884.

McNamara, Robert F. The American College in Rome, 1855-1955. Rochester: The Christopher Press, 1956.

McQuaid, Bernard. The Public School Question. Boston: 1876.

Mead, Edwin. The Roman Catholic Church and the School Question. Boston: Ellis, 1888.

Melville, Annabelle M. John Carroll of Baltimore, Founder of the American Catholic Hierarchy. New York: Charles Scribner's Sons, 1955.

Melville, Annabelle M. Elizabeth Bayley Seton, 1774-1821. New York: Charles Scribner's Sons, 1951.

Melville, Annabelle M. Jean Lefebvre de Cheverus, 1768-1836. Milwaukee: Bruce Publishing Co., 1958.

Messmer, Sebastian G. et al. The Works of the Right Reverend John England. 7 vols. Cleveland: Arthur H. Clark Company, 1908.

Moehlman, Conrad H. The Wall of Separation between Church and State. Boston: Beacon Press, 1951.

Moehlman, Conrad H. School and Church: The American Way. New York: Harper, 1944.

Mosier, Richard D. Making the American Mind: Social and Moral Ideas in the McGuffey Readers. New York: Kings Crown Press, Columbia University, 1947.

Moynihan, James H. The Life of Archbishop John Ireland. New York: Harper & Bros., 1953.

Mueller, Michael. Public School Education. New York: 1873.

Myers, Gustavus. History of Bigotry in the United States. New York: Random House, 1943.

Niedermayer, Andreas. The Council in Baltimore (7th to 21st October, 1866); A Picture of American Church Life by A. Niedermayer. Baltimore: Commercial Ptg. and Sts. Co., 1914.

Nolan, Hugh J. The Most Reverend Francis Patrick Kenrick, Third Bishop of Philadelphia, 1830-1851. Washington: Catholic University of America Press, 1948.

O'Daniel, Victor F., O.P. The Right Rev. Edward Dominic Fenwick, O.P., Founder of the Dominicans in the United States. New York: Pustet, 1920.

O'Dea, Thomas F. American Catholic Dilemma: An Inquiry into the Intellectual Life. New York: Sheed & Ward, 1958.

O'Shea, John J. The Two Kenricks. Philadelphia: J. J. McVey, 1904.'

Pfeffer, Leo. Creeds in Competition: A Creative Force in American Culture. New York: Harper & Bros., 1958.

Power, Edward J. A History of Catholic Higher Education in the United States. Milwaukee: Bruce Publishing Co., 1958.

Reisner, Edward. The Evolution of the Common School. New York: Macmillan Co., 1930.

Religion. Santa Barbara: Center for the Study of Democratic Institutions, 1962.

Roemer, Theodore. The Catholic Church of the United States. St. Louis: B. Herder Book Co., 1951.

Riordan, Michael J. Cathedral Records from the Beginning of Catholicism in Baltimore to the Present Time. Baltimore: Catholic Mirror Press, 1906.

Rothan, Emmet H. The German Catholic Immigrant in the United States: 1830-1860. Washington: Catholic University of America Press, 1946.

Schlesinger, Arthur M. Jr. Orestes A. Brownson, A Pilgrim's Progress. Boston: Little, Brown and Company, 1939.

Shaughnessy, Gerald. Has the Immigrant Kept the Faith? A Study of Immigration and Catholic Growth in the United States 1790-1920. New York: Macmillan, 1925.

Shea, John Gilmary. The History of the Catholic Church in the United States. 4 vols. New York: John G. Shea, 1886-1892.

Shea, John Gilmary. The Life and Times of the Most Rev. John Carroll. New York: John G. Shea, 1888.

Shotwell, John B. A History of the Schools of Cincinnati. Cincinnati: School Life Co., 1902.

Smith, James W. and Jamison, A. Leland (eds.). Religion in American Life. Princeton: Princeton University Press, 1961.

Smith, Sebastian B. Notes on the Second Plenary Council of Baltimore. New York: O'Shea, 1874.

Spalding, John Lancaster. The Life of the Most Reverend M. J. Spalding, D.D., Archbishop of Baltimore. New York: Catholic Publication Society, 1873.

Spalding, John Lancaster. Means and Ends of Education. Chicago: A. C. McClurg and Co., 1897.

Spalding, Martin J. Sketches of the Life, Times, and Character of the Rt. Rev. Benedict Joseph Flaget, First Bishop of Louisville. Louisville: Webb & Levering, 1852.

Spurlock, Clark. Education and the Supreme Court. University of Illinois Press, 1955.

Stanton, Thomas J. A Century of Growth, or the History of the Church in Western Maryland. 2 vols. Baltimore: John Murphy Co., 1900.

Stokes, Anson Phelps. Church and State in the United States. 3 vols. New York: Harper & Bros., 1950.

Sugrue, Thomas. A Catholic Speaks His Mind on America's Religious Conflict. New York: Harper, 1952.

Thayer, Vivian T., The attack upon the American Secular School. Boston: Beacon Press, 1951.

The United States Catholic Almanac; or Laity's Directory, 1833-1837. Baltimore: James Myers, 1833-1837.

The Metropolitan Catholic Almanac, and Laity's Directory, 1838-1854. Baltimore: Fielding Lucas, Jr., 1838-1854.

The Metropolitan Catholic Almanac and Laity's Directory, 1855-1857. Baltimore: Lucas Brothers, 1855-1857.

The Metropolitan Catholic Almanac and Laity's Directory for the United States, 1859-1860. Baltimore: John Murphy and Company, 1859-1860.

Tourscher, Francis E. The Kenrick-Frenaye Correspondence, 1830-1862. Lancaster: Wickersham Printing Co., 1920.

Tussman, Joseph (ed.). The Supreme Court on Church and State. New York: Oxford University Press, 1962.

Walsh, James J. Education and the Founding Fathers of the Republic. New York: Fordham University Press, 1935.

Woywood, Stanislaus. A Practical Commentary on the Code of Canon Law. 2 vols. Edited by Callistus Smith. New York: Joseph F. Wagner, 1948.

Zollman, Carl. Church and School in the American Law. St. Louis: Concordia Publishing House, 1918.

Zwierlein, Frederick J. Letters of Archbishop Corrigan to Bishop McQuaid and Allied Documents. Rochester: Art Print Shop, 1946.

Zwierlein, Frederick J. The Life and Letters of Bishop McQuaid. 3 vols. Rochester: Art Print Shop, 1925-1927.

Theses and Dissertations

Barrett, John D. A Comparative Study of the Councils of Baltimore and the Code of Canon Law. Washington: Catholic University of America Press, 1932.

Balmain, Alexander F. "The History of Catholic Education in the Diocese of Brooklyn." Unpublished Ph.D. dissertation, Fordham University, 1935.

Berry, Cleo C. "Public Schools and Religion: The Opinions of Nine Eminent Educators." Unpublished Ed.D. Dissertation, University of Southern California, 1961.

Boffa, Conrad H. Canonical Provisions for Catholic Schools. Washington: Catholic University of America Press, 1939.

Carlin, Sr. M. Angela. "The Attitude of the Republican Party towards Religious Schools, 1875-1880." Unpublished Master's Thesis, Catholic University of America, 1948.

Carthy, Mother Mary Peter. English Influences on Early American Catholicism. Washington: Catholic University of America Press, 1959.

Casey, Thomas F. The Sacred Congregation de Propaganda Fide and the Revision of the First Provincial Council of Baltimore, 1829-1830. Romae: Apud Aedes Universitatis Gregorianae, 1957.

Chase, Cornelius T. "Roman Catholic Education in the United States." Unpublished Master's Thesis, Hartford, 1938.

Confrey, Burton. Secularism in American Education. Washington: Catholic University of America Press, 1931.

Connaughton, Edward A. A History of Educational Legislation and Administration in the Archdiocese of Cincinnati. Washington: Catholic University of America Press, 1946.

Connally, James F. The Visit of Archbishop Gaetano Bedini to the United States of America, June 1853-February 1854. Romae: Apud Aedes Universitatis Gregorianae, 1960.

Connors, Edward M. Church-State Relationships in Education in the State of New York. Washington: Catholic University of America Press, 1951.

Diffley, Jerome E. "Catholic Reaction to American Public Education, 1792-1852." Unpublished Ph.D. Dissertation, University of Notre Dame, 1959.

Donehoe, Francis J. "Development of American Catholic Theory, Attitudes and Practices with Regard to Public Support for Parochial Schools." Unpublished Ph.D. Dissertation, University of Michigan, 1944.

Elefante, Angela M. "The Rights and Duties of the Independent School in the United States." Unpublished Ph.D. Dissertation, Catholic University of America, 1959.

Ellis, Frederic E. "Attitude of the Roman Catholic Church Towards the Problem of Democratic Freedom and American Public Education as Shown by Selected Writings in Philosophy, the Philosophy of History, and the Philosophy of Education." Unpublished Ph.D. Dissertation, Harvard, 1948.

Fell, Sr. M. Lenore. "The Foundations of Nativism in American Textbooks, 1783-1860." Unpublished Master's Thesis, Catholic University of America, 1941.

Fisher, Charles G. "Archbishop Spalding and the Preparation for the Second Plenary Council of Baltimore." Unpublished Master's Thesis, St. Mary's University, Roland Park, 1950.

Gabel, Richard J. Public Funds for Church and Private Schools. Washington: Catholic University of America Press, 1937.

267

Gobbell, Luther L. "Church-State Relationships in Education in North Carolina Since 1776." Unpublished Ph.D. Dissertation, Yale University, 1934.

Goebel, Edmund J. A Study of Catholic Secondary Education During the Colonial Period up to the First Plenary Council of Baltimore, 1852. New York: Benziger, 1937.

Gordon, John R. "The Battle for Free Schools in the United States. A Sociological Interpretation." Unpublished Ph.D. Dissertation, Texas, 1951.

Hickey, Edward J. The Society for the Propagation of the Faith. Its Foundation, Organization, and Success, 1822-1922. Washington: Catholic University of America Press, 1922.

Howley, Mary C. "The Treatment of Religion in American History Textbooks for Grade Seven and Eight from 1783 to 1956." Unpublished Ed.D. Dissertation, Columbia, 1959.

Jansen, Raymond J. Canonical Provision for Catechetical Instruction. Washington: Catholic University of America Press, 1937.

Johnson, Joseph. "The Development of Certain Legal Issues Concerning the Relationship between Public and Sectarian Education." Unpublished Ph.D. Dissertation, University of Pittsburgh, 1953.

Kaiser, Sr. M. Laurina. The Development of the Concept and Function of the Catholic Elementary School in the American Parish. Washington: Catholic University of America Press, 1955.

Kinzer, Donald L. "The American Protective Association: A Study of Anti-Catholicism." Unpublished Ph.D. Dissertation, Seattle, 1954.

Lawn, Evan. "Fundamental Differences between the Philosophies of Public and Parochial Education--A Socio-Historical Study." Unpublished Ph.D. Dissertation, University of Connecticut,

MacNaughton, Douglas. "The Development of Secularism in Education, Particularly in the Northwest Territory Prior to 1860." Unpublished Ph.D. Dissertation, University of Chicago, 1956.

Murphy, Francis J. <u>Legislative Powers of the Provincial Council</u>. Washington: Catholic University of America Press, 1947.

Nicoletti, James F. "The Attitude of the Church toward the Public School System." Unpublished Master's Thesis, Catholic University of America, 1951.'

Poblete, Elias. <u>The Plenary Council: A Historical Synopsis and A Commentary</u>. Washington: Catholic University of America Press, 1958.

Power, Edward J. "The Educational Views and Attitudes of Orestes A. Brownson." Unpublished Ph.D. Dissertation, Notre Dame, 1949.

Ray, Sr. M. Augustine. <u>American Opinion of Roman Catholicism in the Eighteenth Century</u>. New York: Columbia University Press, 1936.

Reilly, Daniel F. <u>The School Controversy: 1891-1893</u>. Washington: Catholic University of America, 1944.

Roemer, Theodore. <u>Ten Decades of Alms</u>. St. Louis: B. Herder Book Co., 1942.

Roohan, James Edmund. "American Catholics and the Social Question, 1865-1900." Unpublished Ph.D. Dissertation, Yale University, 1952.

Shearer, Donald C. <u>Pontificia Americana: A Documentary History of the Catholic Church in the United States, 1784-1884</u>. Washington: Catholic University of America Press, 1933.

Sokolich, Alexander. <u>Canonical Provisions for Universities and Colleges</u>. Washington: Catholic University of America Press, 1956.

Stauffer, Alvin P. "Anti-Catholicism in American Politics 1865-1900." Unpublished Ph.D. Dissertation, Harvard, 1933.

Widen, Irwin. "Issue of Public Support for Sectarian Schools." Unpublished Ph.D. Dissertation, University of California, Berkeley, 1950.

Will, Robert F. "An Analysis of the Legal Responsibilities of State Departments of Education for Non-Public Schools." Unpublished Ph.D. Dissertation, University of Maryland, 1958.

Yeager, Sr. M. Hildegarde. _The Life of James Roosevelt Bayley, First Bishop of Newark and Eighth Archbishop of Baltimore, 1814-1877_. Washington: Catholic University of America Press, 1947.

Periodicals

Annales d l'Association de la Propagation de la Foi. Paris: L'Oeuvre de la Propagation de la Foi, 1822 ff.

"Archbishop Hughes to Governor Seward on the School Question," _Records of the American Catholic Historical Society of Philadelphia_,XXIII (January, 1912), 36-38.

"Are Our Public Schools Free," _Catholic World_, XVIII (October, 1873), 1-9.

Baisnee, J. A. "The Catholic Church in the United States," _Records of the American Catholic Historical Society of Philadelphia_, LVI (September, 1945; December, 1945), 134-162; 254-292.

Bayma, P. "The Liberalistic View of the Public School Question," _American Catholic Quarterly Review_, II (January, 1877; April, 1877), 1-29; 240-270.

"Best Solution of the School Question," _The Catholic Record_, VI (November, 1873), 46-51.

Brann, H. A. "The Improvement of Parochial Schools," _American Catholic Quarterly Review_, IX (April, 1884), 238-253.

Browne, Henry J. "The Archdiocese of New York A Century Ago A Memoir of Archbishop Hughes 1838-1858," _Historical Records and Studies_, XXXIX-XL (1952), 132-190.

Browne, Henry J. "Public Support of Catholic Education in New York, 1825-1842: Some New Aspects," _Historical Records and Studies_, XLI (1953), 14-41.

Burns, James A. "A History of the Catholic Parochial Schools in the United States," _Catholic University Bulletin_, XII (1906), 434-453.

Campbell, B.U. "Memoirs of the Life and Times of the Most Rev. John Carroll," _United States Catholic Magazine_, III (1884), 32-41; 98-101; 169-176; 244-248; 363-379; 662-669, IV (1845), 249-260; 782-789.

Cassidy, Francis P. "Catholic Education in the Third Plenary Council of Baltimore," _Catholic Historical Review_, XXXIV (October, 1948; January, 1949), 257-304; 414-436.

Conant, James B. "Unity and Diversity in Secondary Education,"
Official Report of the American Association of School
Administrators. Washington, 1952.

"Concordance of the Decrees of the Provincial Councils and
the I Plenary Council of Baltimore with the Decrees of
the II Plenary Council of Baltimore," The Jurist, VI
(January, 1946), 147-148.

Conway, James, "The Rights and Duties of the Church in Regard
to Education," The American Catholic Quarterly Review,
IX (October, 1884), 650-669.

Corcoran, James A. "The Decrees of the Third Plenary Council,"
American Catholic Quarterly Review, VII (April, 1886),
344-355.

Deshon, George. "An Impudent Fabrication Exposed," Catholic
World, XXXIX (1884), 114-119.

"Education and the Republic," Brownson's Quarterly Review,
II (January, 1874), 37-54.

"Educational Problem and Its Solution," The Catholic Record,
II (February, 1872), 193-201.

Elliott, Walter. "A Practical View of the School Question,"
Catholic World, XXXV (April, 1882), 53-63.

Ellis, Frederic E. "Parochial and Public Schools," Educational Forum, XIV (November, 1949), 21-37.

Ellis, John T. "Catholics in Colonial America," American
Ecclesiastical Review, 136 (January-May, 1957), 11-27;
100-119; 184-196; 265-274; 304-321.

Ellis, John T. "The Centennial of the First Plenary Council
of Baltimore," American Ecclesiastical Review, 126 (May,
1952), 321-350.

Evans, J. W. "Catholics and the Blair Education Bill; Federal
Support during the 1880's," Catholic Historical Review,
46 (November, 1960), 273-298.

Fenton, J. C. "Councils of Baltimore and the Catholic Press,"
American Ecclesiastical Review, 136 (February, 1957),
120-131.

Galvin, William. "Ecclesiastical Legislation on Christian
Education with Special Application to Current Problems,"
The Jurist, XIV (October, 1954), 463-480.

Guilday, Peter. "The American Hierarchy of 1846," _American Ecclesiastical Review,_ 114 (May, 1946), 321-326.

Guilday, Peter. "The Sacred Congregation de Propaganda Fide (1622-1922)," _Catholic Historical Review,_ VI (January, 1921), 478-494.

Hald, Henry M. "The Common School Debate of 1840," _Catholic World,_ 136 (October, 1932), 38-44.

Hecker, Issac T. "A New but False Plea for Public Schools," _Catholic World,_ XXXVI (December, 1882), 412-222.

Hecker, Issac T. "Catholics and Protestants Agreeing on the School Question," _Catholic World,_ XXXII (February, 1881), 669-713.

Hecker, Issac T. "The American Side of the School Question," _Catholic World,_ XXX (January, 1880), 515-519.

Hecker, Issac T. "What Does the Public School Question Mean," _Catholic World,_ XXXIV (October, 1881), 84-90.

Helfman, Harold M. "The Cincinnati 'Bible War,' 1869-1870," _The Ohio State Archeological and Historical Quarterly,_ 60 (October, 1951), 369-386.

Insko, W. Robert. "Bishop Smith the Educator," _Historical Magazine of the Protestant Episcopal Church,_ XXII (June, 1953), 191-202.

Klinkhamer, Sr. M. Carolyn. "Historical Reasons for Inception of Parochial School System," _Catholic Educational Review,_ LII (February, 1954), 73-94.

Klinkhamer, Sr. M. Carolyn. "The Blaine Amendment of 1875: Private Motives for Political Action," _Catholic Historical Review,_ XXXXII (April, 1956), 15-49.

Kwitchen, Mother Mary. "Newspaper Comment on the III Plenary Council of Baltimore," _The Jurist,_ VIII (January, 1948), 95-104.

McAvoy, Thomas T. (trans. & ed.). "Bishop Brute's Report to Rome in 1836," _Catholic Historical Review,_ XXIX (July, 1943), 177-233.

McAvoy, Thomas T. "Bishop John Lancaster Spalding and the Catholic Minority (1877-1908)," _Review of Politics,_ XII (January, 1950), 3-19.

McAvoy, Thomas T. "The American Catholic Minority in the Later Nineteenth Century," Review of Politics, XV (July, 1953), 275-302.

McAvoy, Thomas T. "The Anguish of the Catholic Minority," American Ecclesiastical Review, CXXI (November, 1949), 380-385.

McAvoy, Thomas T. "The Catholic Minority in the United States, 1789-1821," Historical Records and Studies, XXXIX (1952), 33-50.

McAvoy, Thomas T. "The Formation of the Catholic Minority in the United States, 1820-1860," Review of Politics, X (January, 1948), 13-34.

Markee, Donald Taylor. "Sectarian Education in America," Phi Delta Kappan, XXXI (January, 1950), 234-247.

Marraro, Howard A. "Rome and the Catholic Church in Eighteenth Century American Magazines," Catholic Historical Review, XXXII (1946), 157-189.

Marshall, T. W. "Secular Education in England and in United States," American Catholic Quarterly Review, I (April, 1876), 278-311.

"Minutes of Roman Meeting Preparatory to III Plenary Council of 1884," The Jurist, XI (1951), 121-132; 302-312; 417-424; 538-547.

Murphy, Robert J. "The Catholic Church in the United States During the Civil War Period (1852-1866)," Records of the American Catholic Historical Society of Philadelphia, XXXIX (December, 1928), 323-344.

Nietz, J. A. "Some Findings from Analyses of Old Textbooks," History of Education Journal, III (Spring, 1952), 79-86.

Onaham, William J. "The Catholic Church and Popular Education," American Catholic Quarterly Review, VIII (April, 1893), 264-281.

Porter, George. "The Decrees of the Council of Baltimore, 1893," The Month, 57 (June, 1886), 153-165.

Power, Edward J. "Brownson's View on Responsibility in Education," Records of the American Catholic Historical Society of Philadelphia, LXII (December, 1951), 221-232.

"Public School System," Brownson's Quarterly Review, III (Oc-
    tober, 1875), 516-538.

Rossi, Peter H. and Rossi, Alice S. "Background and Conse-
    quences of Parochial School Education," Harvard Educa-
    tional Review, XXVII (Summer, 1957), 168-199.

"School Question," Catholic World, XI (April, 1870), 91-106.

"School Systems in America," The Month, VIII (March, 1868), 260-
    276.

Shea, John G. "Catholic Free Schools in the United States--
    Their Necessity, Condition, and Future," American Ca-
    tholic Quarterly Review, XI (December, 1884), 713-725.

Shea, John G. "The Coming Plenary Council of Baltimore,"
    American Catholic Quarterly Review, IX (April, 1884),
    340-357.

Shea, John G. "The Progress of the Church in the United
    States from the First Provincial Council to the Third
    Plenary Council of Baltimore," American Catholic Quar-
    terly Review, IX (July, 1884), 471-497.

Sheedy, Morgan M. "The Catholic Parochial Schools of the
    United States," Report of Commissioner of Education for
    1903, 1079-1101.

"The Anti-Catholic Issue in the Late Election: The Relation
    of Catholics to the Political Parties," American Catholic
    Quarterly Review, VI (January, 1881), 36-50.

"The Bible in the Schools," The Christian World (February,
    1870).

"The Decrees of the Third Plenary Council of Baltimore,"
    American Ecclesiastical Review, XVI (1897), 1-10; 147-
    154; 290-295.

"The School Question," Catholic World, XI (April, 1870), 91-
    106.

"The Second Plenary Council of Baltimore," Catholic World,
    VII (August, 1868), 618-625.

"The Second Plenary Council of Baltimore and Ecclesiastical
    Discipline in the United States," Catholic World, IX (July,
    1869), 497-511.

Tscham, Francis J. "The Catholic Church in the United States, 1852-1868; A Survey," Records of the American Catholic Historical Society of Philadelphia, LVIII (June, 1947), 123-133.

"What Does the Public-School Question Mean?" Catholic World, (October, 1881), 88-89.

The efforts or Archbishop Spalding to make the
Second Plenary Council of Baltimore a model which all
other countries could follow resulted in a much lengthier
codex of legislation. Spalding was not satisfied to
put down in compact form the commands and decrees. He
wished instead to include the reasoning, the philosophical
principles, and the Scriptural arguments involved in the
enactments. Consequently, the legislation loses its
brevity and the decrees take on more and more the tone of
the Pastoral Letters and the sermons which were preached
at the councils. This change of style is not so noticeable
in the educational section as in some other portions but
it does account for the sudden increase of the length of
the decrees without a simultaneous increase in specific
legislation.

The general heading given to the pages of the
educational legislation of the Second Plenary Council is:
De Juventute Instituenda, Pieque Erudienda. The material
is considered under three headings, the most important of
which is chapter 1, which bears the title: De Scholis
Parochialibus ubique fundandis. The decrees included in
the entire educational section follow, along with a
private translation:

Caput I; De Scholis Parochialibus Ubique
Fundandis.

423. Christus Dominus Noster ad Patrem suum
jamjam ascensurus, ex plenaria illa potestate
quae date ei fuerat in coelo et in terra, omnibus Apostolis quos operis sui vicarios his
in terris relinquebat, mandatum illud insigne,
veluti supremae suae voluntatis testamentum
et summi illius amoris, quo in homines flagra-
bat, pignus eximium edixit: "Euntes, docete
omnes gentes." (Matth. xxviii., 19). Quo
quidem divino eloquio, Ecclesia Ejus seipsam
intellexit non solum praeconem ac testem, sed
et cunctorum insuper hominum matrem ac magistram coelitus institutam fuisse. Quamobrem
nullo non tempore summa ubique terrarum cura
invigilavit, ut salutarem doctrinam disseminaret
ac custodiret. Factum inde etiam est, ut omnes
errores tam contra fidem, quam contra morum
honestatem semper impigre debellaverit.
424. Nihil sare in Ecclesia innotescit magis,
aug pulchrius splendescit, quam zelus ille
atque ardor divinus, quo pia illa mater Juventutem, rei Christianae spem firmissimam, semper
et ubique est prosecuta. Memoria enim tenens
et in corde conferens praeclara illa Domini
sui verba, "Sinite parvulos ad me venire,"[1]

---

[1]Translation: As Christ Our Lord was on the point of
ascending to His Father, from the fulness of that power which
had been given to him in heaven and on earth, he proclaimed
to all the Apostles whom he was leaving on this earth as
vicars of his work, that famous command; "Go, teach all
nations," (Matth. xxviii., 19) as a testament of his supreme
will and as an extraordinary pledge of that truly excessive
love which he bore for men. By this divine decree his Church
understood that she herself had been appointed not only the
herald and witness, but also above all the heavenly mother
and teacher of all men. Hence in every age and every place
in the world, she has given great attention to the spread and
protection of the saving doctrine. She has always actively
fought against all errors both against faith and also against
morality, as a consequence of this charge.
424. Nothing is better known in the Church, nothing
shines forth more beautifully than that zeal and divine love
with which that loving mother has always and everywhere
attended Youth, the firmest hope of Christianity. Mindful of
and bearing in her heart those famous words of her Lord,
"Permit the little children to come to me,"

(Matth. xix., 14) nullis unquam laboribus pe-
percit, ut tenellum illum hominum florem ab
omni vitiorum afflatu arceret, et ab omni labe
erroris incolumem servaret. Hince sacri Antistites, jam inde ab exordiis Ecclesiae, collatis viribus magis magisque allaborarunt, ut
Christianam Juventutem tum in scholis tum extra
scholas rite erudirent atque pie educarent.
Quam profecto Juventutis institutionem, ut omni
discrimini subducerent, gymnasia circumquaque
excitavere, privilegiis amplissimis auxerunt,
et per varios scholarum gradus ad summum usque
artium atque scientiarum fastigium evehere non
dubitarunt. Ex quibus gymnasiis quot quantaque
beneficia quam uberrimi fructus in civilem so-
cietatem, atque adeo in ipsam Ecclesiam redun-
darint, neminem praeterire arbitramur.
425. Itaque non possunt hujus Plenarii Concilii Patres ultro non agnoscere palamque pro-
fiteri, curam teneriori aetati atque adoles-
centiae Christianis moribus informandae impen-
dendam, inter praecipuas sollicitudinis Pastoralis
partes recenseri; eoque magis, quo hodierni
Religionis nostrae inimici suas omnes artes
conferre connituntur, ut juvenum animos vel a
prima aetate depravent.[1]

---

[1](Translation continued): (Matth. xix., 14) she has
never spared any efforts to guard that delicate flower of man
from every breath of imperfection, and to preserve it safe
from every stain of error. Hence the holy Bishops from the
very beginnings of the Church with concerted efforts have
labored more and more to instruct correctly and to train
religiously Christian youth both inside and outside the
schools. As a matter of fact, they have set up everywhere
institutions to lead the education of youth away from every
hazard, they have strengthened these institutions with very
broad privileges, and they did not hesitate to build them
through the various levels to the highest peak of the arts
and sciences. We feel that no one can ignore the many and
great benefits, the very rich fruits which have redounded
to civil society and to the Church itself from these
schools.
425. Accordingly, the Fathers of this Plenary Council must
recognize and openly profess that the care which is to be
expended in the formation of the younger children and
adolescents in Christian morality, is numbered among the
principal functions of Pastoral care; and this is the more
so, because the current enemies of our religion are striving
to bring all their wiles to bear in order to corrupt the
minds of youth even from their earliest years.

426. Experientia siquidem diuturna satis su-
perque probavit, quam gravia sint mala, quam
intrinseca etiam pericula, quae Juventuti Catholicae ex frequentatione scholarum publicarum
hisce in regionibus plerumque obveniunt. Vi
enim systematis apud illas obtinentis, nequaquam fieri potest quin simul in magnum fidei
morumque discrimen juvenes Catholici adducantur.
Neque alia profecto ex causa repetendi videntur
progressus, quos exitialis illa Indifferentismi,
ut vocant, labes hactenus in hac regione maximos
habuit, habetque in dies; illa quoque morum
corruptela, qua vel tenerrimam apud nos aetatem
passim infici ac perdi non sine lacrymis vide-
mus. Consuetudo enim eorum, qui aut falsam
aut nullam religionem colunt, quotidiana etiam
auctorum lectio et meditatio, qui Sanctissimam
Religionem nostram et instituta, immo coelites
ipsos incessunt, rodunt, nigroque sale adsper-
gunt, paullatim in puerorum Catholicorum animis
vim ac virtutem verae Religionis elevant. Deinde
condiscipuli, quibus utuntur, iis plerumque
sunt moribus et exemplis, ea loquendi agendique
nefaria licentia, ut hoc commercio et usu fami-
liari nostris adolescentibus, (licet domi optime
institutis) pudor omnis ac pietas, quasi cera ad-
moto igne, cito absumatur ac pereat. Neque deces-
sores nostros hujusmodi mala et pericula latuerunt,
ut ex hisce eorum decretis videre est:

---

[1](Translation continued): 426. For daily experience
enough and more than enoght proves how serious are the evils,
how intrinsic are the dangers which more and more come into
the way of Catholic Youth from attendance at public schools
in those areas. It can surely happen by the force of the
system existing among them that often Catholic Youth will
be exposed to great danger to faith and morals. And not
merely for the sake of repetition, we see the strides which
that taint of deadly Indifferentism, as they call it, has
up to this time made and daily continues to make in this
area. We see also the corruption of morals by which we
tearfully notice that even the youngest among us are infected
and destroyed. For the habit of those who foster either a
false religion or none at all, of daily reading and medi-
tating on authors who attack, slander and sprinkle with foul
wit our most Sacred Religion and teachings, yea even the
Saints themselves, gradually weakens in the minds of Catholic
children the force and virtue of true Religion. Their fellow-
students, with whom they are in close association, are by
their habits and examples, by that lawless freedom of speaking
and acting, such that by this close contact and intercourse
with our youngsters, (even though excellently trained at
home), all shame and sense of piety is quickly consumed and
destroyed, just like wax in the presence of fire. The evils
of this kind were not unknown to our predecessors as is clear
from their decrees:

427. Quoniam quamplurimos adolescentes ex
Catholicis parentibus praesertim pauperibus
ortos, in multis provinciae hujus locis exposi-
tos esse, et adhuc exponi constat magno fidei
amittendae periculo, vel morum corruptelae,
ob inopiam talium magistrorum quibus tantum
munus tuto committi possit; necessarium omnino
censemus ut scholae instituantur, in quibus
juvenes edoceantur fidei morumque principia,
dum literis imbuuntur. (Balt., Num. 33).

428. Cum non raro plura reperiantur in libris
qui in scholis plerumque adhibentur, quibus
principia fidei nostrae impugnantur, dogmata
nostra perperam exponuntur, et ipsa historia
pervertitur, qua ratione puerorum animi erroribus imbuuntur, in animarum damnum gravissimum;
postulat tun religionis studium, tum Juventutis recta educatio, et ipsam Foederatae Americae decus, remedium aliquod tanto malo afferri. (Ibid., 34).

429. Cum constet publicae educationis rationem
plerisque in his Provinciis ita iniri, ut hae-
resibus inserviat, puerorum Catholicorum mentibus sensim sine sensu falsis sectarum principiis
imbutis, monemum pastores, ut omni quo valent
studio Catholicorum puerorum Christianae et[1]

---

[1](Translation continued): 427. Since it is evident
that very many of the young, the children of Catholic parents,
especially the poor, have been exposed and are still exposed
in many places of this province, to great danger of the loss
of faith or the corruption of morals, on account of the lack
of such teachers as could safely be entrusted with so great
an office, we judge it absolutely necessary that schools
should be established in which the young may be taught the
principles of faith and morality, while being instructed
in letters. (Balt., No. 33).
428. Since it frequently happens that many things are
found in the books used in most schools by which the principles of our faith are attached, our dogmas explained
falsely and even history perverted, the minds of youth imbued with errors and very grave harm done to their souls,
the zeal for religion, the proper education of youth and
even the glory of the United States demand that some remedy
be offered for such an evil. For this reason we decree
that, as soon as possible, books, completely cleansed of
error, in which nothing is contained which could bring forth
hatred of the faith or ill-feeling, be edited. (Ibid., 34).
429. Since it is clear that the purpose of public education
in very many of these Provinces is so constructed as to
favor heresies, the minds of Catholic children being gradually filled without their knowing it with the false
principles of the sects, we warn the pastors that will all
possible zeal they look after the Christian and Catholic

Catholicae educationi prospiciant, et diligenter
invigilent, ne versione protestantica biblio-
rum utantur, vel sectarum cantica aut preces
recitent. Ideo invigilandum erit, ne in publicas scholas libri vel exercitia hujusmodi
introducantur, cum fidei pietatisque discrimine. Constanter autem et moderate hisce sectarum conatibus ubique resistendem est, eorum
qui auctoritate valent opportunum adhibere
remedium implorato auxilio. (Balt., Num. 54).
430. Optimum vero, immo unicum quod superest
remedium quo gravissimis hisce malis atque
incommodis occurratur, in eo situm videtur,
ut in singulis dioecesibus, unamquamque prope
ecclesiam, Scholae erigantur, in quibus juventus
Catholica tam literis ingenuisque artibus, quam
Religione ac probis moribus imbuatur. Quod jam
a Patribus superioris Concilii Plenarii sapi-
enti consilio provisum fuit:

Hortamur episcopos, et, attentis gravissimis malis quae ex juventute haud rite instituta sequi solent, per viscera misericordiae
Dei obsecramus, ut Scholas unicuique ecclesiae
in eorum dioecesibus annexas instituendas curent;
et si opus fuerit, et rerum adjuncta sinant,[1]

---

[1](Translation continued):   education of the Catholic
young, and that they be alertly watchful so that they do not
use protestant versions of the bible or recite songs or
prayers of the sects. Therefore, they will have to be
vigilant that books or exercises of this kind not be introduced into the public schools, with danger to faith and
piety. Moreover constantly and with moderation they must
everywhere resist these attempts of the sects, imploring
the help of those who have authority to use a fitting
remedy. (Balt., No. 54).
430. It seems that the best, or rather the only, remedy
that remains by which these very serious and troublesome
evils can be met is that in every diocese, next to each
and every church, Schools be erected in which the Catholic
youth may be imbued with literature and the fine arts as
well as with Religion and good morals. This was already
provided for in the wise admonition by the Fathers of
the previous Plenary Council:

We exhort the bishops, and in view of the very great
evils which usually result from the defective education of
youth, we beseech them through the bowels of the mercy of
God to see that schools are established in connection with
the churches of their dioceses; and if it be necessary and

provideant ut ex redditibus ecclesiae cui
Schola annexa sit, idonei magistri in ea
habeantur. (Ibid., 90).
431. Decessorum igitur nostrorum vestigiis
inhaerentes, Pastores animarum vehementer monemus, ut pro viribus operam suam conferant ad
Scholas Parochiales, ubicumque fieri potest,
extruendas. Hisce in Scholis, sub Pastorum
oculis ordinatis, vitabuntur pericula quae
gymnasiis publicis inhaerere jam diximus; de-
fendentur pueri ab illo indifferentismo adeo
nunc grassante; viam Catholicam insistere,
jugumque Domini ab adolescentia portare addi-
scent.
432. Quod ut facilius praestetur, magnopere
commendamus multiplicationem adhibitarum pluribus jam in locis Sodalitatum sive Congregationum
piarum utriusque sexus, quae, juxta peculiaris
sui instituti regulas, pueros puellasque tum
primis literarum ac artium rudimentis imbuere,
tum praesertim coelestis doctrinae pabulo vel
ab ipsis quasi incunabulis reficere et enu-
trire satagant.
433. Quod si ob defectum hujusmodi Sodalitatum, saecularibus hominibus munus instituendae
pueritiae committendum sit, ii tantum ad hoc[1]

[1][Translation continued]: circumstances permit,
to provide, from the revenues of the church to which the
School is attached, for the support of competent teachers. (Ibid., 90).
431 Therefore following the examples of our predece-
sors, we strongly urge the Pastors to apply their efforts
in accord with their resources to construct Parochial
Schools, wherever it can be done. In these Schools, under
the careful scrutiny of the Pastors, shall be avoided the
dangers which we have already said inhere in the public
schools; the children shall be protected from that indifferentism now so rampant; they shall learn to walk in
the Catholic way and to bear the yoke of the Lord from
their youth.
432. That such matters may be more easily accomplished,
we strongly recommend the increase of Pious Societies or
Congregations of both sexes, which are already employed
in several places, which religious according to the regulations of their individual institutes, are busily engaged
in teaching boys and girls the first principles of literature and arts and in restoring and nourishing them, as it
were from their very cradles, with the food of heavenly
doctrine.
433. If because of the lack of Congregations of this kind,
the task of instructing the young must be assigned to lay
teachers, only those should be chosen for this purpose

operis eligantur, qui non tantum scientia prae-
stent, sed, etiam fide, moribus ac vita proba-
tissima inter caeteros emineant. Quod de mu-
lieribus quoque dictum volumus, quibus insti-
tuendarum puellarum cura credatur.
434. In re tanti momenti, serio etiam parentes
monendi sunt, ut proli suae magis magisque
invigilent, et pro recta ejus educatione diligenter consulant ac sedulo laborent; cum suis
Pastoribus pie conspirent, suasque opes generose diffundant, ut Scholae Catholicae Parochiales quantocius erigantur ac sustententur.
435. Cum autem omnibus in paroeciis Scholae
exclusive Catholicae, propter rerum angustias,
nondum haberi queant, et nullibi sit locus pro
institutione quotidiana et necessaria nisi in
gymnasiis publicis, eo magis oportet omnes
cautelas adhibere, ut exinde quam minimum detrimentum juventus Catholica patiatur. Hunc
in finem Catecheses et Scholae doctrinae Christianae instituantur. Pueros puellasque in pro-
priam ecclesiam Dominicis et aliis diebus fes-
tivis, et quandoque etiam seapius, Pastores con-
vocent, ut eos elementa Christianae doctrinae
studiose et diligenter edoceant.[1]

---

[1](Translation continued): who excel not only in
knowledge, but also stand out among the rest in faith,
morals and a most blameless life. The same holds for women
to whom the care of instructing girls is entrusted.
434. In a matter of such great importance, the parents
must also be seriously warned to be more and more watchful
over their children, and carefully to look to and assiduously
work for the proper education of their children; let them
cooperate religiously with their Pastors and generously
spread their efforts so that Catholic Parochial Schools
may as soon as possible be erected and supported.
435. Since however in all parishes exclusively Catholic
schools cannot yet be provided because of financial
reasons, and since there is no other place for the
necessary and daily instruction except in the public schools,
all precautions must be taken so that the Catholic children
suffer in them the least possible harm. Toward this end
Catechetical Instruction and Schools of Christian doctrine
shall be provided. Let the Pastors call together the
boys and girls into their own churches on Sundays and
other feast days, and occasionally even oftener, to
teach them zealously and carefully the elements of Christian
doctrine.

436.   Quod quidem non solum a patribus maxime
commendatum atque usitatum fuit, sed etiam saepius gravissimisque adjectis poenis, praesertim
tribus hisce saeculis, quae disciplinam resti-
tutam subsecuta sunt, plurimorum Pontificum
atque Synodorum legibus constitutum. Inter
praeclaros piissimi hujus moris atque instituti
restitutores ac vindices, eminuit S. Carolus,
Ecclesiae Mediolanensis Antistes, cujus hac in
re labores, consilia, ac praecepta digna sunt,
quae ab omnibus animarum Pastoribus assidue
perlegantur. Ecclesiae igitur monitis ac praeceptis obtemperet animarum moderator; ac sanctorum hominum, immo ipsius Christi Pastoris op-
timi exemplo animatus parvulos, spem commissi
sibi gregis singulari amore prosequatur, summa
cura custodiat, indefessa vigilantia et sollicitudine a luporum ac tartarei praedonis insidiis et incursibus defendat ac tueatur. Pulcher-
rimum illum integritatis et innocentiae florem,
atque ineffabile, quo fruuntur, baptismalis
gratiae donum, sanctum in illis inviolatumque,
quasi oculi sui pupillam, servandum ipse curet.
Eos ita instituat atque assuefaciat, ut Dei de-
mum et atria sancta Ejus libenter frequentent;[1]

---

[1] (Translation continued): 436. This has not
only been especially recommended and followed by the
fathers, but has also been decided by the decrees of many
Popes and by synods, rather frequently with grave penalties
attached, espcially in these three centuries which have
followed the restored discipline. Outstanding among
the famous restorers and protectors of this most pious
custom and undertaking was St. Charles, Bishop of Milan,
whose efforts, plans and precepts in this matter are worthy
of careful reading by all Pastors of souls. Therefore let
the director of souls comply with the admonitions and commands of the Church; and, animated by the example of holy
men, even of Christ himself, the most perfect shepherd,
let him with special love attend to the little children,
the hope of the flock entrusted to him; let him watch over
them with the greatest care, and let him with indefatigable
watchfulness and care defend and protect them from the
snares and attacks of wolves and infernal robbers. Let
him see to it that the most beautiful flower of purity and
innocence and the unspeakable gift of baptismal grace,
which they enjoy, may be preserved in them untouched, as
the apple of his eye. Accordingly let him instruct and
accustom them to visit frequently the house of God and His
sacred dwellings;

ibique congregatos sanctis vitae morumque
praeceptis imbuat. Tenellis adhuc eorum animis
ea instillet fidei ac pietatis rudimenta, quae
postea aetate adultis firmamento ac robori,
tutissimoque contra pravas doemonis ac malorum
hominum insidias praesidio sint futura.
437. Parentes omnibus, quibus poterit, modis
inducat, ut partes suas agant. Eos hortamentis
excitet, minis terrefaciat, precibus exoret,
ut liberos stato catecheseos tempore ad ecclesiam mittant. Hos autem ad alacrius adsistendum
discendumque munusculis et praemiis alliciat.
Quod enim quotidie faciunt haereseos magistri,
ut pueros Catholicos ad suas scholas trahant,
veneno erroris imbuant, atque infortunio mac-
tent sempiterno; id Dei sanctissimaeque nostrae
Religionis minister non studiose ac diligenter
praestabit, ut suos servet, neque ex iis, quos
dedit Christo sui Pater, perdat quemquam?
(Joan. xvii., 12; xviii., 9).
438. Neque hoc muneris per alios, ut negligen-
tiores solent, sed per sese ipse exequatur.
Onus enim pueros Christianae fidei rudimentis
instituendi adeo est cum pastorali officio[1]

---

[1](Translation continued): let him steep them,
gathered together there, in the holy commandments of life
and in morality. In their yet tender souls let him instill
those fundamentals of faith and piety which will later in
adult life be the support and strength, the safest protection against the depraved ambushes of the devil and of
wicked men.
437. Let him induce the parents with every means of
which he is capable to do their parts. Let him stir them
up with exhortations, let him instill fear with threats,
and let him entreat them with prayers to send their children
to Church for catechechical instructions at the proper time.
Moreover, let him entice the children with little presents
and rewards to come more quickly and to learn. Every day
the teachers of heresy do this to draw the Catholic children
to their schools, in order to steep them in the poison of
error and to inflict them with eternal punishment; will not
the minister of God and our most holy Religion carefully
and diligently do the same in order to preserve his own and
not lose any one of those whom the Father has given to his
Anointed One? (John, xvii., 12; xviii., 9).
438. Nor should he accomplish this task through others,
as they are wont to be rather negligent, but he should do
it himself. The burden of instructing the children in the
fundamentals of the Christian faith is so joined to the

conjunctum, ut qui ex ignavia vel desidia id ferre
nolit, aut in alios reliciat, violati officii
poenas vitare nullo modo possit. Quod disertis
verbis omnibus, ad quos spectat, in memoriam
revocatur a Patribus Concilii Plenarii superioris.
(Decr. 89, jam supra cit., in Tit. iii).
439. Dum pueros ad divinarum rerum scientiam
educare studet, omnem in eo operam ponat, ut,
quod in Ecclesia Catholica laudat Augustinus
(S. Aug. de Moribus Eccles. Cath., Lib. i., Cap.
30, Ed. Maur., i. 708), "pueros pueriliter doceat;" ea scilicet facilitate et simplicitate,
quae eorum imbecillitatem et imperitiam deceat.
Altissima fidei mysteria ita explicet, ut eorum
aetati atque ingenio se accommodet. Etiamsi,
quod saepe evenit, adulti haud pauci catechesos
tempore dicentem in templo circumstent, numquam
ipse verbis aut loquendi modis exquisitis et
elegantioribus utatur; sed ea tantum adhibeat,
quae simplicia, clara, et apertissima sint,
quaeque ab omnibus, etiam rudioribus, facile
intelligantur. "Qui docet," monet apposite Augustinus (De Doctrina Christ., Lib. iv., Cap. 9,
§§ 23, 24, ed. cit.,iii, 73), "non curet quanta
eloquentia doceat, sed quanta evidentia.[1]

---

[1](Translation continued): pastoral office that he
who is unwilling from laziness or apathy to carry it out,
or hands it over to others, can in no way avoid the punishments of his violated trust. This is called in very eloquent
words to the attention of those to whom it pertains by
the Fathers of the previous Plenary Council. (Decr. 89,
already cited, in Title iii).
439. While he is striving to train the children in the
knowledge of divine things, let him place great importance
on this point, which Augustine praises in the Catholic
Church, (S. Aug. de Moribus Eccles. Cath., Lib. i., Cap.
30,Ed. Maur., i. 708), that "he teach the children in
a childlike manner;" that is, with that ease and sim-
plicity which suits their lack of knowledge and inex-
perience. He should so explain the deepest mysteries
of the faith that he accommodates himself to their age and
ability. Even if, as often happens, many adults are present
in the Church while he is giving the catechetical instructions, he should never use words or methods of
speaking that are high-flown and lofty, but he should
use only those words and phrases that are simple, clear,
intelligible, and which are understood by all, even the
less cultivated. "He who teaches," St. Augustine aptly
warns, (De Doctrina Christ., Lib. iv., Cap. 9, §§ 23, 24,
ed.cit., iii. 73), "should not be concerned as to how
eloquently he teaches, but how clearly.

Cujus evidentiae diligens appetitus aliquando
negligit verba cultiora, nec curat quid bene
sonet, sed quid bene indicet atque intimet quod
ostendere intendit. * * * * Quid enim prodest lo-
cutionis integritas, quam non sequitur intellec-
tus audientis, cum loquendi omnino nulla sit
causa, si quod loquimur non intelligunt, propter
quos ut intelligant loquimur?"
440. Sedulo laborent animarum Pastores, ut
parentes, qui ipsorum curae concrediti sunt,
liberos suos qui ad annos discretionis perve-
nerint ad Sanctae Eucharistiae et Confirmationis
Sacramenta suscipienda rite paratos adducant;
et ad hunc finem obtinendum, saepius per annum,
praesertim appropinquante Paschali tempore,
populum publice in templis moneant de gravissimo hoc officio, quod qui non servaverint
parentes se maximo salutis amittendae periculo
exponunt, ac proinde a Sacramentis arcendi sunt,
donec resipiscentes officio suo satisfecerint.
(Cf. Conc. Cincinnat. Prov. II., an. 1858,
Decr. 12.).
441. Curent etiam animarum Pastores, ut quotannis
Ordinarios certiores faciant de numero eorum, qui
superiori anno prima vice ad Sacram Synaxim ad-
missi fuerint. (Ibid.).[1]

---

[1](Translation continued): Having cultivated a desire
for this clarity of speech, he sometimes neglects more re-
fined words, and is not concerned with that which sounds
good, but rather with that which properly indicates and
intimates that which he intends to demonstrate. * * * * *
For of what use is a correctness of speech which the in-
telligence of the listener cannot follow, since there is
no reason at all for speaking if those, on whose account
we speak in order that they may comprehend, do not understand that which we say."
440. Let the Pastors of souls see to it with all care,
that the parents who have been entrusted to their charge,
present those children who have reached the age of reason
properly prepared for the reception of the Sacraments of
Holy Communion and Confirmation. To secure this end, let
them rather frequently during the year, especially as the
Easter season approaches, publicly warn them in the Churches
of this very serious duty; those parents who have not fulfilled this duty expose themselves to grave danger of losing
their eternal salvation, and hence they are to be barred
from the reception of the Sacraments until, repentant, they
have fulfilled their obligation. (II Prov. Con. Cin., 1858,
Decree 12.).
441. Let the Pastors of souls see to it that annually they
inform the Ordinaries of the number of those who made their
First Communion during the previous year. (Ibid.).

442. Omnibus animarum curam gerentibus in
Domino injungimus, ut saltem quater unoquoque
anno, et praesertim, si fieri possit, Quatuor
Temporum feriis, pueros omnes spirituali ipsorum
regimini commissos, qui nondum S. Eucharistiae
participes facti sunt, in unum colligant, et
per aliquot dies Doctrinam Christianam diligenter edoceant, Eos, qui ad septennium per-
venerint, ad Confessionem accedere curent; qui
vero id aetatis attigerint, ut Panem coelestem
discernere valeant, ad primam Communionem, omni
adhibita diligentia, disponantur. (Cf. Conc.
Prov. Cincinnat. III., an. 1861, Decr. 2).

CAPUT II. De Scholis Industriae, Seu Reformatoriis
           Constituendis.

443. Perpetuus ille humani generis hostis, qui ab
ipso mundi exordio cum semine mulieris exercet ini-
micitias, Christi corpus, quod est Ecclesia, nequit
quidem violare ac perdere: at calcaneo tamen ejus
insidiatur, et nonnulla saltem membra vulnerare,
et in interitum secum rapere quotidie studet.
Quod eum felici nimis successu agere, non sine
acerbo animi dolore fatere cogimur. Inter alia
vero hujus generis sane luctuosa, quae quotidie
ante oculos obversantur, illud maxime deplorandum[1]

---

[1](Translation continued): 442: We enjoin on all who in
the Lord have the care of souls, that at least four times a year,
and particularly during the Ember Days if that is convenient, that
they gather together all the children entrusted to their
spiritual guidance who have not yet become sharers of the Holy
Eucharist, and for several days carefully instruct them in
Christian Doctrine. They are also to see to it that those who
have reached their seventh year confess their sins; and that
those who have reached the age when they are able to appreciate
the Eucharistic mystery, be with all possible care prepared
for their first holy Communion.

Chapter II: The Establishment of Industrial Schools, or
             Reformatories.

     That never-ending enemy of the human race, who from
the beginning of time exercises enmities with the seed of the
woman, can never, to be sure, injure or destroy the body of
Christ, which is the Church; but he does lie in wait for her
heel, and he daily strives to wound at least

est, quod parvulos nostros, sacro baptismi
fonte renatos, Deoque ob innocentiam et sancti-
tatem acceptissimos, a sinu et complexu Ecclesiae
matris avellit, et ad sua castra transfert, ut
de filiis hostes, de piis sanctisque impios
faciat ac profanos. Atque hoc quidem cum per
se ipse efficere nequaquam possit, nullo negotio
inter mortales invenit, quorum ope et auxilio
efficiat. Adsciscit enim sibi homines aut haeresis
labe infectos, aut religionis omnis osores et
contemptores, quibus in nefario hoc opere sociis
et adjutoribus utatur.
444. Atque hi quidem sunt, qui puellas et pueros
Catholicos, aut parentibus vita functis orbatos
aut a dyscolis derelictos, quasi lupi agnos
nacti, statim arripiunt et in domos Refugii
dictas conjiciunt; ubi, velut in carcere quodam
inclusi, ita caute custodiuntur, ut nec a con-
junctis quidem reperiri et dignosci queant. Quin
et ipsa nomina misellis istis mutantur, ne forte
patriae religionis memoriam aliquando excitare
possint. Aluntur splendide quidem, si prioris
conditionis ratio habeatur; educantur tamen
sedulo ad haeresim, ad avitae fidei odium et
detestationem, ad interitum animae sempiternum.[1]

---

[1](Translation continued): some of the members and to drag
them into ruin with himself. That he does this with too much
success, we are forced to confess with bitter sorrow of
spirit. Among other tragic occurrences of this kind which
are daily brought to our attention, that practice which
snatches our little ones, reborn at the sacred font of baptism,
most acceptable to God because of their innocence and holiness,
from the bosom and embrace of mother Church, and conveys
them to his camp, that he may make enemies of sons, impious
and profane ones of the pious and holy, must be especially
deplored. And since he can in no way accomplish this by
himself he has found with no trouble at all among mortals
those with whose help and assistance he can accomplish this
end. He has taken to himself men either infected with
the stain of heresy or else haters and despisers of all religion, whom he uses as associates and helpers in this
wicked work.
444. These are the officials who, just as the wolves fell
upon the lambs, immediately snatch and cast into homes called
Refuges, those Catholic boys and girls who have lost their
parents by death, or who have been abandoned by cruel parents;
there, as if locked up in jail, they are so closely guarded
that they cannot be found and recognized even by close
friends. On the contrary even the names of these miserable
little ones are changed, lest perchance at some time or other
they might be able to revive the memory of their ancestral
religion. They are well cared for if comparison is made

Atqui haec omnia specioso philanthropiae nomine
geruntur; jamdiu enim apud istos homines obsolevit
praeclarum illud nomen Christianae charitatis.
445. Ad mala haec praecavenda et avertenda, vix
ullum in civitatum legibus praesidium sperari
potest; quinimmo, his saepe improbi homines
ad haec scelera patranda ac tuenda foedissime
abutuntur. Quamobrem nonnulli jam Episcopi,
charitate et misericordia permoti, in suis
dioecesibus pias domos erexerunt, aut jam
erectas in hunc usum converterunt, ut in eas
pueri, quorum religio aut animae salus peri-
clitatur, recipiantur, ut a lupis rapacibus
tuti serventur, et Christianae fidei morumque
principia addiscant. Vocantur idcirco Domus
Refugii seu Protectionis, at frequentius
Scholae Industriae; ibi enim docentur pueri
agriculturam, aut fabriles aliasque vulgares
artes, quibus olim exercendis sibi victum
honeste comparare possint. Appellantur etiam
nonnumquam Scholae seu Domus Reformatoriae;
quoniam in eas aliquando recipiuntur pueri,
qui forte malis parentum ac propinquorum
exemplis aut incuria a recto tramite aberrarunt,
quos tamen tempore et diligenti opera adhibita
emendatum iri sperari merito possit.[1]

---

[1](Translation continued): with their former condition;
but they are carefully educated to heresy, to the hatred and
detestation of their ancestral faith, and to the eternal loss
of their souls. All these things are done under the
specious name of philanthropy; since for quite some time
now that marvelous term, Christian charity, has gone out of
use among men of that type.
445. Little help can be expected from the laws of the states
in averting and preventing these abuses; on the contrary,
depraved men frequently use these laws most detestably to
achieve and maintain these very crimes. Consequently, several
Bishops, moved by charity and mercy, have already erected in
their dioceses pious houses, or they have converted to this
use houses already in existence, so that children, whose
religion or salvation is endangered, might be received into
them, in order that they may be preserved safe from ravenous
wolves and learn therein the principles of Christian faith and
morals. For this reason they are called Houses of Refuge or
Protection, or frequently Industrial Schools; for there the
youngsters are taught agriculture, carpentry and other
useful arts, by means of which they may be able sometime to
earn for themselves an honest living. They are also sometimes called Schools or Houses of Reform, because boys are
occasionally brought into them, who by the bad example or
negligence of parents or relatives have strayed from the

446. Episcopos igitur enixe hortamur, ut omni
qua possint, cura et sollicitudine, tenellos hosce
Christiani gregis agnos ab avidis circumcursantium
luporum faucibus defendant. Pias hujusmodi Industriae seu Refugii Domus ubique constituant;
idque praesertim majores prope urbes, ubi major
est periflitantium numerus. Laudandi quidem
sunt, qui summam in eo industriam ponunt, ut
magnifica e marmore templa ubique in Dei
honorem et cultum extruantur. At longe melior
atque utilior, in his vivis et electis lapidibus
(Miss., in De. Eccles., in Postcomm.) ad
aeternum Divinae Majestatis habitaculum prae-
parandis, labor et cura impenditur.

Caput III.   De Universitate Literarun Fundanda.

447. Praeter plures, quae Dei O. M. beneficio
in hac regione existunt, minores Scholas, in
quibus Religionis ac literarum elementa pueris
traduntur, habentur etiam Scholas majores, seu
Collegia, in quibus, in adultioris aetatis com-
modum, dum literae artesque ingenuae plenius ac
perfectius docentur, Catholicae quoque doctrinae
capita fusius atque uberius explicentur. Quod
quidem maximopere commendandum ducimus; virosque[1]

---

[1](Translation continued):   straight path; given time
and careful assistance, there is hope that they will be
corrected.
446.   Therefore we strongly urge the Bishops to protect
with every care and solicitude of which they are capable
these tender lambs of the flock of Christ from the jaws
of the bloodthirsty wolves who lurk everywhere.   They
are to establish Pious Houses of Work or Refuge everywhere, especially near the larger cities where the danger
is greatest.   To be sure, we must praise those who have
put all their effort into building magnificent temples
of stone for the honor and glory of God; but far greater
and more useful labor is expended in preparing these
living and chosen stones for the eternal dwelling place
of the Divine Majesty.   (Post., Mass of Church Dedication).

Chapter III.   The Founding of a University of Letters.

447.   Besides the many elementary schools which, through
the kindness of Almighty God, already exist in this area,
in which the fundamentals of religion and literature are
taught to youngsters, we must likewise consider higher
schools or Colleges, in which, in accordance with the more
advanced age of the students, the sources of Christian
doctrine are explained more fully and completely, along
with literature and the natural arts.

illos pios et eruditos, qui in hac palaestra
huc usque com laude desudarunt atque elaborarunt,
de Christiana republica optime meritos esse
praedicamus. Quantum enim ab eorum opera
pendeat, is facile intelliget, qui ex hisce
Academiis et Collegiis eos adituros sciat,
qui deinceps Sacrorum ministerio forte se
addicant; qui in foro, in curia, in magistratu
aliquando versentur.
448. Singulari Dei beneficio nobis obtigit,
ut clericorum Collegia non solum domi, sed etiam
in Europa habeamus. Atque ante omnia commemorandum
est Collegium Americanum in Urbe Sancta, omnium
matre atque principe, prope ipsam Apostolicae
veritatis Cathedram constitutum; quod SSmi.
Domini Nostri Pii· PP. IX. paternae munificentiae
acceptum referri debet. Hoc profecto, ut, quotquot sumus hujus regionis Episcopi, tueamur,
foveamus, ornemus, et quantum in nobis est
collatis consiliis opibusque amplificemus,
tum aequitas, tum grati animi officium
postulat. (Vide quae hac super remonet
S. Cong. P. F., in Instructione Generali,
art. 20, supra.)[1]

---

[1](Translation continued): We consider this practice highly
commendable; and we proclaim that those holy and learned
men who have exerted themselves and have labored in this
school with honor are most deserving in the Christian state.
How much depends on their work can easily be understood by
those who know that from these Academies and Colleges will
come forth those who in the future will dedicate themselves
to the Sacred Ministry, and also those who will be actively
engaged in the business world, the courts and in politics.
448. By the singular blessing of God it has been our good
fortune to have a College of Clerics not only here at home
but also in Europe. Above all, we must call to mind the
American College in Rome, the mother and head of all,
established near the very throne of Apostolic truth; this
foundation must be attributed to the paternal generosity
of our most Holy Father, Pope Pius IX. Justice and gratitude
demand, as many bishops as we are in this area, that we
protect, cherish, adorn and, as far as possible, even enlarge
it. (Cf. the remarks of the Sacred Congregation of the Propagation
of the Faith in their General Instruction, quoted above.)

449. Commemorari quoque debet Collegium alterum pro nostrae regionis Missionariis, prope
celeberrimum illud literarum scientiarumque
domicilium, Universitatem Lovaniensem, ab
Episcopis Belgii constitutum. Cujus jam
fructus plurimos ac saluberrimos percepimus.
Novennio enim, ex quo fundatum est, plusquam
quinquaginta Missionarios ad nos misit, qui
in Vinea Domini excolenda laborarent.
450. Neque ultimo loco praetereundum est
Collegium Omnium Sanctorum, viginti fere ante
annis, Drumcondrae prope Dublinium in Hibernia
erectum. Cujus Collegii praesidibus et doc-
toribus gratias et habemus, et hanc nacti occasi-
onem palam agimus maximas, eo quod pro nostris
dioecesibus haud paucos sacerdotes maxima bene-
volentia et liberalitate educarint.
451. Atque utinam in hac regione Collegium unum
maximum, sive Universitatem habere liceret, quod
Collegiorum horum omnium, sive domesticorum sive
exterorum, commoda atque utilitates complecteretur;
in quo, scilicet, literae et scientiae omnes, tam
sacrae quam profanae traderentur! Utrum vero
Universitatis hujusmodi constituendae tempus
advenerit, necne, Patrum judicio, rem totam
maturius posthac perpendentibus, relinquimus.[1]

---

[1]Concilii Plenarii Baltimorensis II., pp. 218-228.
(Translation continued): We must also mention the other College
for Missionaries of our area, founded by the Bishops of Belgium,
near that famous house of letters and science, the University
of Louvain. We have already received its many and salutary
fruits, for in the nine years since its foundation it has
sent more than fifty Missionaries into the Vineyard of the
Lords.
450. Finally, we must not pass over the College of All
Saints. It was erected nearly twenty years ago at Drumcondra,
near Dublin, in Ireland. We owe a great debt of gratitude
to the presidents and teachers of this School, and on this
occasion we openly thank them for having with the greatest
generosity and kindness educated many priests for our
dioceses.
451. And would that we might have in this area one really
great College or University, which would embrace the advantages and conveniences of all these Colleges, whether
at home or abroad, in which all the letters and sciences,
both sacred and profance, might be taught. Whether the time
has arrived for establishing a University of this kind or
not, we leave to the judgment of the Fathers, who will
examine the whole problem in the future.

APPENDIX II

III Plenary Council Decrees

Titulus VI: De Catholica Juventutis Institutione

Caput I: De Scholis Catholicis, Praesertim De
                 Parochialibus

#1   De Summa earum necessitate

194. Si ullo unquam tempore, certo hac nostra
aetate Ecclesia Dei et spiritus saeculi de
educatione juventutis mirando quodam et acer-
rimo conflixere duello. Homines enim spiritu
mundano penitus imbuti, jam multis ab annis,
nullum non movent lapidem, ut Ecclesiae quod
ipsa a Christo accepit (Matth. xxviii. 19.;
Marc. x, 14) Catholicam juventutem docendi
munus eripiant, et in manus societatis civilis
tradant vel subdant gubernii saecularis potes-
tati. Nec mirum hoc. Ex quo enim nequissimi
illi spiritus indifferentismi, naturalismi et
materialismi multorum animos ita invaserunt,
ut finem ac felicitatem hominis non nisi in
hac vita temporali et mundo materiali quaeri
et inveniri posse somnientur; ea sane educa-[1]

---

[1]Translation:

Title VI: On the Catholic Instruction of Youth

Chap. I: On Catholic Schools, Especially Parochia Schools

#1:   On their absolute necessity

194. If ever in any age, then surely in this our age, the
Church of God and the spirit of the world are in a certain
wondrous and bitter conflict over the education of youth.
Men, completely imbued with the spirit of the world, have
for many years left no stone unturned in order to snatch
away that which the Church received from Christ (Matt. 28,
19; Mark 10, 14); that is, the duty of teaching Catholic
youth, and to turn this duty over into the hands of civil
society or to subject it to the power of secular rule. Nor
is this any wonder. For those most ruinous movements of
indifferentism, naturalism and materialism have so invaded
the minds of many that they foolishly imagine that the
goal and happiness of man cannot be sought or found except
in this passing life and material world;

tionis ratio, quae hominem etiam ac praecipue
ad vitam futuram et beatitudinem aeternam eri-
gere et dirigere intendit, aliis quidem stulta
et inutilis, aliis vero vel perniciosa et abol-
ends esse videatur necesse est. Ecclesia autem,
cujus haec potissimum est missio super terram,
ut singulos homines, in baptismate Christo
renatos, jam a primo rationis usu in viis veritatis et justitiae ad finem supernaturalem
adducat, nequaquam sinere potest, ut parentes
Catholici quorum tum jus tum officium naturale
et divinum est Christianae filiorum suorum
educationi consulere, educationem mere saecularem ipsis procurent, quippe quae eis media
ad ultimum finem suum cognoscendum et assequen-
dum necessaria suppeditare minime possit.
195. Inter eos, qui hanc educationem mere saecularem strenue advocant, non pauci quidem
inveniuntur, qui nec religioni ullam damnum
afferre, nec juventuti pericula parare velint.
Attamen ex ipsa rei natura sequitur, et tris-
tissima etiam experientia comprobatur, educationem mere saecularem paulatim ita degenerare,
ut fiat irreligiosa et impia, adolescentium
fidei et moribus maxime perniciosa. Si enim
juxta verba Christi: "Nemo potest duobus[1]

---

[1](Translation continued):   consequently, that
principle of education which intends to arouse and direct
man particularly to his future life and eternal happiness
must necessarily seem to some foolish and useless, and
to others, ruinous and something to be destroyed. The
Church, whose primary mission here on earth is to lead
each man, reborn in the baptism of Christ, from the very
first awakenings of reason to his supernatural end along
the paths of truth and justice, cannot in any way allow
Catholic parents whose right and natural and divine duty
it is to look to the Christian education of their children,
to obtain a merely secular education for them. Secular
education cannot furnish the necessary means for the
recognition and attainment of their final end.
195. Among those who strongly advocate this merely
secular education are many who wish neither to bring any
harm to religion nor to afford dangers to young people.
From the very nature of the case, however, it follows that
a merely secular education gradually breaks down so that it
becomes irreligious and wicked, and especially dangerous
to the faith and morals of the young. This point has been
demonstrated from sad experience. For if according to the
words of Christ: "No one can serve two masters;

dominis servire: aut enim unum odio habebit,
et alterum diliget; aut unum sustinebit, et
alterum contemnet" (Matth. vi. 24); si porro,
juxta aliud ejusdem divinae Sapientiae oracu-
lum, "Qui non est mecum, contra me est" (Luc.
xi. 23); si denique Christus passim docet spir-
itum mundi odio quodam implacabili asseclas
suos adimplere contra eos, qui Spiritu Dei
aguntur; vix potest, non fieri, ut juvenes
spiritu saeculari a pueritia imbuti, non tantum
obcaecati mundi amatores, sed eo ipso etiam
contemptores Christi et adversarii Ecclesiae
sensim sine sensu plerumque evadant. Claris-
simis a tem tam hostium quam domesticorum fidei
testimoniis docemur numerum eorum, qui ob hanc
inter alias principalem causam, quod educatione
mere saeculari instituti fuerint, ab Ecclesia
defecerunt, tam ingentem esse, ut inimicis
quidem gaudendi, nobis autem dolendi locum ac
rationem nimis abundanter praebeat.
196. Itaque parentes Catholicos non solum paterno amore hortamur, sed iis etiam omni qua
valemus auctoritate praecipimus, ut dilectissi-
mae proli suae, a Deo sibi datae, Christo in
baptismate renatae, et coelo destinatae, educationem vere Christianam et Catholicam procurent
eamque totam ac toto infantiae et pueritiae
tempore a periculis educationis mere saecularis defendant et in tuto collocent;[1]

---

[1](Translation continued): for either he will hate
the one and love the other; or else he will stand by the one
and despise the other" (Matth. vi. 24); if further, according
to the other utterance of the same Divine Wisdom, "He who
is not with me is against me" (Luc. xi. 23); if, finally,
Christ in various places teaches that the spirit of the
world fills its followers with a certain inexorable hatred
of those who are led by the Spirit of God' it can hardly
fail to happen that the young, steeped in the secular spirit
from childhood, generally become by degrees and without
their being aware of it not only lovers of the blind world,
but by that very fact also haters of Christ and opponents of
the Church. We are taught by the clearest testimony of as it
were household enemies that the number of those who have de-
fected from the Church chiefly for this reason, among others,
that they have been instructed in a merely secular education,
is so great that only too abundant an opportunity and basis
for rejoicing is given to the enemy, but for us only occasion for sorrow.
196. And so we exhort Catholic parents not only because of
our paternal love but we also admonish them with all the authority of which we are capable, to provide for that most beloved
offspring given them by God, reborn to Christ in Baptism, and
destined for heaven, a truly Christian and Catholic education, and to defend their children completely during the entire time of their infancy and childhood from the dangers of
a purely secular education, and to place it in safe hands;

atque ideo eam in scholas parochiales vel alias
vere Catholicas mittant, nisi forte Ordinarius
in casu particulari aliud permitti posse judicet.
197. Has quidem esse scholas in quibus parentes
permulti saltem si non omnes et jure suo utentes
et officio obsequentes, Christianam prolis suae
educationem quaerere debeant et invenire possint,
jam Patres Conc. Plen. Balt. I. lucidis verbis
statuerunt. Decreto enim XIII. dicunt: "Hortamur Episcopos, et attentis gravissimis malis
quae ex juventute haud rite instituta sequi
solent, per viscera misericordiae Dei obsecramus,
ut scholas uniquique ecclesiae in eorum dioecesibus annexas instituendas curent; et si opus
fuerit et rerum adjuncta sinant, provideant ut
redditibus ecclesiae cui schola annexa sit, idonei
magistri in ea habeantur." Patres vero Conc. Plen.
Balt. II., No. 430, docuerunt: "Optimum vero,
immo unicum quod superest medium, quo gravissimis
hisce malis atque incommodis [scilicet exitiali
indifferentismi labi et morum corruptelae (No.
426) summo cum dolore deploratis] occurratur, in
eo situm videtur, ut in singulis dioecesibus,
unamquamque prope ecclesiam scholae erigantur in
quibus juventus Catholica tam literis ingenuisque artibus quam religione ac probis moribus
imbuatur."[1]

---

[1](Translation continued): Let them, therefore, send
their children to parochial or other truly Catholic schools,
unless perhaps the Ordinary, in a particular instance, judges
that other arrangements can be tolerated.
197. That these are the schools in which at least very many
if not all parents, using their own rights and following
their duty, must seek and find a Christian education for
their children was already decided by the Fathers of the
1st Plenary Council of Baltimore in clear fashion. In Decree 13 they say: "We exhort the Bishops, and in view of
the very grave evils which usually result from the defective
education of youth, we beseech them through the bowels of the
mercy of God to see that schools are established in connection with the churches of their dioceses; and if it be
necessary and circumstances permit, to provide from the
revenues of the church to which the school is attached,
for the support of competent teachers." In addition, the
Fathers of the Second Plenary Council of Baltimore, no.
430, stated: "It seems that the best, or rather the only,
remedy that remains by which these very serious and troublesome evils [that is, the deadly blight of indifferentism
and the corruption of morals (no. 426) both of which are
deeply deplored] can be met is that in every diocese, next
to each and every church, schools be erected in which the
Catholic youth may be imbued with literature and the fine
arts as well as with religion and good morals.

Sacra etiam Congregatio de Propaganda Fide,
die 24 Nov. 1875, ad Episcopos nostros instruc-
tionem S. Cong. Sancti Officii misit, (Vide in
Appendice, p. 279) quo Sacrorum Antistites monen-
tur, quacumque possint ope atque opera commissum
sibi gregem ab educatione mere saeculari arcere.
Esse "autem ad hoc omnium consensu nil tam
necessarium, quam ut Catholici ubique locorum
proprias sibi scholas habeant, easque publicis
haud inferiores. Scholis ergo Catholicis sive
condendis ubi defuerint, sive amplificandis
et perfectius instruendis parandisque, ut institutione ac disciplina scholas publicas adae-
quent omni cura prospiciendum" esse.
    Denique in medium proferre juvat Epistolam
Encyclicam Leonis PP. XIII. ad Episcopos Galliae
diei 8. Febr. hujus anni 1884, qua necessitas
educationis Christianae in scholis Catholicis
tam moderatissimis verbis quam solidissimis
rationibus a summa auctoritate docetur. "Interest quam maxime suscentam e coniugio Chris-
tiano sobolem mature ad religionis praecepta
erudiri et eas artes quibus aetas puerilis ad
humanitatem informari solet cum institutione
religiosa esse conjunctas. Alteras sejungere
ab altera idem est ac reipsa velle ut animi
pueriles in officiis erga Deum in neutram partem[1]

[1](Translation continued): The Sacred Congregation of the
Propagation of the Faith, on the 24th of Nov., 1875, sent to our
Bishops an instruction of the S. Cong. of the Holy Office in
which the Bishops are advised to protect the flock entrusted
to them from a merely secular education with whatever power and
effort they can. (They warned them) that "there is
nothing according to common consent more necessary than that
Catholics everywhere have their own schools, and that these
be by no means inferior to the public schools. Therefore they must with all care look either to the establishment
of Catholic schools where they are lacking, or to their enlargement and more perfect equipping and furnishing, so that they may
be equal to the public schools in instruction and discipline."
    Finally, it helps to bring to mind the Encyclical letter
of Pope Leo XIII to the Bishops of France on the 8th of Feb. of
this year, 1884, in which the necessity of Christian education in
Catholic schools is taught by that highest authority in very restrained words as well as with most basic reasons. "It is
important that the offspring of a Christian marriage as much as
possible be exposed early in life to the precepts of religion and
that those arts by which little children are accustomed to be
fashioned in the humanities be connected with religious instruction.
To separate the one from the other is the same as to wish that the
young minds might be moved in their duties toward God in neither direction:

moveantur: quae disciplina fallax est, et
praesertim in primis puerorum aetatulis per-
niciosissima, quod revera viam atheismi minit,
religionis obsepit. Omnino parentes bonos
curare oportet, ut sui cujusque liberi cum
primum sapere didicerunt, praecepta religionis
percipiant, et ne quid occurrat in scholis
quod fidei morumve integritatem offendat. Et
ut ista in instituenda sobole diligentia ad-
hibeatur, divina est naturalique lege constitutum, neque parentes per ullam causam solvi
ea lege possunt. Ecclesia vero, integritatis
fidei custos et vindex quae delata sibi a Deo
conditore suo auctoritate debet ad sapientiam
Christianam universas vocare gentes, itemque
sedulo videre quibus excolatur praeceptis in-
stitutisque juventus quae in ipsius potestate
sit, semper scholas quas appellant mixtas vel
neutras aperte damnavit, monitis etiam atque
etiam patribusfamilias, ut in re tanti momenti
animum attenderent ad cavendum. Quibus in
rebus parendo Ecclesiae, simul utilitati
paretur, optimaque ratione rei publicae con-
sulitur. Etenim quorum prima aetas ad religionem
erudita non est, sine ulla cognitione adolescunt
rerum maximarum quae in hominibus alere virtutum[1]

---

[1] (Translation continued): This teaching is false and is
especially destructive in the earliest ages of the children, because
by truly building the road of aetheism, it renders inacces-
sible that of religion. Good parents must by all means see to it
that each and every one of their children, as soon as they are able
to reason, learn the precepts of religion, and see to it
that nothing happens in the schools that offends the integrity
of faith or morals. That such care should be shown in the instruction of the children, has been established by divine and natural law,
nor can parents for any reason be relieved of this duty. Indeed,
the Church, the guardian and protector of the integrity of the
Faith which by the authority given it by God, its founder, must
call all nations to Christian wisdom, and likewise must carefully
see to it that the young who are in her power are ennobled by these
precepts and instructions, has always openly condemned the schools
which are called mixed or neutral. The heads of families
have time and time again been warned that in a matter of such
great importance they should take special care to be on guard.
By obeying the Church in these matters, usefulness is served and
for the loftiest reason consideration is had for the common good,
for those whose earliest years have not been enriched in matters
of religion, grow to adolescence without any knowledge of the most
important things which in men can nourish zeal for virtue and can
alone curb the appetites opposed to reason.

studia et appetitus regere rationi contrarios
solae possunt. Cujusmodi illae sunt de Deo
Creatore notiones, de Deo judice et vindice,
de praemiis poenisque alterius vitae expec-
tandis, de praesidiis coelestibus per Jesum
Christum Allatis ad illa ipsa officia diligenter sancteque servanda. His non cognitis,
mala sane omnis futura est animarum cultura:
insueti ad verecundiam Dei adolescentes nullam
ferre possunt honeste vivendi disciplinam,
suisque cupiditatibus nihil unquam negare ausi,
facile ad miscendas civitates pertrahentur."
198. Attamen quamvis necessitas et obligatio
juventutem Catholicam in scholis Catholicis
instituendi ex dictis luce clarius eluceat,
aliquando contingere potest -- sicut etiam instructio modo laudata innuit -- "ut parentes Catholici
prolem suam scholis publicis committere in
conscientia possint. Id autem non poterunt,
nisi ad sic agendum sufficientem causam habeant, ac talis causa sufficiens in casu aliquo
particulari utrum adsit necne, id conscientiae
ac judicio Ordinariorum relinquendum erit; et[1]

---

[1](Translation continued); Of this latter kind are those
notions of God the Creator, of God the judge and avenger, of the rewards and punishments to be expected in the other life, of the
heavenly aids brought through Jesus Christ for preserving carefully and with holiness those very obligations. If these are
not known, then the cultivation of souls will be completely
evil: unaccustomed to respect for God, the adolescents cannot
stand any training for an honorable life, and never having dared
to deny any of their desires, they will easily be induced to
confound states."
    198. Although from what has been said, the
necessity and obligation of instructing Catholic youth in
Catholic schools is clearer than light, it can sometimes happen -- just as the instruction just praised intimated -- "that
Catholic parents can in conscience commit their children to
public schools. They cannot do this, however, unless they have sufficient reason for so acting. Whether
such a sufficient reason in any particular instance is present
or not, will have to be left to the conscience and judgment
of the Ordinary;

tunc ea plerumque aderit quando vel nulla
praesto est schola Catholica vel quae suppe-
tit parum est idonea erudiendis convenienter
conditioni suae congruenterque adolescentibus.
Tunc autem ut scholae publicae in conscientia
adiri possint, periculum perversionis cum pro-
pria ipsarum ratione plus minusve nunquam non
conjunctum opportunis remediis cautionibusque
fieri debet ex proximo remotum."

Cum igitur ob causam sufficientem et ab
Ordinario probatam, parentes ad scholas publicas filios mittere velint, dummodo necessariis
cautionibus proxima pericula removeantur, stricte praecipimus ne quis sive Episcopus sive
presbyter, quod Pontifex per Sacram Congregationem diserte vetat, hujusmodi parentes a
sacramentis quasi indignos sive intentis minis
sive actu ipso repellere audeat. Quod multo
magis de pueris ipsis intelligendum est. Quare
pastores animarum dum fideles sibi commissos
de scholarum harum periculis monent, summopere
caveant ne immodico zelo ducti sapientissima
Sanctae Sedis consilia et praecepta verbis aut
factis violare videantur.[1]

---

[1](Translation continued): this reason will generally
be present when that which is at hand is ill-suited for properly
or suitably instructing the youths in accord with their development. Before they can in conscience enter the public schools, fitting
remedies and precautions must be taken to render remote the proximate danger of perversion which is more or less always connected
with the very nature of such schools."

Since therefore for a sufficient reason, approved by
the Bishop, parents may wish to send their children to public
schools, provided that the immediate dangers are removed by
the necessary precautions, we strictly enjoin that no one whether Bishop or priest, because the Pope through the Sacred Congregation clearly forbids it, dare keep from the Sacraments
by rigorous threats or action parents of this kind as though
unworthy. This is much more the case in regard to the children
themselves. Wherefore, let pastors of souls be exceedingly cautious
while they warn the faithful committed to their care of the
dangers of these schools, lest, influenced by excessive zeal,
they seem by words or deeds to violate the very wise counsels
and commands of the Holy See.

199. Quibus omnibus bene perpensis statuimus
et decernimus:
    I. Prope unamquamque ecclesiam ubi nondum
existit, scholam parochialem intra duos annos
a promulgatione hujus Concilii erigendam et
in perpetuum sustentandam esse, nisi Episcopus
ob graviores difficultates dilationem conce-
dendam esse judicet.
    II. Sacerdotem, qui intra hoc tempus
erectionem vel sustentationem scholae gravi
sua negligentia impediat, vel post repetitas
Episcopi admonitiones non curet, mereri remo-
tionem ab illa ecclesia.
    III. Missionem vel paroeciam quae sacer-
dotem in erigenda vel sustentanda schola ad-
juvare ita negligat, ut ob hanc supinam neg-
ligentiam schola existere non possit, ab
Episcopo esse reprehendendam ac quibus effi-
cacioribus et prudentioribus modis potest, in-
ducendam ad necessaria subsidia conferenda.
    IV. Omnes parentes Catholicos prolem suam
ad scholas parochiales mittere teneri, nisi
vel domi vel in aliis scholis Catholicis Christianae filiorum suorum educationi sufficienter
et evidenter consulant, aut ob causam sufficientem, ab Episcopo approbatam, et cum opportunis[1]

---

[1](Translation continued): Having carefully in-
vestigated all these matters, we decide and decree:
    I. Near each church, where it does not exist,
a parochial school is to be erected within two years from the
promulgation of this Council, and is to be maintained in perpetuum, unless the Bishop, on account of grave difficulties,
judges that a postponement may be allowed.
    II. A priest who, by his grave negligence, prevents
the erection of a school within this time, or its maintenance, or who, after repeated admonitions of the Bishop,
does not attend to the matter, deserves removal from that
church.
    III. A mission or a parish which so neglects to assist
a priest in erecting or maintaining a school, that by reason
of this supine negligence the school is rendered impossible,
should be reprehended by the Bishop and, by the most effi-
cacious and prudent means possible, be induced to contribute
the necessary support.
    IV. All Catholic parents are bound to send their
children to the parochial schools, unless either at home or
in other Catholic schools they may be sufficiently and evidently certain of the Christian education of their children,
or unless it be lawful to send them to other schools on
account of a sufficient cause, approved by the Bishop, and
with opportune cautions and remedies.

cautionibus remediisque eos ad alias scholas
mittere ipsis liceat. Quaenam autem sit
scholas Catholica Ordinarii judicio definiendum relinquitur.

§ 2. De viis ac mediis Scholas Parochiales
quam maxime Promovendi.

200. Si ex una parte conscientias sacerdotum,
fidelium atque imprimis parentum Catholicorum
strictissime in Domino decretis supra datis
oneramus, ex altera parte hoc etiam Nostrum
esse et intimis cordibus sentimus et expressis
verbis profitemur, scilicet pro viribus nostris providere et efficere, ut parentes Catholici non scholas qualescunque, sed bonas et
efficaces "publicis scholis," ut instructio
S. Congregationis monet, "haud inferiores" pro
prole sua invenire possint. Itaque aliqua media proponere ac mandare placet, quibus adhibitis scholae parochiales ad eum utilitatis
et perfectionis gradum eleventur, quem tum
honor Ecclesiae, tum salus non solum aeterna
sed etiam temporalis puerorum, tum denique
generosa parentum devotio pleno jure postulant
ac merentur. Haec autem media ea praecipue
esse videntur, quibus efficiatur ut tum sacerdotes, tum laici, tum denique ludimagistri of-[1]

---

[1](Translation continued): As to what is a Catholic school,
it is left to the judgement of the Ordinary to define.

§ 2. Concerning the ways and means of improving the
parochial schools.

200. If on the one hand we, in the Lord, by the decrees given above place a very strict burden on the consciences
of priests, faithful and especially Catholic parents, on the
other hand, we feel in our inmost hearts and profess with
unmistakable words that this also is our duty, that in accord
with our strength we see to it and effect that Catholic parents can find for their children not just any schools, but
good and efficient ones by no means, as the Sacred Congregation
warns, inferior to the public schools. And so we are pleased
to propose and command some means by which the parochial
schools can be raised to that level of usefulness and perfection which both the honor of the Church and not only the
eternal but also the temporal salvation of the children, and,
finally, the wholehearted devotion of the parents in full accord
with the law, demand and deserve. However these means seem to
be principally those by which it is made possible that priests,
laity and the teachers best understand and most faithfully
fulfill their duties toward the schools.

ficia sua erga scholas et optime intelligant
et fidelissime adimpleant.
201. Et primo ad sacerdotes quod spectat, statuimus ut jam in seminariis candidati S. Theologiae sedulo edoceantur, unum ex praecipuis
sacerdotum officiis, praesertim hisce nostris
temporibus, esse Christianam juventutis institutionem, eamque sine scholis sive parochialibus sive aliis vere Catholicis non esse possi-
bilem. Itaque in studiis psychologiae, peda-
gogiae et theologiae pastoralis relatio specialis
habeatur ad puerorum institutionem. Alumni
etiam modum et methodum addiscant, qua catechismum et historiam sacram pueris lucide et solide
explicare valeant.
   Sacerdotes vero in cura animarum saepe
saepius de gravissimo suo erga scholas officio
in colloquiis et collationibus cum fratribus
consilia conferant. Scholas suas sicut pupil-
las oculorum suorum diligant, eas frequenter,
unamquamque partem earum semel saltem in heb-
domade invisant et inspiciant, puerorum moribus
invigilent, zelum eorum congruis mediis stimu-
lent, catechismum et historiam sacram ipsi per
se doceant, aut certe ut a magistris sodalibus
congregationum rite doceatur, efficiant;[1]

[1](Translation continued): First with regard to that which
pertains to the priests, we have decided that already in the seminaries the candidates for Sacred Theology should be zealously
taught that one of the principal duties of priests especially in
these our times, is the Christian instruction of youth, and that
this is not possible without schools whether parochial or other
truly Catholic schools. And so in the studies of psychology,
pedagogy and pastoral theology, special direction is to be given
to the instruction of children. Likewise let the students learn
the manner and method by which they can explain to the children
clearly and solidly the catechism and sacred history.
   Priests entrusted with the care of souls should rather
frequently compare ideas concerning their very serious duty
toward the schools in talks and meetings with their associates.
Let them cherish their schools as the apple of their eyes,
let them visit and look into them frequently, every part of them
at least once a week; let them watch over the morals of the
children, stir up their zeal with appropriate means. They themselves should teach catechism and sacred history, or certainly
see to it that they are correctly taught by teachers who are
members of a congregation;

ceteris studiis autem attentos oculos adver-
tant, examinationibus publicis semel vel etiam
bis in anno scholas suas notitiae fidelium
subjiciant ac favori commendent. Operam dent
ut in scholis adhibeantur semper libri a Catholicis scriptoribus concinnati. Sanctis motivis
ducti haec omnia curent, insuper scientes non
fore, ut ad rectoratum inamovibilem vel aliud
munus promoveantur, si partes suas ergo scholas
adimplere neglexerint.
202. Ad laicos quod attinet, hortamur et mandamus ut illorum mentes et ab Episcopo et a
sacerdotibus ita instruantur, ut scholam parochialem quasi partem essentialem parochiae habere assuescant, sine qua vel ipsa parochiae
in futuro existentia periclitetur. Plane igitur
et solide doceantur scholam minime esse opus
quoddam supererogatorium a sacerdote sive ad
zelum suum superabundantem probandum, sive
saltem ad tempus jucunde et honeste terendum
sibi ipsi electum, sed onus et officium ab Ecclesia sacerdoti impositum et ab eo religiose
exequendum, sed non sine adjutorio laicorum.[1]

---

[1](Translation continued): in addition, let them turn
their attention to the other branches of knowledge; let them
submit their schools to the attention of the faithful by
public examinations once or even twice a year, and let them
recommend these schools for approval. They are to do their
utmost to see to it that only books prepared by Catholic
writers are used in the schools. Inspired by holy motives,
let them be solicitous for all these things; in addition,
let them be aware that they will not be promoted to irre-
movable pastorates or other offices if they have neglected
their duties toward the schools.
202. As to the laity, we exhort and command that they
be so instructed by the Bishop and by the priests so that
they regard the parish school as an essential part of the
parish, without which the very existence of the parish in
the future will be threatened. Let them, therefore, be
taught clearly and convincingly that the school is by no
means a work of supererogation, taken up as an outlet for
the superabundant zeal of the priest, or as a pleasant and
proper occupation, but that it is a burden and a duty laid
upon the priest by the Church; a duty which is to be faithfully taken up by him and carried by him, but not without the
aid of the laity.

305

Nec minori zelo ac prudentia e mentibus laicorum
erronea illa opinio eradicetur qua opinantur,
curam scholae ad illam tantum paroeciae partem
pertinere, quae directe et actualiter ea pro sua
prole utatur, imo vero obviis argumentis ipsis
demonstretur, fructus et benedictiones quae ex
fide moribusque in scholis parochialibus conser-
vatis derivantur, in bonum totius communitatis
redundare. Quibus omnibus efficietur, ut laici
ad paroeciam pertinentes post ecclesiam parochialem
nullum alium locum in majori pretio habeant ac
majori sollicitudine prosequantur, quam scholam
parochialem, tamquam fidei morumque conserva-
torium ac juventutis, quae omnibus gaudio et
solatio future sit, seminarium.

Laici competentem et generosam sustentationem
scholis suppeditent. Itaque unitis viribus stu-
defunt, ut parochiae sumptibus et expensis pro
scholis incurrendis semper pares sint. Commone-
fiant fideles "sive pastoralibus litteris sive
concionibus sive privatis colloquiis, * * sese officio suo graviter defuturos, nisi omni qua possunt cura impensaque scholis Catholicis providerint.
De quo potissimum monendi erunt quotquot inter
Catholicos ceteris praestant divitiis ac auctoritate apud populum." (Instr. S. C.) Parentes[1]

---

[1](Translation continued): Let no less zeal and prudence be employed in rooting out the false idea that only
those whose children attend the school have a stake in it'
rather let the clergy show, as they easily can, that the
benefits to faith and morals which result from the parish
schools redound to the good of the whole community. After
the church, let the faithful assign the place of honor to
the school as a most powerful factor in the preservation of
faith and morals, and as the nursery of youth, destined
to prove later to us all a source of joy and consolation.

The laity are to give adequate and generous support
to the schools. And so with united strength, they will be
zealous in seeing to it that the parishes shall be equal
to the costs and expenses of these schools. Let the faithful
be reminded "whether through pastoral letters or sermons or
private discussions, * * that they will seriously fail in
their duty unless with all care they provide for the upkeep
of Catholic schools. Those among the Catholics who sur-
pass the others in wealth and influence have particularly
to be reminded of this duty." (Instr. S. C.).

igitur pro rerum facultate parvulam illam
mensilem contributionem, quae pro singulis
pueris exigi solet prompte et libenter sol-
vant. Cetera autem parochiae membra redditus
ecclesiae, in quantum pro scholarum sustenta-
tione opportunum vel necessarium sit, creare
et augere ne renuant. Omnes vero, sive parentes, sive alia familiarum capita, sive juvenes,
suis propriis opibus praediti, parati sint
nomina dare alicui societati pro unaquaque
paroecia maxime commendandae, in plures jam
introductae et ab ipso Summo Pontifice jamjam
uberrime benedictae,in qua, quamvis modicis,
regularibus tamen contributionibus scholas
adjuvent, easque, si non omnino, saltem in
partem gratuitas (free schools) reddant. Opibus autem ad hunc sanctissimum finem generose
ab omnibus collatis, hoc etiam efficietur, ut
externus scholarum splendor et internum earum
ornamentum crescere, numerus magistrorum com-
mode augeri, scholares in classes minus nume-
rosas dividi singulaeque classes aptius inter
se distingui et secundum gradus disponi possint;[1]

---

[1](Translation continued): Therefore, in accordance with
their means, parents are to pay promptly and freely that
small monthly contribution which is customarily demanded for
each child. However, the rest of the members of the parish
are not to refuse to produce and increase the revenues of the
Church insofar as is fitting or necessary for the support
of the schools. Let everyone whether parents, or other
heads of families, or the young who have their own source of
income, be prepared to join some society especially recommended for each parish, particularly one already introduced
and very richly blessed by the Holy Father himself, in which
they might render help to the schools with modest but regular
contributions and make these schools if not completely, at least
partially, free schools. With the resources generously gathered
by all for this very sacred purpose, this also will be effected,
that the external glory of the schools and their internal
luster will be enabled to grow, the number of teachers can
be increased, the pupils can be divided into less crowded classes
and the individual classes can be more suitably distinguished
from one another and distributed according to grades;

quae omnia mirum in modum cooperabuntur, ut
scholae nostrae ad altiorem perfectionis gradum
promoveantur.

Laicis etiam jura quaedam et privilegia
per statuta dioecesana accuratius definienda,
quoad scholas concedantur; salvis juribus ec-
clesiasticis quoad magistros instituendos vel
dimittendos, necnon quoad disciplinam, et di-
rectionem doctrinae.

203. Quoniam vero status et incrementum scholarum nostrarum maxime ab idoneitate magistrorum dependet, summa cura in eo ponenda est,
ut non nisi boni et idonei praeceptores iis
praeficiantur. Itaque statuimus ac mandamus,
ut nemo ad munus docendi in schola parochiali
in futuro admittatur, nisi qui praevio examine
se habilem et idoneum probaverit.

Episcopi igitur intra annum a promulgatione Concilii unum vel plures sacerdotes rerum
ad scholas pertinentium peritissimos nomina-
bunt, qui "Dioecesanam Commissionem Examina-
tionis" constituent. Nominabuntur usque ad
revocationem, et nominati Episcopo in manus
solemniter promittent, se munere suo juxta
normam ab Episcopo sibi tradendam et ad finem,
ob quem examen instituitur, pro viribus asse-[1]

---

[1](Translation continued): All this will be marvelously
co-ordinated so that our schools may be promoted to a loftier degree
of perfection.

Certain rights and privileges must be more
accurately defined for the laity through the diocesan statutes, in as far as they are granted to the schools; safeguard-
ing the rights of the Church, the rights and privileges of
the schools must be defined insofar as the hiring and firing of
teachers is concerned and the correctness of doctrine.

203. Since the status and growth of our schools depend especially on the fitness of the teachers, the greatest
care must be exercised that none but good and competent teachers are set over them. And so we decree and command, that no
one in the future will be admitted to the position of teaching
in a parochial school unless he has by a previous examination
proved himself suitable and competent.

Therefore the bishops, within a year of the promulgation
of this Council, shall name one or more priests who are very
well versed in matters pertaining to schools, to form a
"Diocesan Commission of Examination." They shall be appointed
until recalled, and those named shall solemnly promise the Bishop that they will perform their task according to the norms to
be given them by the Bishop and to attain the end for which the
examination is established in accord with their abilities.

quendum esse functuros. Hujus commissionis
erit omnes magistros ac magistras, sive religiosos pertinentes ad congregationem aliquam
dioecesanam, sive saeculares, qui munere docendi in scholis parochialibus in futuro fungi
cupiunt, examinare, eisque, si idoneos repererint,
testimonium idoneitatis vel diploma praebere,
sine quo nulli sacerdoti fas erit magistrum vel
magistram ullam (nisi jam ante celebrationem
Concilii docuerint) pro schola sua conducere.
Quod diploma ad quinque annos ac pro omnibus
dioecesibus valebit. Quo tempore elapso, alterum et ultimum examen a magistris requiretur.
Iis autem, quos in uno vel altero examine idoneos non repererint, diploma nequaquam dabunt,
sed ad examen anni sequentis eos relegabunt.

Hoc examen semel in anno instituetur; pro
sodalibus ex congregationibus dioecesanis in
domibus et temporibus de quibus examinatores
cum superioribus convenerint; pro saecularibus
tempore et loco ab examinatoribus designandis.
Materiae et quaestiones pro examine in scriptis
conficiendo a commissariis conjunctim praepara-
buntur et die examinis vel ab uno ex ipsis vel
ab alio sacerdote a praeside commissionis deputato,[1]

[1](Translation continued): It will be the task of this
commission to examine all the teachers, whether religious
belonging to some diocesan congregation or secular, who desire
in the future to teach in the parochial schools, and if they
find them suitable to give them evidence of competency or a
diploma, without which diploma no priest has the right to
hire for his school any teacher (unless they have already taught
before the deliberations of the Council). This diploma will be
valid for five years and for all dioceses. When that time has
elapsed, another and final examination will be required of the
teachers. Moreover a diploma will by no means be given to
those whom they do not find competent in one or the other
examination, but they will relegate these persons to the
following year's examination.

This examination will be set up once in a year; for
members of a diocesan congregation, in houses and at times
agreed upon by the examiners and the superiors; for seculars,
at a time and place to be designated by the examiners. The
materials and questions for the written examination will be
prepared jointly by the commissioners, and on the day of the
examination either by one of their own number or by another
priest appointed by the president of the commission,

in epistola sigillo praesidis munita et coram
examinandis aperienda proponentur, qui sub
oculis commissarii vel deputati solutiones
et responsa exarabunt. Scripta parte examinis
ab examinatoribus cognita et recensita, examen
orale quam primum habebitur coram tota commis-
sione. Antequam e loco examinis discedant,
examinatores triplicem elenchum conficient
eorum qui in examine satisfecerunt, quorum
unum pro sodali congregationis dioecesanae
tradent ejusdem superiori, aut ipsi candidato
si sit saecularis; alterum apud praesidem commissionis retinebunt; tertium autem ad cancel-
larium dioecesis transmittent.

Quando regularibus aut congregationibus
quae suos habent superiores vel suas modera-
trices generales juxta constitutiones a S.
Sede approbatas, scholae parochiales commis-
sae sunt, et Episcopus vel ex visitatione
scholarum juxta const. Romanos Pontifices instituta, vel aliunde probatum habeat, alicubi
ad docendum destinari magistros aut magistras
ex istis congregationibus impares suo muneri,
monebit superiorem ut intra congruum tempus
provideat; quod si superior neglexerit, S.[1]

---

[1](Translation continued): they will be produced in a
letter protected by the seal of the president, and opened in
the presence of the ones to be examined; these latter shall
write their solutions and answers under the surveillance of
the commissioner or delegate. When the written part of the
examination has been examined and reviewed by the examiners,
an oral test will be conducted as soon as possible before the
entire commission. Before they leave the place of the examination, the examiners shall prepare a summary in triplicate
of those who have done satisfactorily in the examination. One
of these lists they will give to the superior for a member of a
diocesan congregation, or to the candidate himself if he is
a secular; the second will be kept by the president of the
commission; the third they will send to the chancery of the
diocese.

When parochial schools have been assigned to regulars
or congregations which have their own superiors or their own
moderators general according to constitutions approved by the
Holy See, the Bishop, should he from a visitation of the schools
according to the approved constitution Romanos Pontifices, have
knowledge that in some places there are teachers from those
congregations who are unequal to the task and are appointed
to teach, he shall warn the superior to rectify the situation
within a reasonable time;

Congregationi nuntiandum est, ut opportunis
remediis succurrat. Si in committendis scholis
parochialibus certae pactiones ab Ordinariis
quoad magistrorum aut magistrarum designationem
et romotionem, aut methodum docendi scientias
profanas cum superioribus congregationum initae
sint aut in futurum ineantur, illae omnino
serventur.

204. Praeter hanc commissionem ad magistros
examinandos pro tota dioecesi institutam,
Episcopi pro locorum et linguarum diversitate
plures "Commissiones Scholarum," ex uno vel
pluribus sacerdotibus compositas ad scholas
in civitatibus et districtibus ruralibus ex-
aminandas constituent. Munus autem harum com-
missionum erit, semel vel etiam bis in anno
unamquamque scholam districtus sui visitare
et examinare et accuratam de statu scholarum
relationem ad praesidem commissionis dioecesanae pro notitia et actione Episcopi trans-
mittere.

205. Ut autem sufficiens numerus magistrorum
Catholicorum semper praesto sit, singuli vero
eorum ad sacrum et sublime juventutis instituendae munus optime parati, monemus ut Episcopi[1]

---

[1](Translation continued): if the superior neglects
to do so, this neglect must be reported to the Sacred Congregation so that it may take appropriate action. If in assigning the
parochial schools, definite agreements have either already been
entered into by the Ordinaries or should be entered into in the
future with the superiors of the congregations, regarding the
appointment or removal of teachers or method of teaching the
profane sciences, those agreements are to be kept in their
entirety.

204. Besides this commission established to examine teachers for the whole diocese, the Bishops in proportion to the diversity of places and languages, shall establish several "School
Commissions" made up of one or more priests to examine the
schools in city and rural districts. Moreover it will be the
duty of these commissions once, or even twice a year, to visit
and examine each and every school in their district and to send an
accurate report of the condition of the schools to the president
of the diocesan commission for the information and action of the
Bishop.

205. In order that there may always be on hand a sufficient number of Catholic teachers, each one of them well prepared
for the sacred and sublime duty of instructing the young, we
warn the Bishops whose concern it is,

quorum interest, vel ipsi per se, vel, si
opus sit, etiam invocata auctoritate S. Congregationis, agant, cum superioribus congregationum, muneri in istis scholis docendi dedica-
tarum, ut quantum fieri potest scholae quae
dicuntur Normales, ubi nondum existunt et earum
necessitas apparet, instituantur in domibus
opportunis, in quibus juniores ab expertis et
naxime idoneis magistris in diversis disciplinis
et scientiis, in methodo et paedagogia ceteris-
que ad utile scholae regimen pertinentibus pro-
tracto temporis spatio et diligentia vere religiosa instruantur.
206. Si autem, sicut jam alicubi factum est,
sacerdotes sive saeculares sive regulares in
pluribus provinciis nostris scholas normales
ad magistros laicos vere Catholicos instituendos
erigant easque bene regant, sane opus faciunt
omni laude et auxilio dignum.
207. Haec omnia ab iis quorum interest, imprimis
a sacerdotibus, viris laicis, magistris et parentibus Catholicis omni qua par est reverentia
ponderentur et zelo religioso observentur, ut
scholae nostrae parochiales magis magisque et
numero et valore crescant, ac non tantum Eccle-[1]

---

[1](Translation continued): either themselves, or if there
is need, even calling upon the authority of the S. Congregation,
to agree with the superiors of congregations dedicated to the
taks of teaching in those schools, to establish in their proper
houses as soon as it can be done, normal schools where they do
not yet exist and where their necessity is evident. In these
schools for an extended period of time and with truly religious
solicitude, the younger members shall be instructed by experienced and especially competent teachers in the different dis-
ciplines and sciences, in method, teaching skill and other matters relating to the beneficial guidance of the school.
206. If however, as has already in some places been
done, priests whether secular or regular, should erect and properly conduct in our several provinces normal schools for
training truly Catholic lay teachers, they are indeed performing
a task worthy of every praise and assistance.
207. All these things should be considered with all
appropriate reverence and observed with religious enthusiasm
by those whose concern it is, especially by priests, lay men,
teachers and Catholic parents, that our parochial schools may
more and more grow both in number and excellence, and that they
may daily become not only for the Church but also for the State

possint. Nimis frequenter enim accidit, ut ii
qui pueri pii ac puri e sinu familiae Christianae ed de sub tecto scholae Catholicae in
collegia acatholica transeunt, scientia quidem
inflati, caritate vero, i.e. fide moribusque
Christianis privati revertantur.
209. Monemus igitur et in Domino obsecramus
fideles nostros, ut unitis viribus felicem
illum rerum statum accelerent, quo academiae,
collegia, universitates Catholicae tam nume-
rosa sint tamque excellentia, ut omnes ad unum
juvenes Catholici omnia quae ipsis addiscenda
vel a parentibus proponuntur, vel ipsi sibi
eligunt, in scholis Catholicis invenire possint!
210. Quod ut quam primum eveniat, parentes in
Domino hortamur, ut adolescentes suos, quibus,
scholis parochialibus absolutis, superiorem
educationem procurare velint, in Catholicas
scholas superiores jam nunc existentes mittant.
Si vero scholae Catholicae filiis suis pro
speciali quem sequuntur studiorum cursu desint
eosque ob hanc causam in scholas acatholicas
mittere cogantur, enixe eos monemus, ut fidei
morumque pericula a filiis suis quam longis-
sime removeant, verbi Domini semper memores:[1]

---

[1](Translation continued): Too often it happens
that those who, as God-fearing and pure youths, pass from
the bosom of the Christian family and from under the roof
of a Catholic school into non-Catholic colleges, become
puffed up by knowledge and, deprived of love, that is,
of faith and Christian morals, are doomed to fall.
209. Therefore we advise and beseech our faithful in the
Lord that with combined efforts they hasten that happy
state of affairs when Catholic academies, colleges and
universities will be both so numerous and so excellent
that all Catholics to a man can find in the Catholic
schools all the things which they or their parents feel
should be learned or which they themselves elect.
210. To bring this about as soon as possible, we exhort
parents in the Lord to send their children for whom they
wish to provide a higher education to the already existing
Catholic high schools when the parochial course has been
completed. If Catholic schools are not available for
their children in the special course of studies that they
are following and they are forced to send them to non-
catholic schools for this reason, we strenuously urge
them to remove as far as possible from their children
the dangers to faith and morals, mindful always of the
saying of the Lord:

siae, sed etiam reipublicae honor et decus,
spes et columna in dies magis evadant.

Caput II. De Superioribus Scholis Catholicis.

208. Cum in dies augeatur numerus juvenum Catholicorum, qui vel opibus vel ingenio vel
utroque praestantiores scholis parochialibus
absolutis ad altiorem educationis cursum ad-
spirant, pauca quaedam de superioribus scholis
Catholicis addere placet. Alii namque pueri
Catholici mentes oculosque ad sacrum ministerium
attollunt; alii liberalem, quam dicunt, profes-
sionem sibi adipiscendam proponunt. De iis,
qui ministerio sacro sese mancipare desiderant,
in collegiis et academiis Catholicis ac seminariis
clericorum jam satis ample provisum est; ceteris
vero plures, meliores ac tutiores viae ad fines
suos assequendos omnino sunt aperiendae. Utinam
jam nunc, quod certo venturum esse speramus,
res ita disponi et stabiliri possint, ut juvenes Catholici ex Catholicis scholis elementari-
bus in Catholicas scholas superiores intrare et
per eas ad metam desideriorum suorum accurrere[1]

---

[1](Translation continued): a thing of respect, pride,
hope and support.

Chapter II. On Catholic High Schools

208. Since daily the number of Catholic youth is on
the increase, who, more outstanding because of wealth or talent
or both, aspire to a higher course of study than that of strictly
parochial schools, we are pleased to add a few ideas about
Catholic High schools. Some Catholic young men raise
their minds and eyes to the sacred ministry; others propose to
obtain for themselves what they call a liberal profession. For
those who wish to attach themselves to the sacred ministry
sufficient provision has already been made in the Catholic
colleges, academies and seminaries of the clerics; but for the
rest better and safer ways of attaining their goals must be
wholly opened up. Would that already now, a fact that we certainly hope will come about, matters could be so arranged and
established, that Catholic youths could from Catholic elementary schools enter Catholic high schools and through them
reach the goal of their ambitions.

"Quid prodest homini, si mundum universum
lucretur, animae vero suae detrimentum patiatur." (Matth. xvi. 26).
211. Eos vero ex fidelibus nostris, qui copia
rerum temporalium ditati sunt, per viscera
misericordiae Dei rogamus ac pro Catholici
hominis honore obsecramus, ut ad collegia Catholica fundanda augendaque thesauros suos
aperiant, hoc potissimum fine, ut adolescentibus pauperioribus, qui ingenio, indole moribusque futurae bonitatis, utilitatis, imo
forte excellentiae solida indicia prae se fe-
runt, viae aditusque patefiant. Summo cum
gaudio jam compertum habemus in nonnullis dioecesibus viros Catholicos nobiles, generosos
hoc caritatis vere Catholicae opere studiosae
juventutis gratias, omnium bonorum plausum,
Summi Pontificis approbationem, nec non Dei
O. M. benedictionem sibi meruisse. Utinam
in omnibus dioecesibus viri ditiores nobilis-
simum eorum exemplum imitentur, et ita quidem,
ut in futuro necessarium non sit, quod in
praeterito non sine rubore fieri debebat, scilicet viros Catholicos monere, ut ab iis qui
foris sunt, vel etiam ab ipsis inimicis Ecclesiae partes suas hac in re discant.[1]

---

[1](Translation continued): "What does it profit a
man if he gain the whole world and suffer the loss of his
soul?" (Matth. 16, 26).
211. Indeed we ask through the bowels of the mercy of
God those of our faithful who have been enriched with an
abundance of this world's goods and we beseech them for the
honor of the Catholic name to open their treasures for the
founding and enlargement of Catholic colleges, especially
so that a way and means of entrance may be given to the
poorer youths who through talent, character and morals
show sound indications of future goodness, usefulness and
perhaps even excellence. We have already with the greatest
joy found in several dioceses that noble Catholic men,
magnanimous for this work of truly Catholic charity, have
merited for themselves the thanks of eager youth, the
approval of all good men, the approbation of the Holy
Father, and the blessing of Almighty God. Would that in
all the dioceses the more wealthy men would imitate their
most noble example, so that in the future it would not
be necessary to repeat that which in the past could only
be done with great shame; namely, the warning of Catholic
men to learn their duties in this matter from those who
are not of the flock or who are even among the very
enemies of the Church.

212. Moderatores denique et professores collegiorum nostrorum gravissimi ac sanctissimi
muneris sui semper memores esse in Domino hortamur. Ipsis enim commissi sunt ii, qui Ecclesiae et reipublicae plus ceteris aut honori
et saluti aut pudori et periculo futuri sunt.
Eorum enim discipuli hominum minus cultorum
erunt duces et directores; scriptis et verbis,
in cathedra et in rostris, in foliis publicis
et conciliis privatis, scientiis et commerciis,
in omnibus denique vitae viis et circumstantiis
aliorum mentes dirigent et ad partes et consilia
sua, aut bona et utilia, aut mala et nociva,
adducent. Tales autem optimis in adolescentia
sua imbuendos esse principiis optimisque cogi-
tandi, dicendi, agendique rationibus, majoris
quam dici potest est necessitatis. "Adolescens,"
enim, "juxta viam suam, etiam cum senuerit non
recedet ab ea." (Prov. xxii. 6). Praeceptores
igitur moribus eorum sedulo invigilent. Non
solum curent ut inter collegiorum muros a malo
arceantur, sed etiam ab illecebris, quae in
civitatibus et oppidis vicinis existunt, eos
maxima cura custodiant nec proinde eos in civitates et oppida exire permittant, nisi magnis
cum cautionibus pro morum ipsorum incolumitate.[1]

---

[1](Translation continued): 212. Finally we exhort in
the Lord the directors and professors of our colleges to be
ever mindful of their most serious and sacred duty. For to
them have been entrusted those who will be for the Church and
State more than others either for honor and welfare or for shame
and danger. For their pupils will be the leaders and directors
of less educated men; in writings and discourses, in the professors' chair and in the pulpit, in public papers and private
meetings, in the sciences and business, finally, in all the ways
and circumstances of life, they shall direct the minds of others
and lead them to their own designs and plans, either good and
useful or bad and harmful. Moreover it is of greater need than
can be mentioned that such people must be imbued in their youth
with the best principles and the loftiest ideals of thinking,
speaking and acting. For "train a boy in the way he should
go; even when he is old, he will not swerve from it." (Prov.
22,6). Therefore let the teachers carefully look out for their
morals. Let them not only see to it that they are protected
within the walls of the colleges but also let them guard them
from the allurements which exist in the cities and neighboring
towns with the greatest care, and they shall not permit
them to go out into the cities and towns except with great
caution for the safety of their morals.

In doctrina Christiana autem per totum studiorum curriculum non obiter et cursivo quodam
modo, sed apprime et solide eos instruant.
Armatura veritatis ita eos induant et obarment,
ut nullo vitae tempore errorum insidiis et
telis succumbere, sed econtra ipsos debellare
et devincere fortiter possint. Suas quisque
igitur vires summamque ambitionem omnes eo
dirigant, ut discipuli sui in artibus et scientiis alumnis vel optimae cujusvis scholae
acatholicae sint aequales, morum vero probi-
tate ac puritate omnibus antecellant. In tam
arduo labore ne animo unquam deficiant! Pro
honore enim Dei et Ecclesiae gloria, pro salute
societatis humanae et rei publicae incolumitate
se certare sciant, nec unquam gloriosissima
illa verba prophetae ab oculis amittant: "Qui
autem docti fuerint, fulgebunt quasi splendor
firmamenti; et qui ad justitiam erudiunt multos, quasi stellae in perpetuas aeternitates."
(Dan. xii. 3).
213. Pro rerum nostrarum adjunctis et civilis
societatis in his regionibus permistione saepe
contingit, ut parentes acatholici pueros et puellas suas nostris scholis superioribus commit-
tant, quae ideo fiunt scholas plus minusve mixtae.[1]

---

[1](Translation continued): Moreover they are to instruct
them in Christian doctrine through the entire course of their
studies, not incidentally and in some hurried manner, but completely and solidly. Let them so clothe and arm them with
the armour of truth that at no time in their lives can they
succumb to the snares and weapons of error but on the contrary
can bravely fight against and overcome them. Therefore let
each one so direct his forces and highest aspirations that
his pupils may be in the arts and sciences equal to the gradu-
ates of even the best non-Catholic school, and excel all
in uprightness and purity of morals. In such a difficult task
let them never fail in courage! For the honor of God and
glory of the Church, for the salvation of human society
and for the safety of the state, let them know how to assert
themselves and never lose sight of those most glorious words
of the prophet: "But they that are learned shall shine as the
brightness of the firmament; and they that instruct many to
justice, as stars for all eternity." (Dan. 12, 3).
    213. In view of the circumstances of our situation and
the mixture of civil society in these areas, it often happens
that non-catholic parents entrust their boys and girls to our
high schools and they therefore become more or less mixed
schools.

Constat enim multos acatholicos etsi rei Catholicae fautores minime esse velint, sacerdotes tamen nostros et religiosos, ac praecipue religiosas, tanta fiducia dignos habere,
ut sub eorum directione et protectione, doctrina et exemplo prolem suam in tuto collocatam
esse credant. Quamvis alienos recipere non
absolute prohibeamus, enixe tamen superiores
hortamur ut moribus omnium alumnorum eo reli-
giosius invigilent, quo magis permixti sunt,
ut non solum Catholici ab acatholicis nullum
detrimentum, sed nec acatholici a Catholicis
ullum scandalum patiantur.
    Alumni Catholici vero in his scholis mix-
tis majori quo fieri potest studio in operibus
pietatis et devotionis exerceantur et in omnibus rebus divinis tam lucide ac solide instruantur, ut periculum indifferentismi, si forte
ex tam arcto cum acatholicis commercio oriri
videatur, prorsus tollatur. Disputationes de
rebus religiosis, absentibus ac insciis magistris, ne habeantur, per regulas scholae stricte
prohibeatur. Non enim strepitu verborum et
argumentorum certamine, sed potius precibus[1]

---

[1](Translation continued): It is evident that many
non-catholics, even if they in no way wish to be patrons of
things Catholic, consider our priests and religious, especially
religious sisters, worthy of such great trust that they believe
their children have been safely placed under their direction
and protection by teaching and example. Although we do not
absolutely forbid them to receive outsiders, nevertheless we
strongly urge superiors to look after the morals of their
students the more religiously the more mixed they are, not
only that Catholics may suffer no harm from the non-catholics,
but also that the non-catholics suffer no scandal from the
Catholics.
    Indeed Catholic students in these mixed schools must
be trained with all possible zeal in works of piety and
devotion and must be instructed so clearly and fully in all
divine matters that the danger of indifferentism is completely taken away if from such close contact with non-
catholics it may seem perhaps to arise. Arguments on religious
matters, when the teachers are absent and not aware of them,
are not to be held, and are to be strictly forbidden by the
rules of the school.

et virtutum exemplis praeceptorum et alumnorum
catholicorum, qui speciali quodam modo sunt
proles benedicta et proprius Ecclesiae fructus,
efficietur, ut ii qui foris sunt, ad unitatem
Ecclesiae revertantur, verbo Salvatoris ducti:
"Omnis arbor bona fructus bonos facit." (Matth.,
vii., 17).[1]

---

[1](Translation continued): For it is not by the sound
of words and the clash of arguments, but rather by the prayers
and by the example of the virtue of Catholic teachers and
students, who in some special way are the blessed offspring
and special fruit of the .hurch, that those who are outside
the fold will be led to return to the unity of the Church,
inspired by the word of the Savior: "Every good tree bears
good fruit." (Matth. 7, 17).

The Latin text has been taken from: Acta et Decreta
Concilii Plenarii Baltimorensis Tertii. A.D. MDCCCLXXXIV.
Praeside Illmo, ac Revmo, Jacobo Gibbons, Archiepiscopo Balt.
et Delegato Apostolico (Baltimorae: typis Joannis Murphy et
Sociorum, 1894), pp. 99-114.

THE AMERICAN CATHOLIC TRADITION

An Arno Press Collection

Callahan, Nelson J., editor. **The Diary of Richard L. Burtsell, Priest of New York.** 1978

Curran, Robert Emmett. **Michael Augustine Corrigan and the Shaping of Conservative Catholicism in America, 1878-1902.** 1978

Ewens, Mary. **The Role of the Nun in Nineteenth-Century America** (Doctoral Thesis, The University of Minnesota, 1971). 1978

McNeal, Patricia F. **The American Catholic Peace Movement 1928-1972** (Doctoral Dissertation, Temple University, 1974). 1978

Meiring, Bernard Julius. **Educational Aspects of the Legislation of the Councils of Baltimore, 1829-1884** (Doctoral Dissertation, University of California, Berkeley, 1963). 1978

Murnion, Philip J., **The Catholic Priest and the Changing Structure of Pastoral Ministry, New York, 1920-1970** (Doctoral Dissertation, Columbia University, 1972). 1978

White, James A., **The Era of Good Intentions: A Survey of American Catholics' Writing Between the Years 1880-1915** (Doctoral Thesis, University of Notre Dame, 1957). 1978

Dyrud, Keith P., Michael Novak and Rudolph J. Vecoli, editors. **The Other Catholics.** 1978

Gleason, Philip, editor. **Documentary Reports on Early American Catholicism.** 1978

Bugg, Lelia Hardin, editor. **The People of Our Parish.** 1900

Cadden, John Paul. **The Historiography of the American Catholic Church: 1785-1943.** 1944

Caruso, Joseph. **The Priest.** 1956

Congress of Colored Catholics of the United States. **Three Catholic Afro-American Congresses.** [1893]

Day, Dorothy. **From Union Square to Rome.** 1940

Deshon, George. **Guide for Catholic Young Women.** 1897

Dorsey, Anna H[anson]. **The Flemmings.** [1869]

Egan, Maurice Francis. **The Disappearance of John Longworthy.** 1890

Ellard, Gerald. **Christian Life and Worship.** 1948

England, John. **The Works of the Right Rev. John England, First Bishop of Charleston.** 1849. 5 vols.

Fichter, Joseph H. **Dynamics of a City Church.** 1951

Furfey, Paul Hanly. **Fire on the Earth.** 1936

Garraghan, Gilbert J. **The Jesuits of the Middle United States.** 1938. 3 vols.

Gibbons, James. **The Faith of Our Fathers.** 1877

Hecker, I[saac] T[homas]. **Questions of the Soul.** 1855

Houtart, François. **Aspects Sociologiques Du Catholicisme Américain.** 1957

[Hughes, William H.] **Souvenir Volume. Three Great Events in the History of the Catholic Church in the United States.** 1889

[Huntington, Jedediah Vincent]. **Alban: A Tale of the New World.** 1851

Kelley, Francis C., editor. The First American Catholic Missionary Congress. 1909

Labbé, Dolores Egger. **Jim Crow Comes to Church.** 1971

LaFarge, John. **Interracial Justice.** 1937

Malone, Sylvester L. **Dr. Edward McGlynn.** 1918

The Mission-Book of the Congregation of the Most Holy Redeemer. 1862

O'Hara, Edwin V. **The Church and the Country Community.** 1927

Pise, Charles Constantine. **Father Rowland.** 1829

Ryan, Alvan S., editor. **The Brownson Reader.** 1955

Ryan, John A., **Distributive Justice.** 1916

Sadlier, [Mary Anne]. **Confessions of an Apostate.** 1903

Sermons Preached at the Church of St. Paul the Apostle, New York, During the Year 1863. 1864

Shea, John Gilmary. **A History of the Catholic Church Within the Limits of the United States.** 1886/1888/1890/1892. 4 Vols.

Shuster, George N. **The Catholic Spirit in America.** 1928

Spalding, J[ohn] L[ancaster]. **The Religious Mission of the Irish People and Catholic Colonization.** 1880

Sullivan, Richard. **Summer After Summer.** 1942

[Sullivan, William L.] **The Priest.** 1911

Thorp, Willard. **Catholic Novelists in Defense of Their Faith, 1829-1865.** 1968

Tincker, Mary Agnes. **San Salvador.** 1892

Weninger, Franz Xaver. **Die Heilige Mission** *and* **Praktische Winke Für Missionare.** 1885. 2 Vols. in 1

Wissel, Joseph. **The Redemptorist on the American Missions.** 1920. 3 Vols. in 2

The World's Columbian Catholic Congresses and Educational Exhibit. 1893

Zahm, J[ohn] A[ugustine]. **Evolution and Dogma.** 1896